Two Centuries
OF
AUSTRALIAN
POETRY

Two Centuries
OF
AUSTRALIAN
POETRY

Edited by
MARK O'CONNOR

OXFORD
UNIVERSITY PRESS

MELBOURNE

OXFORD UNIVERSITY PRESS AUSTRALIA

Oxford   New York   Toronto
Delhi   Bombay   Calcutta   Madras   Karachi
Petaling Jaya   Singapore   Hong Kong   Tokyo
Nairobi   Dar es Salaam   Cape Town
Melbourne   Auckland
and associated companies in
Berlin   Ibadan

OXFORD is a trade mark of Oxford University Press

©This collection Mark O'Connor, 1988
First published 1988
Reprinted 1988

National Library of Australia
Cataloguing-in-Publication data:

Two centuries of Australian poetry.

  Includes index.
  ISBN 0 19 554772 1.

  1. Australian poetry. 1. O'Connor, Mark, 1945–

A821'.008

Designed by Jennifer Johnston
Illustrated by Kevin Burgemeestre
Cover illustration by Jennifer Johnston
Set in 9/11 Baskerville by Post Typesetters, Queensland
Printed by Impact Printing, Melbourne
Published by Oxford University Press,
253 Normanby Road, South Melbourne, Australia

CONTENTS

To the Reader   xi
To the Teacher   xv

1 EUROPEAN CONTACT   1

The Conquest   *Les A. Murray*   2
Child with a Cockatoo   *Rosemary Dobson*   4
From Five Visions of Captain
    Cook   *Kenneth Slessor*   5
The Kangaroo   *Barron Field*   6

2 THE ABORIGINAL WORLD   11

Lament for the Drowned   *Mary Durack*   14
    Country
The Evening Star   *from 'Song Cycle of the*
                                    Moon-Bone', Wonguri-
                                    Madjigai People, trans. by
                                    R. M. Berndt   17
We Are Going   *Oodgeroo of the tribe*
                                    Noonuccal   18
'Consultation'   *Kevin Gilbert*   19
Shells   *Selwyn Hughes*   20
Wanna Be White   *Charmaine Papertalk-Green*   20

3 WHITE ON BLACK   25

The Last of His Tribe   *Henry Kendall*   26
At Cooloolah   *Judith Wright*   27
Brown, Black and White   *John Manifold*   28
At an Exhibition of Historical
    Paintings, Hobart   *Vivian Smith*   28
From The Buladelah-Taree
    Holiday Song Cycle   *Les A. Murray*   30

4 BECOMING A NATION 33

Jim Jones	*Anonymous*	35
The Old Prison	*Judith Wright*	36
Bullocky Bill	*Anonymous*	37
Harry Pearce	*David Campbell*	38
The Shearer's Wife	*Louis Esson*	39
Sweeney	*Henry Lawson*	40
Ned's Delicate Way	*Henry Lawson*	42
From The English Queen	*Henry Lawson*	42
Wine Tasting	*Michael Dransfield*	43
The Australian Dream	*David Campbell*	44

5 THE AUSTRALIAN VERNACULAR 49

Folklore	*Les A. Murray*	51
Life-Cycle	*Bruce Dawe*	52
The Breach	*Les A. Murray*	53
And a Good Friday Was Had by All	*Bruce Dawe*	55
Reverie of a Mum	*Nancy Keesing*	56
You're Great	*John Jenkins*	59

6 ACCEPTING A LANDSCAPE 63

A Dedication	*Adam Lindsay Gordon*	65
Fire in the Heavens, and Fire along the Hills: *From* The Quest of Silence	*Christopher Brennan*	66
Crow Country	*Kenneth Slessor*	66
South of My Days	*Judith Wright*	67
Mangrove	*John Blight*	68
Terra Australis	*James McAuley*	69
Egrets	*Judith Wright*	69
Drought in the Mallee, 1940	*Barbara Giles*	70
The Cycads	*Judith Wright*	70
A Kangaroo	*Robert Gray*	71
The Beginning	*Mark O'Connor*	72

7 MIGRANT EXPERIENCE 77

Smugglers · *Maria Lewitt* · 79
The Exile · *J. J. Encarnação* · 80
From Prague, 1968 · *Kevin Hart* · 80
Freedom Fighter · *Antigone Kefala* · 81
Bonegilla 1961 · *Manfred Jurgensen* · 82
Migrant Woman on a
   Melbourne Tram · *Jennifer Strauss* · 83
Post Card · *Peter Skrzynecki* · 84
Mute Conversations:
   Conversazioni Mute · *Paolo Totaro* · 86
Postponement (Anavolee) · *Dimitris Tsaloumas* · 89
Be Good, Little Migrants · *Uyen Loewald* · 89

8 WAR 95

Epitaph, World War I · *C. R. Jury* · 97
Adieu... · *Anonymous* · 97
Inscription for a War · *A. D. Hope* · 97
The Regulars · *Alan Gould* · 98
Beach Burial · *Kenneth Slessor* · 99
Christ at Gallipoli · *Geoff Page* · 100
Pozières Cemetery · *Mark O'Connor* · 100
1915 · *Roger McDonald* · 102
Brothers · *Geoff Page* · 103
Weapons Training · *Bruce Dawe* · 104
Homecoming · *Bruce Dawe* · 105

9 URBAN LIFE AND WORKPLACES 109

Late Ferry · *Robert Gray* · 110
Prosperity · *Michael Dransfield* · 111
The Meat Works · *Robert Gray* · 112
Lines from a Factory · *Marion Alexopoulous* · 113
Doctor to Patient · *Bruce Dawe* · 115
Living Dangerously · *Dorothy Hewett* · 116
That Which We Call a Rose · *Michael Dransfield* · 117

10 TRADITIONAL VERSE 121

The Convicts' Rum Song	*Anonymous*	124
The Bystander	*Rosemary Dobson*	124
The Brides	*A. D. Hope*	125
Louise and Alessandro:		
From Letter from Rome	*A. D. Hope*	126
The Scarecrow	*Rosemary Dobson*	129
An Art of Poetry	*James McAuley*	130
Brindabella	*Douglas Stewart*	131
Lament	*Douglas Stewart*	132
The Bulldozer: *From* Machine		
Portraits with Pendant		
Spaceman	*Les A. Murray*	132
The Big Web	*Bruce Beaver*	133
Generations	*Evan Jones*	133

11 FREE VERSE 137

After the 'Ball'	*Lilian Tait*	140
Note on Rhyme	*Anna Wickham*	141
Mangoes	*Richard Tipping*	141
Mort aux Chats	*Peter Porter*	142
The Gull's Flight	*Nigel Roberts*	143
The Night-Ride	*Kenneth Slessor*	143
A Victorian Hangman Tells his		
Love	*Bruce Dawe*	144
Garrakeen	*Rex Ingamells*	145
Petit Testament	*Ern Malley (James McAuley*	
	and Harold Stewart)	145
Bringing the Cattle	*Robert Gray*	147
Snake	*David Campbell*	148

12 YOUNG AND OLD 153

The Old	*Kevin Hart*	154
Parents	*Vincent Buckley*	155
Weights	*Les A. Murray*	155
Father and Child	*Gwen Harwood*	156
Because	*James McAuley*	158
Naked Girl and Mirror	*Judith Wright*	160
Lake in Spring	*Judith Wright*	161

13 PEOPLE 165

Cricket	*Peter Kocan*	166
Ladies and Gentlemen	*Kate Llewellyn*	166
The Fishermen at South Head	*Les A. Murray*	167
Painter of Antwerp	*Rosemary Dobson*	168
For David Campbell	*A. D. Hope*	169
Near the School for Handicapped Children	*Thomas W. Shapcott*	172

14 WOMEN'S EXPERIENCE 177

The Edge	*Rosemary Dobson*	179
Once When She Thought Aloud	*Dorothea Mackellar*	179
Smalltown Dance	*Judith Wright*	180
Emily Brontë	*Alison Croggon*	181
Woman to Man	*Judith Wright*	181
Woman to Child	*Judith Wright*	182
Andromeda	*Diane Fahey*	183
Breasts	*Kate Llewellyn*	184
Five Days Late	*Geoffrey Lehmann*	185
Theatre	*Kate Llewellyn*	186
In the Park, Looking	*Barbara Giles*	187
Play Group	*Doris Brett*	188
In the Park	*Gwen Harwood*	189
Couples	*Kate Jennings*	190

15 LOVE 195

Love's Coming	*John Shaw Neilson*	196
Love and Complacency	*Geoffrey Dutton*	197
Finished	*Kate Llewellyn*	198
Sassy	*Kate Llewellyn*	198
Pas de Deux for Lovers	*Michael Dransfield*	199
A Simple Story	*Gwen Harwood*	200
Time of Waiting	*Geoffrey Dutton*	201
Vows	*Ada Cambridge*	201
Going Down. With no permanence	*Vicki Viidikas*	202
Stars	*David Malouf*	203

16 MORTALITY   207

To Kill an Olive   Mark O'Connor   208
Popular Statesman   Vincent Buckley   208
Meditation on a Bone   A. D. Hope   209
Ulinda   David Campbell   210
Starting from Central Station David Campbell   210
Green Hands   David Campbell   211
To David Campbell   Philip Martin   211
Song be Delicate   John Shaw Neilson   212
Mid-Channel   Gwen Harwood   213
Goya Paints a Portrait of a
    Child   John Griffin   214
The Apparition   Chris Wallace-Crabbe   215
Death: *From* Letters to Live
    Poets   Bruce Beaver   216
The Electors   John Griffin   217
Individualist   B. R. Whiting   217
Brother and Sisters   Judith Wright   218

17 THE WORLD WITHIN   223

Faith   Ada Cambridge   224
The Inspector of Tides   Michael Dransfield   224
The Land I Came Thro' Last   Christopher Brennan   225
Sea Children   Randolph Stow   226
So Quietly   Keith Harrison   227
The Wandering Islands   A. D. Hope   228
Poetry and Religion   Les A. Murray   229
Third Song of Pop-Eye the
    Sailorman   Hal Colebatch   230
Semi-conductors are also
    Semi-insulators   R. G. Hay   230

18 WORLD IN PERIL—THE FUTURE   235

Package for the Distant Future	*Sylvia Kantarizis*	237
Your Attention Please	*Peter Porter*	238
Death of a Whale	*John Blight*	239
Natural Increase: *From* Conversation with Calliope	*A. D. Hope*	241
The Future	*Les A. Murray*	242
A Document	*Judith Wright*	243
Outback	*Michael Dransfield*	244

Biographical Notes   249
Acknowledgements   253
Index of Titles and First Lines   257
Index of Poets   262

TO THE READER

In our culture, many of the truths of life are hidden or are covered over by banalities. What does it feel like to bear a child? to lose your parents? to lie on your deathbed? to have a mystical experience? to be old and unloved (or young and unloved)? or loved for the first time by someone outside your own family? All of these experiences may be expressed, and discovered, in poetry. In poetry you can stand with Lilian Tait beside the body of a rape victim, or overhear Michael Dransfield lament how he surrendered his will to heroin, or listen to Dorothea MacKellar talking about a man she 'couldn't bear out of my sight'. If you want to know what it is that people really think and feel, one way is to read the poets.

Poetry is also one of the things that make nations different. Being an Englishman, a Greek, a German or an Italian would mean something different if poets like Shakespeare, Homer, Goethe or Dante had not existed. Similarly, the poets in this book have helped determine what it means to be Australian.

Few of us will ever meet any of our ancestors from generations older than our grandparents, or at most great-grandparents; but in an anthology like this the Australians of the past can speak to you—not as elderly relatives, but as persons at the height of their vitality.

Sometimes you will meet people who thought and felt very much as you would. Sometimes you will find that their different world gave them different emotions and attitudes, ones which you can understand only by entering that world. You will meet young men like Adam Lindsay Gordon, to whom horse-riding was a passion; optimistic or disillusioned bushmen; and pioneer women with enduring hearts and far-reaching minds. You may also meet Aboriginal ancestors to whom this land was the temple of a complex religion that is now almost forgotten. You will find poets speaking of many of the high points of Australian history, but also of many forgotten byways.

WHAT POETRY DOES

Poetry can capture the private world of one person, or the larger world of a nation. It is memorable and evocative speech. Poetry is what we produce on those rare occasions when we feel strongly and truly, or when we think over something that has been happening to us and suddenly it all makes sense, and the perfect words for the occasion rise to our lips.

Most people produce only fragments of poetry, scattered throughout their lives. Certain people, however, the ones we commonly call poets, have the knack of weaving these fragments into larger poems which can express whole chunks of their lives, and of ours.

For instance, in 'The Fishermen at South Head' Les Murray describes a cliff-top in Sydney 'where the suicides come by taxi'. Those six words paint a scene. After all, if someone has decided to jump off a cliff, they might as well spend their money on a taxi. Perhaps you get a quick picture of a white-faced girl, paying off the driver before she walks to the cliff. You may wonder what the driver thinks, or says, and your own emotions, as you read, may be a mixture of pity and wry understanding. In fact, those few words are concentrated poetry: a great chunk of knowledge and feeling has gone into them. (It is in this sense that Richard Tipping once wrote: 'Poems are the tomato-paste of literature'.) Of course, these six words are only a small sliver out of the poem, just as the suicides are only one of many realities, some good, some bad, and some neutral, that enter into the poet's vision of that place.

One of the tests of a poem is that its words stick in your mind and get richer the more you think about them. Often the quiet poems are the ones that do it. A flashy poem that seems wonderfully clever at first may die on a second reading, while one that seemed a bit odd or obscure the first time may come to mean much more on the second or third reading.

Les Murray's line about the suicides proves that poetry need not be 'beautiful'. It does have to be interesting and resonant. Its words have to have 'echoes', and it has to make us feel we have captured some part of the truth about our world. After all, advertising jingles are designed to be memorable, and evocative—'Let your teeth go far/into a crunchy Fred Nurk's yum-yum bar!'. But because they tell us only what it suits the advertiser to have us think, we cannot value them as poetry. This is not to say that some popular songs, including rock songs, cannot be a kind of poetry. Everyone can think of some that are.

POETRY AND EXPERIENCE

A good poem, like a good song, does not simply create a world of its own: it opens out onto the real world. It makes sense on the page, but often its real power cannot be felt until you've had the experiences it describes. (That is why sometimes you have to take it on trust that a particular poem is good.) A good poem will grow as your own experience of life grows. Sometimes you will meet experiences first in your own life—including frightening and unsettling ones—and then discover that a poet in this book has already written about them and proved that it is possible to understand and control them. Other times you will meet experiences first in poetry, and later discover them in life.

The poetry of your own country is like a bank balance that was put there by your family and your ancestors: you get it simply by being born. It is a stock to which many people contribute, but from which each receives more than he or she could possibly add. Some people are lucky enough to be bilingual or trilingual, and have the key to two or more such stocks.

The poet is a creator of meaning. He or she invents words or phrases that help us grasp the patterns of our lives. That is why poets are often cult figures.

POETRY THEN AND NOW

We value the masterpieces of the past; but we also need the news of today. Good poets usually write about their own times; their inspiration comes from here and now. But 'here' and 'now' have a way of turning into 'over there' and 'back then'. The things that are 'common knowledge' change so fast. If you were to write a satire on today's prime minister, in five years' time it would need footnotes! Poets have been writing poetry for so many centuries that most of the world's great poetry is about things that happened long ago. This is a pity, because, as we all know, nothing spoils a poem, or a joke, like having to explain the point.

That problem is at its worst when you study poetry in school, because when you are in senior high school, you probably don't remember many world events that are more than ten years old, and you probably haven't visited many of the foreign countries that are mentioned in poems.

To make things worse, Australian students have often been made to concentrate on British rather than Australian poetry. It was said that this was because Australian poetry was not good enough; but the real reason may have been a 'colonial cringe'—the feeling that everything was better in Britain, the motherland, than it was in a primitive place like Australia.

In this anthology all the poets are Australian, and many of them are still alive and writing about what happens now. Except perhaps for some of the Aboriginal songs, even the oldest poems are only about 200 years old. Two hundred years is time enough for a lot of things to change. In one Henry Lawson poem, a girl's lover is drowned when his horse is swept away in a flooded river. Today she might lose him in a car accident, but in Australia even the things that have gone are still part of our recent past. 'The past is another country'—it has also what made us what we are.

POETRY AND OBSCURITY

When you read some of the earliest poems in this book, you will notice that the English language and its literary habits were a little different from today's usage. In general, however, you'll find it much easier to get the point of older Australian poems than of older English ones.

There are no deliberately obscure poems in this anthology. Earlier this century many people had the idea that it was 'modern' for poetry to be full of far-fetched ideas and eccentric wording. That idea was never very popular in Australia, and is now itself old-fashioned. If some of the poems here are complex or difficult, it is with the complexity and difficulty of real life, not with that irritating difficulty that comes from a writer trying to be impressive without quite knowing what he or she means. Yet no good poet pretends that the world is simpler (or better) than it is.

This anthology is divided into sections, so that you can investigate them one at a time. Later, when you are familiar with Australian poetry as a whole, you may prefer to take each poem as it comes, but the sections can be a help when starting out. For instance, you may have a problem understanding vernacular poetry, or perhaps you cannot yet see the point of free verse, or of traditional ballads, but this way you will know that you have a problem with free verse or ballads or whatever, not with poetry in general.

Some of the later sections deal more with the world of a person's inner self. The early sections start almost where a history book would, with the discovery of Australia by seafaring nations, and then with its colonization by England.

Notes to the Poems

If you want to read ahead and separately from the rest of the class, there are notes at the end of each section to help with some of the poems.

One reason this book needs to have notes is that Australia is such a diverse country, and is inhabited by groups of people from most of the other countries on earth. Some people grow up among apple trees and lilac bushes, others among mangoes and bougainvillea. Some come from happy families, and others have terrible ones. Each generation, of course, grows up into a different world from the world in which their parents were young. That is why all good poetry needs some footnotes for people from other places, climates, and times.

CREATIVE WRITING

The study of other Australian poets may help you to write poetry yourself. Good poets create something that is evocative, not only for themselves, but also for others. How can you learn to recognize when you yourself have achieved this? There is no sure way, because poetry is an art, like conversation. You can always sharpen that skill by reading and discussing with others the work of your favourite poets. If this anthology has been well selected, you should find in it some of the best that has been said and thought in the last two hundred years by wise or sensitive men and women on this continent.

Mark O'Connor

TO THE TEACHER

For most teachers an anthology is rather like a mine. It contains some dross, large amounts of middling ores, a little high-grade ore, and occasional specks of pure gold. These last are the few poems whose power and vitality will charm even the most cynical student or jaded class.

My aim has been to present an anthology that is, as far as possible, all gold. It should represent at least the major authors, styles, and periods of Australian poetry. And it should help to free the teacher from the chore of panning through a pile of books in the school library to find material for that afternoon's class—or through a still larger pile to assemble a course.

THEMATIC ARRANGEMENT

Many teachers of poetry like to follow up themes. Too often at present they must be content to discover middling examples of contemporary Australian verse which connect with something the class has already studied. I believe that this is to starve in the midst of plenty. The 'relevant' but inferior poem may provide a quick diversion for a dull afternoon, but unless it has those deep provocative qualities which make good literature, it will never be remembered after school is out; and it will not give students that sudden illumination, which often comes only late in secondary school, as to what poetry is and why it should matter to them.

Of course any anthology may chance to provide the teacher with the perfect poem for a given theme. For instance Alison Croggon's 'Emily Brontë' may follow upon a reading of *Wuthering Heights*. However, the poems in this book should be 'relevant' in a more reliable and regular way because, after being first selected for quality, they have been organized into groups around major themes like War, Aborigines, Becoming A Nation, The World Within, Women's Experience, and Migration. A class which has already learned a term like 'ticket-of-leave' or 'triangles' in one poem of the convict era will benefit in confidence by meeting the same term a couple of pages later, rather than fifty or one hundred pages later as might happen in an anthology organized in order of authors' birthdates.

In the past many Australian school anthologies used mainly older British (and sometimes Irish and American) poetry. No other English-speaking country was commonly included. This was due partly to a lingering 'colonial cringe' and partly to the high cost of permission fees for living authors. In the worst cases a mere handful of Australian poems were provided as a kind of afterthought.

This sort of mixed anthology, being drawn from five centuries and three continents, covered such a range of experiences that it was not very useful to classify the poems by subject. The artificiality or antiquated nature of much of the language added to the problem. The alternative of classification by style (ballad, sonnet, etc.) is undermined by the fact that much of the best Australian poetry, since the time of Kenneth Slessor, has been written in free verse.

Moreover, the most common reason students fail to respond to poetry is that they do not feel or recognize the experiences it describes. An anthology should be structured to minimize this risk. In general, this is better done by classifying poems according to what they are about rather than how they are shaped. The alternative approach tends to lose the pupil who is not very literary. This is precisely the group most at risk.

It is the great advantage of an anthology containing only poems written in one country—and most of them within the last two centuries—that it can be readily organized to convince even the most unliterary pupil that poems are about real experience. National parochialism, however, is not the aim. The notes and activities at the end of each section suggest comparisons with the major poets of other English-speaking countries, and not merely with those of Britain and the United States. There are also cross-references to *Seven Centuries of Poetry in English* (ed. J. Leonard, OUP, 1987) which draws on poets from many countries, and to *The New Oxford Book of Australian Verse* (chosen by Les A. Murray, OUP, 1986).

This anthology reveals how the English language, and the people who wrote and spoke it, adapted (or were adapted to) the most alien continent they ever conquered. It is a story that does not lead to a happy ending or, indeed, to any single ending. Migrant poetry, confessional poetry, feminist poetry, and confident vernacularism are all equally legitimate endings, or progress reports. Hence the anthology is divided into sections, each focusing on a single issue. Collectively they will give the student a working knowledge of the major elements of Australian poetry to date. It is true the experienced reader needs no such artificial structure, but it is clear that beginners do. Later they may look back from the heights and smile at the rungs by which they climbed. Nonetheless, a good final-year class should be versatile enough to take poems as they find them; and there are many poems, especially in the later sections, that sprawl across several categories. The notes at the end of each section also suggest other ways of linking poems from different sections; and the index of poets makes it easy to follow the work of a major poet like Judith Wright or Gwen Harwood through several sections.

FREE VERSE

Free verse is a special issue that receives a section to itself. Its introduction early in this century did more than any other change to alienate the traditional readers of poetry. Many critics and anthologists believed or hoped it would run its course and pass away; but today it has become the dominant form in English-speaking countries, and an increasing number of readers have come to accept and like good free verse.

Yet it is still almost impossible to find a coherent account of what it is, how it works, or why most poets have chosen to use it. No amount of working up to free verse through study of couplets, ballads and sonnets can substitute for this understanding. For lack of it, teachers are sometimes left feeling a little lost when the pupil asks some perfectly reasonable question like 'What's the difference between free verse and prose?' or 'How do you know when to end a line?'. Both the Traditional Verse and the Free Verse sections suggest answers to these questions, and provide material for further investigations.

SELECTION OF POEMS AND POETS

Some anthologists prefer to reduce the complexities of twentieth century styles, and offer senior students simplified poems—sometimes little more than creative writing exercises—for study. I have rejected this approach, and assumed that students must have the best. I have also asked of each poem: is this likely to interest, and excite, and also extend the imagination of an adolescent reader? Hence some poets, like Michael Dransfield, receive more space than they might in an anthology selected purely on merit. I have also asked myself if some interesting discussion is likely to come out of each poem included. I have favoured poems which express the main themes of Australian history, geography and society, and have regretfully passed over many excellent poems which are perhaps a little too private or self-contained, or depend too fully on adult experiences, to be ideal for teaching purposes.

Where merit was equal I have tried to give preference to more contemporary poems, remembering that older poems are well represented in older anthologies. Names such as Wright, Hope, Dawe, Murray, Harwood, Dobson, Campbell and others inevitably dominate an anthology chosen on merit, but newer voices, such as those of Dransfield, Gray, Llewellyn, Page, Alexopoulos, Kefala, Hart, Fahey, Giles and Brett, are also to be heard. I regret that Bruce Dawe's contractual arrangements allow only six of his poems to appear in a given anthology.

I am well aware that 'new' poems initially demand more effort than those old favourites for which the teacher may need to do little more than polish up last year's notes, but I believe the new pieces here will soon enthuse both teachers and students, and that many will soon themselves become old favourites.

The anthology includes a number of regional poems. All have been selected on merit. (A good anthology is a meritocracy, not a house of representatives.) They will give students in most areas a taste of the satisfactions of having one's own local poetry, as well as the possible struggle of having to deal with someone else's hometown references.

Much of the most exciting and accessible Australian poetry has appeared in the last two or three decades. Between 1970 and 1980, for instance, over 200 Australian poets published well over 400 books of verse. Unfortunately the best work was often lost to sight in an avalanche of mediocre poetry made available by new and cheaper printing technologies. The years after 1970 are an area into which many teachers have made their own somewhat haphazard forays. There are as yet few anthologies to mark the way, and those which have appeared have often been uncritical or contained material unsuitable for schools. One problem is that young poets had few sources of advice; hence even the better poems often contain unintelligible lines which are simply blunders by the poet. Such poems can be risky in the classroom. They may demoralize the student who has just begun to believe he or she could read poetry; and they may embarrass the teacher who is unable to explain them.

Yet the alternative of sticking to safe poems in the older anthologies is no longer acceptable. In the 1970s Australian schools discovered Bruce Dawe, and by the early 1980s Les Murray. Since then many other talented poets of both sexes and of many different beliefs, styles, backgrounds and personalities have emerged, and can no longer be ignored. Female experience, migrant experience, and traditional Aboriginal culture, to name only three crucial areas, demand proper attention. And some poets of an older generation, like A. D. Hope, have gone on writing powerfully into the 1980s. What is needed is a general anthology that includes both the older and younger contemporary poets. Teachers and students alike deserve access to the poetry of their own time.

How then to design an anthology that is mainly 'gold'? One answer is obvious: ask the teachers. In the preparation of this anthology, teachers were asked to send in their own favourite classroom-tested poems other than standard anthology pieces. Many of these new favourites are included here.

Notes, Activities and Other Features

For each section I have suggested certain possible activities which the teacher may use or ignore at will. In devising these I have used my own experience as a working poet. Texts are viewed not as flawless or mysteriously unimprovable masterpieces but as compromises between what the author wanted to say and what the language and culture of the time allowed him or her to think or say. The questions suggested for discussion will occasionally imply serious faults—obscurity, unintended ambiguities, clumsy compromises—in some poems. This approach will benefit those courses which include a creative writing strand.

The preface entitled 'To the Reader' offers some ideas which, while not new to the teacher, may help to overcome obstacles and put poetry in a new light for the student.

Allusions and references are a special problem for students of poetry. Even the most intelligent adolescent tends to have a smaller range of general knowledge than an adult. If the students are one day to begin reading modern poetry on their own, and for their own pleasure without depending on the teacher, then they need every help. I have tried to solve this with a system of notes. It should not be assumed that the information to be found in them is all that might usefully be known about the points annotated. Though the anthology is designed primarily for use in the later years of secondary school in Australia, I have kept in mind that it may also be used in tertiary courses in Australian literature. I have taken especial pains with contemporary poems, knowing that some teachers will be meeting them for the first time, and will have no inherited body of knowledge from their own student days. Factual explanations and glosses can remove many barriers; and I believe they can do no harm provided one remembers that the poetry is often in the part you can't explain, and that no two people respond to a text in quite the same way.

Difficulties of interpretation (as opposed to factual allusions) are often answered only by implication, or by some indication of a direction in which to look. This has the advantage of not specifying correct or 'official' answers, which may stultify individual response. Poetry as a school subject is like sex education: we seek to facilitate, not intrude.

The sections may be studied in any order. Some teachers may wish to begin with the major issues of style and tone (Free Verse, Traditional Verse, Vernacular). Others may wish to follow historical order, or at least to get the story moving with European Contact. Others again may be more interested in following up particular authors, or poems that relate to art, or landscape, and so on. The anthology offers the teacher maximum flexibility and independence, but with a structure to fall back on if desired.

Throughout the notes, a single asterisk (*) beside a title or list of titles indicates poems which can be found in *The New Oxford Book of Australian Verse*, chosen by Les A. Murray, Oxford University Press, 1986. A dagger (†) indicates poems in *Seven Centuries of Poetry in English*, edited by John Leonard, Oxford University Press, 1987. Most of the poems recommended as possible 'poems for further study' will be found in these two anthologies.

Useful anthologies containing recent verse include *The Penguin Book of Modern Australian Verse* (edited by H. P. Heseltine, 1981), *The Penguin Book of Australian Women Poets* (edited by Susan Hampton and Kate Llewellyn, 1986), *The Penguin Book of Contemporary British Verse* (edited by Blake Morrison and Andrew Motion, 1982), *The Golden Apples of The Sun* (edited by Chris Wallace-Crabbe, Melbourne University Press, 1981), *Cross Country* (edited by John Barnes and Bruce McFarlane, Heinemann, 1984), and *The Heritage of Australian Poetry* (edited by Geoffrey Dutton, Currey, rev. 1984). *The Younger Australian Poets* (edited by Robert Gray and Geoffrey Lehmann, Hale & Iremonger, 1983) attempts to chart the work of younger Australian poets up to about 1982. Useful articles and information on many themes and authors can be found in *The Oxford Companion to Australian Literature*.

Mark O'Connor

1

EUROPEAN CONTACT

When groups of black and white men confronted each other near what is now Sydney in 1788 they did so as proud equals. Even in military power they were surprisingly well matched, since the spears of stone-age warriors were often quicker and more reliable than the slow-firing muskets of the British marines. Neither race could understand the other's culture or language. Les Murray's 'The Conquest' captures this moment of equal status when Governor Phillip 'proffers cloth and English words', and the tribesmen 'defy him in good Dhuruwal' (their native language).

The balance did not last long. The Aboriginal tribes were quite unprepared for the British landing which was the inevitable result of increasing foreign interest in Australia. Ships from Japan, China, and Portugal may have explored Australia centuries earlier, and Macassan fishermen from Indonesia certainly visited northern Australia each year. By the early seventeenth century Dutch captains had mapped and sometimes landed on the barren west coast of Australia, which they knew as the South Land or New Holland. Their merchant ships came to use it as a navigational aid, turning north when they sighted Australia en route to Indonesia.

Events such as these had not changed Australia. In 1788 Governor Phillip arrived at Sydney Harbour with high ideals, fretful troops, and a fleet of ships laden with convicts. It was a scene that was to be repeated at other landing spots which today are major cities. Australia, that vast time capsule, was at last to be conquered and 'civilized'.

The Conquest

Phillip was a kindly, rational man:
Friendship and Trust will win the natives, Sir.
Such was the deck the Governor walked upon.

One deck below, lieutenants hawked and spat.
One level lower, and dank nightmares grew.
Small floating Englands where our world began.

And what was trust when the harsh dead swarmed ashore
and warriors, trembling, watched the utterly strange
hard clouds, dawn beings, down there where time began,

so alien the eye could barely fix
blue parrot-figures wrecking the light with change,
man-shapes digging where no yam roots were?

The Governor proffers cloth and English words,
the tribesmen defy him in good Dhuruwal.
Marines stand firm, known warriors bite their beards.

Glass beads are scattered in that gulf of style
but pickpockets squeal, clubbed in imagination
as naked Indians circle them like birds.

They won't Respond. They threaten us. Drive them off.
In genuine grief, the Governor turns away.
Blowflies form trinkets for a harsher grief.

As the sickness of the earth bites into flesh
trees moan like women, striplings collapse like trees—
fever of Portsmouth hulks, the Deptford cough.

It makes dogs furtive, what they find to eat
but the noonday forest will not feed white men.
Capture some Natives, quick. Much may be learned

indeed, on both Sides. Sir! And Phillip smiles.
Two live to tell the back lanes of his smile
and the food ships come, and the barracks rise as planned.

And once again the Governor goes around
with his Amity. The yeasts of reason work,
triangle screams confirm the widening ground.

No one records what month the first striped men
mounted a clawing child, then slit her throat
but the spear hits Phillip with a desperate sound.

The thoughtful savage with Athenian flanks
fades from the old books here. The sketchers draw
pipe-smoking cretins jigging on thin shanks

poor for the first time, learning the Crown Lands tune.
The age of unnoticed languages begins
and Phillip, recovering, gives a nodded thanks.

McEntire speared! My personal huntsman, Speared!
Ten Heads for this, and two alive to hang!
A brave lieutenant cools it, bid by bid,

to a decent six. The punitive squads march off
without result, but this quandong of wrath
ferments in slaughters for a hundred years.

They couldn't tell us how to farm their skin.
They camped with dogs in the rift glens of our mind
till their old men mumbled who the stars had been.

They had the noon trees' spiritual walk.
Pathetic with sores, they could be suddenly not,
the low horizon strangely concealing them.

A few still hunt way out beyond philosophy
where nothing is sacred till it is your flesh
and the leaves, the creeks shine through their poverty

or so we hope. We make our conquests, too.
The ruins at our feet are hard to see.
For all the generous Governor tried to do

the planet he had touched began to melt
though he used much Reason, and foreshadowed more
before he recoiled into his century.

Les A. Murray

Child with a Cockatoo

Portrait of Anne, daughter of the Earl of Bedford,
by S. Verelst

'Paid by my lord, one portrait, Lady Anne,
Full length with bird and landscape, twenty pounds
And framed withal. I say received. Verelst.'

So signed the painter, bowed, and took his leave.
My Lady Anne smiled in the gallery
A small, grave child, dark-eyed, half turned to show
Her five bare toes beneath the garment's hem,
In stormy landscape with a swirl of drapes.
And, who knows why, perhaps my lady wept
To stand so long and watch the painter's brush
Flicker between the palette and the cloth
While from the sun-drenched orchard all the day
She heard her sisters calling each to each.
And someone gave, to drive the tears away,
That sulphur-crested bird with great white wings,
The wise, harsh bird—as old and wise as Time
Whose well-dark eyes the wonder kept and closed.
So many years to come and still, he knew,
Brooded that great, dark island continent
Terra Australis.

                    To those fabled shores
Not William Dampier, pirating for gold,
Nor Captain Cook his westward course had set
Jumped from the longboat, waded through the surf,
And clapt his flag ashore at Botany Bay.
Terra Australis, unimagined land—
Only that sulphur-crested bird could tell
Of dark men moving silently through trees.
Of stones and silent dawns, of blackened earth
And the long golden blaze of afternoon.
That vagrant which an ear-ringed sailor caught
(Dropped from the sky, near dead, far out to sea)
And caged and kept, till, landing at the docks,
Walked whistling up the Strand and sold it then,
The curious bird, its cynic eyes half-closed,
To the Duke's steward, drunken at an inn.

And he lived on, the old adventurer,
And kept his counsel, was a sign unread,
A disregarded prologue to an age.
So one might find a meteor from the sun
Or sound one trumpet ere the play's begun.

Rosemary Dobson

From *Five Visions of Captain Cook*

Cook was a captain of the Admiralty
When sea-captains had the evil eye,
Or should have, what with beating krakens off
And casting nativities of ships;
Cook was a captain of the powder-days
When captains, you might have said, if you had been
Fixed by their glittering stare, half-down the side,
Or gaping at them up companionways,
Were more like warlocks than a humble man—
And men were humble then who gazed at them,
Poor horn-eyed sailors, bullied by devils' fists
Of wind or water, or the want of both,
Childlike and trusting, filled with eager trust—
Cook was a captain of the sailing days
When sea-captains were kings like this,
Not cold executives of company-rules
Cracking their boilers for a dividend
Or bidding their engineers go wink
At bells and telegraphs, so plates would hold
Another pound. Those captains drove their ships
By their own blood, no laws of schoolbook steam,
Till yards were sprung, and masts went overboard—
Daemons in periwigs, doling magic out,
Who read fair alphabets in stars
Where humbler men found but a mess of sparks,
Who steered their crews by mysteries
And strange, half-dreadful sortilege with books,
Used medicines that only gods could know
The sense of, but sailors drank
In simple faith. That was the captain
Cook was when he came to the Coral Sea
And chose a passage into the dark.

How many mariners had made that choice
Paused on the brink of mystery! 'Choose now!'
The winds roared, blowing home, blowing home,
Over the Coral Sea. 'Choose now!' the trades
Cried once to Tasman, throwing him for choice
Their teeth or shoulders, and the Dutchman chose
The wind's way turning north. 'Choose, Bougainville!'
The wind cried once, and Bougainville had heard
The voice of God, calling him prudently
Out of the dead lee shore, and chose the north,
The wind's way. So, too, Cook made choice,
Over the brink, into the devil's mouth,
With four months' food, and sailors wild with dreams
Of English beer, the smoking barns of home.
So Cook made choice, so Cook sailed westabout,
So men write poems in Australia.

Kenneth Slessor

The Kangaroo

mixtumque genus, prolesque biformis

Virgil, *Aeneid VI*

Kangaroo, Kangaroo!
Thou Spirit of Australia,
That redeems from utter failure,
From perfect desolation,
And warrants the creation
Of this fifth part of the Earth,
Which should seem an after-birth,
Not conceiv'd in the Beginning
(For GOD bless'd His work at first,
And saw that it was good),
But emerg'd at the first sinning,
When the ground was therefore curst;—
And hence this barren wood!

Kangaroo, Kangaroo!
Tho' at first sight we should say,
In thy nature that there may
Contradiction be involv'd,
Yet, like discord well resolv'd,
It is quickly harmoniz'd...

Thy fore half, it would appear,
Had belong'd to some 'small deer',
Such as liveth in a tree;
By thy hinder, thou should'st be
A large animal of chace,
Bounding o'er the forest's space;—
Join'd by some divine mistake,
None but Nature's hand can make—
Nature, in her wisdom's play,
On Creation's holiday.

For howsoe'er anomalous,
Thou yet art not incongruous,
Repugnant or preposterous.
Better-proportion'd animal,
More graceful or ethereal,
Was never follow'd by the hound,
With fifty steps to thy one bound.
Thou can'st not be amended: no;
Be as thou art; thou best art so.

When sooty swans are once more rare,
And duck-moles the Museum's care,
Be still the glory of this land,
Happiest Work of finest Hand!

Barron Field

NOTES

'The Conquest'
st. 2: What do these deck-levels suggest about British society?
st. 3: Aborigines often mistook whites for the pallid ghosts of their own dead, and tried to welcome them.
st. 4: Which race is looking at which?
st. 5: **Dhuruwal**: The **Dh** stands for a voiced *th* sound like the one in English *this,* as opposed to the true or unvoiced *th* sound as in *thick* or *thistle.*
st. 12: **striped men**: Why are the convicts so called?
st. 14: **Crown Lands tune**: i.e. the notion that their land belonged to the British government which could sell it to private individuals
st. 15: **My personal huntsman**: What does this suggest about Phillip's attitudes?
st. 16: **quandong**: (pron. quondong) a bright red native stone-fruit sometimes fermented to give alcohol
st. 21: **his century**: the eighteenth century or Age of Reason
Companion Piece: Murray's long poem 'Immigrant Voyage' deals with the experiences of more recent immigrants to Australia.

'Child with a Cockatoo'
The sulphur-crested cockatoo's range includes the north-eastern Australian coast from Darwin eastward to NSW and then as far south and west as Adelaide.

From **'Five Visions of Captain Cook'**
krakens... nativities... warlocks... daemons... sortilege: The new science of navigation seemed no different from magic to the ordinary sailors.
Class Activity: Research the history and associations of these words in the largest dictionary you can find. How much does this knowledge add to your reading of the poem?
chose the wind's way: Earlier navigators, by following the winds, had largely missed the fertile east coast of Australia.

'The Kangaroo'
mixtum genus prolesque biformis: 'mixed race and compound offspring' ... **animal of chace** and **followed by the hound**: The British upper classes had a passion for hunting. **duck-moles the Museum's care**: i.e. when black swans and platypuses have been almost shot out.

ACTIVITIES

1   Which themes or ideas are common to one or more poems in this section? Can you divide the poems clearly into positive and negative views of European contact?

2 A class of foreign students writes to you saying that they are studying one of the poems in this section, but can't understand it, adding 'Perhaps we just don't know enough about Australia'. Write back to them, explaining whatever they would need to know.

3 Divide into groups and read Murray's 'The Conquest' carefully. Try to work out the main historical events, or supposed events, to which he refers. What are the stages by which the truce between the English and the Aborigines breaks down? In which lines does Murray present events from the Aboriginal view, and in which from the English? Make a list of any points you feel you still need to find out about in order to understand the poem completely. Then see if other groups, your teacher, or reference books can supply the answers.

4 'The learned judge's poem tell us more about the limits of his traditional education than about the kangaroo.' Is this a fair assessment of 'The Kangaroo'?

5 **Library Project**: Divide into groups, each of which investigates the opening chapters of one of the standard histories of Australia. Can you identify the episodes Murray picks out? Find out how similar to Murray's is their account of Governor Phillip's character, and of black–white relationships in 1788–89. Can you detect any differences between a historian's and a poet's eye for historical events?

6 **Library Project**: Using a good encyclopedia, investigate eighteenth-century attitudes to colonies, 'noble savages', and native peoples, especially in literature and art. Or find out about the resort-town of Bath where Arthur Phillip took a house when he retired from the navy and 'recoiled into his century'.

Relevant poems from other sections

'At an Exhibition of Historical Paintings, Hobart'. Most of Sections 6 and 7.

Poems for further study

*'The Great South Land', Rex Ingamells; 'There is a Place in Distant Seas', Richard Whately; 'Van Diemen's Land', Allen Afterman; 'Five Visions of Captain Cook' (full text); 'Rottnest Island', Nicholas Hasluck; 'Colonial Nomenclature', John Dunmore Lang.

2

THE ABORIGINAL WORLD

The Aborigines have lived in Australia for at least 40,000 years. They had no crops or herds, but were skilled hunters and food gatherers. They lived in small bands, and each band had a territory through which it followed a regular path each year to places where food was abundant in season. For some bands this territory was no more than thirty kilometres across.

Like most nomadic peoples, they were egalitarian, without kings or chiefs. Their society was largely non-competitive, and the social organization involved sharing food and possessions. They gathered food and created objects; but unlike Europeans, they worked only as necessary, not in order to 'get ahead'. The land was their 'spirit country', and they had duties to it—for instance to participate in ceremonies that they believed kept the world going and animals and plants reproducing. They commonly practised birth control or infanticide, and rarely suffered from famine. In 1788 their lives were probably easier and less laborious than those of the average European peasant.

There was no single Aboriginal nation, or language, or religion. Instead there were hundreds of 'tribes', of languages, and of sacred legend-cycles or 'Dreamings'. Yet the various Aboriginal peoples had much in common.

For instance, their world, unlike ours, was not global or national but overwhelmingly local. They knew their territory intimately, and where to find food, water, and shelter in it. An Aboriginal might spend a lifetime gathering knowledge about an area we would drive across in half an hour today without remembering or noticing anything. Their songs and legends—like those of the ancient Greeks, and like the stories of the Old Testament—are full of local place names. To the Aborigines names were half magic. To name a place or a person was, in a way, to conjure them up.

They put great energy into their religious ceremonies, which were bound up with territory. They generally believed, as old Jilligan puts it in 'Lament for the Drowned Country', that 'only spirit can make country', and that not only the shape of the land but the laws and customs by which people should live had been laid down forever by ancestral spirits. Most tribes believed the world was made not by a single god, but by a number of these ancestral creation-spirits during the primal creation period, the so-called 'Dreamtime'. For instance, a water-filled rock-hole in the desert might be the work of the great Rainbow Serpent, who had created it with a flick of his tail back in the Dreamtime. Their land was an intricate pattern of sacred and significant places. (A Christian, a Jew, or a Muslim might get something of this sense today by living in a place like Jerusalem.) They often believed in re-incarnation.

The Aborigines' songs, like the 'Song Cycle of the Moon-Bone' were never written down. Just as the story of the Trojan War was preserved in ancient Greece for something like 500 years before people discovered writing, so the great Aboriginal songs were memorized and passed down.

They are often secret—indeed, people have been speared for revealing them—and anonymous; yet they may belong to particular persons or groups. They are not poems for the page, but songs designed to accompany ceremonial dancing and sometimes the hypnotic music of clap-sticks or didgeridoo. Songs of many regions have been lost when the last people who knew them by heart died out. Stripped to bare words in a white man's book, they are only shadows of themselves, but still powerful. As well as the major song-cycles, there are also shorter, more personal, and non-sacred kinds of song.

When you first encounter traditional Aboriginal songs, you will find you have to work hard at understanding them because they contain so many unfamiliar names and ideas. After working through two or three, the next ones will be surprisingly easy.

Today, Aborigines have begun to write poems for the page, and often directly in English. Such poems often express anger and regret at what Aborigines have suffered in the past two centuries.

When white settlers first moved into an area, they usually took over the wells or springs, and restricted the Aborigines' access to essential food and shelter areas and to their sacred sites. Once the whites were dominant, Aborigines who tried to resist were usually 'dispersed' or massacred by the police. Unable to follow their traditional migrations through land that was increasingly blocked by farms, they were reduced to hangers-on of white settlements. In their humiliation they often took heavily to alcohol. Mary Durack's 'Lament for the Drowned Country' gives a vivid sense of what it meant to one Aboriginal woman to be deprived of the lands which were the centre of her world.

More recent humiliations came early in the twentieth century when Aborigines, who by then were regarded as a social nuisance, were rounded up in several states and moved forcibly to camps on islands or in remote areas. There they lost contact with their spirit country; and, because they had to live with Aborigines from many other language-groups, the children often forgot their real languages in favour of Pidgin-Creole or English. Pidgin is not 'bad English' but one of the 'unnoticed languages' of Australia. Until recently most communication between blacks and whites took place in some form of it.

Unfortunately, as a result of having mainly each other to talk to, the Aborigines developed special kinds of Pidgin-influenced English that most non-Aborigines have trouble understanding. This means that English-speaking Aborigines today often suffer the same language problems as migrants. Even as late as 1980, much of the best poetry in English about Aboriginal experience was not by Aborigines but by Europeans. However, this is rapidly changing.

After the second world war, the Aborigines suffered a more subtle kind of persecution, as white Australians sought to populate what they perceived as an empty continent by inviting in European immigrants. Unlike the Aborigines, the migrants were soon offered Australian citizenship, while Aborigines were divested of still more of their lands, especially in the north. In 1967 a referendum granted the Aborigines Australian citizenship. Since then, in some northern areas they have become a political force, and have regained parts of their traditional lands that had remained with the Crown.

Lament for the Drowned Country ✩

You hear them kids over there laugh this old woman?
'She mad, old Maggie. She sit there fishing all day—
talk to myself and when she got a catch she let him go.
We *seen* her let'em go.
Mad Maggie! Mad Maggie! Poor old *Jilligan, Numbajina,*
Mad Maggie. You look now—she let that fish go...

They can laugh at me, old Maggie, old *Jilligan*—
Numbajina skin woman belong *Mirriwung* tribe.
I don't expect young people understand—
not these days—understand. They got different singing—
all that pop-song—good too! I like'm too.
And all that cowboy picture—Red Indian fella...
Well that all right. That good too. When I been young girl
I ride like cowboy with them cattle, all same man—
only nothing Indian—nothing feather. Aboriginal different.
He only sing out 'Yakai! Yakai!' Like-a-that.
Djoalung—blackfellow people—more quiet people—my people.
I got to remember that *Djoalung*, that dreamtime people
I got to remember *Moolarli, Bilbilji, Yarralong,*
I got to remember *Beermun, Gudwirri*—big spirit song men.
I got to talk them old fellas—send 'em that message.

I sit along river coming down from my born country.
That heart place! I got to talk to that water.
I got to tell that fish: 'You go back—go back now—
talk strong my country. You tell him that spirit can't leave 'em.
You tell him—Wait! Hang on! *This not the finish*!
Bilbilji, grasshopper fella on top that mountain—
you tell him: Don't go away. You tell him my old man
still got him that corroboree where him lift him wing
Brrr! Brrr! Brrr! He keep that corroboree—can't lose'm'.
Moolarli—Oooo—strong fellow that one for making country.
All that good spring water for wallaby, cattle, everything—
Moolarli make'm. You know that old station waterhole?

In-bulling-burry we call'm. Whiteman call'm *Argyle*.
Well, that where 'im come from first time. Nothing whiteman
when *Moolarli* jump up from waterhole, move round in
      whirlwind
like helicopter. (*You-eye*, he got that helicopter first time—
before whiteman). He got spear like lightning—flash one—like
      fire.

All right, one day he come along—only billabong that time—
nothing river. He see old Jabiroo alonga water—
fishin', fishin', fishin',—gobble'm up, gobble'm up.
He talk: 'Yakai! Old Jabiroo, my friend, gooday!'
Jabiroo don't talk nothing. He just go gobble'm, gobble'm.
He don't talk properly: 'Yakai, my friend *Moolarli*, my mate.
You come now, must be hungry, you tuck out fish, we split'm'.
No, 'im don't talk nothing. Just go on tuck in, gobble'm up,
gobble'm up.

Well *Moolarli* know that not properly way, blackfella law.
Man can't fill'm up own stomach, 'nother fella go hungry.
Man got to think about 'nother fella first time. *Moolarli* talk:
'I teach this Jabiroo lesson. He got to learn sometime!
All right—you know Moolarli got that spear—that lightning?
Well, he pick'm up and he chuck'm—wheew! crackin' like thunder
and that range behind billabong come tumble down, make way for
        gorge
for river and he talk: 'Come on you fish, turtle, everysing,
you can go now, you free. That Jabiroo fella can't catch you,
you can swim away now down to salt water coast country'.
Then he talk along salt water crocodile: 'You can come up now,
camp on river, sleep in that shade place along paperbark'.
My people reckon we can't play round with country.
Only spirit can make him. That dangerous business.

Well, whiteman got different way from blackfella. He reckon:
'No, we don't want spirit. We got *ingineer*. Clever fella properly.
We got plenty man, tomahawk, truck, tractor, dynamite.
WHOOSH! We seen that big smoke come up. Everysing—
ground, tree, rock, shake like the finish coming.
Bird sing out—Carrr! Carrr! Carrr! Cattle, horse, kangaroo,
fright—gallop, gallop, nobody can't stop 'em.
By'n'bye, when 'im settle down—no more mountain that side—
no more goanna dreaming place. All that finish'.

Well, *Moolarli* got only *one spear* when he make that gorge first
        time.
He push that storm water down long way, away along coast.
He don't want to drown my country—(my born country).
Before, when I catch a fish, I cook 'em straight away,
I call my family: 'You come now! We got good tucker!'
Only now, today, when I take away hook I don't hurt 'im.
He go 'flap-flap' in my hand and I talk this way:

'You go back up there, that old station—Argyle station—
(poor fella my old boss, my old missus. Nothing left that house
where I sweep'm every day!) You look out that house—you look
        out
windmill, tank, garden, kitchen, saddle shed.
You look out that store, that camp down there along crossing.
You look out that horse paddock, yard, mustering camp
        everywhere,
plain country ranges. You look out that limestone pocket
where I come from my mummy—that place where I lie along
        coolimon.
(Poor fella my old mummy, pass away long time ago).
You tell him, my country—*me*, old Maggie, old *Jilligan*—
she can't forget 'im, my country, she all day heart-crying.
You tell my country that secret. You tell him old Maggie,
old *Numbagina* woman belong *Mirriwung—she got that dream*.
You tell him *hang on!* Old *Jilligan* see what going happen
long time, might be close up, might be fifty, t'ousand year.
I think them old spirit fellows gone fast asleep'.

Well, one day him going wake up again... *Bilbilji*, that
        grasshopper,
that locust, he wake up on top that high place, that mountain,
and you hear'm wing like long time ago, make: Brrr! Brrr! Brrr!
And *Yarralong*, that snake fella (look out all-about
piccaninny spirit) he get fed up too much water.
He stretch himself—ough! ough! ough! then he jump up rainbow,
storm clouds come coming, big, high, everywhere,
thunder hard-talking all around sky.
Then *Moolarli* come along in whirlwind like helicopter,
pick up him spear, that lightning and WHEEW! straight through
that wall, that top-dam place—WHOOSH! like dynamite.
All that flood water go jump through Kangaroo Pocket,
Down that dingo dreaming place, way down past Lomargin,
Push down that water-trap, that bridge close up Bandicoot,
Ivanhoe crossing, *Djigamurri, Bullgoomurri*, that Carlton
        country—
Swoosh down, lose'm in that big salt water.
And that the finish all that *ingineer* business.
Old Maggie, old *Jilligan*, she tell that fish:

'You bring this message my country, down there underneath.
You tell him *hold on*! Some day that dream coming true—
then he can stretch out and dry himself, my country.
He can breathe that air, he can open him up eye.
Bye'n'bye the grass come back again, tree, spinifex,
all them lizard and snake and wallaby, bandicoot, porcupine,
flying fox—all that good bush tucker—everysing come back.
And bird too—big mob brolga—dance like that—
and Jabiroo, emu, cockatoo—poor fella—I watch'm
flyin' over, lookin' down—Carrr! Carrr! What all that water?
What happen this good country? (That born place, my country.)
Little fish, you tell him—*me*, old Maggie, old *Jilligan*
heart-crying my born country. I got him here—
inside my heart, can't lose'm. I got that dream,
that message. You talk my country: Hold on!
Some time you gonna look out that sun again. You gonna
find all that moon and star. You gonna feel that warm wind
     blowing.
You gonna look-out that sky!'

Mary Durack

The Evening Star

From *Song Cycle of the Moon-Bone*

Up and up soars the Evening Star, hanging there in the sky.
Men watch it, at the place of the Dugong and of the Clouds, and of
    the Evening Star.
A long way off, at the place of Mist, of Lilies and of the Dugong.
The Lotus, the Evening Star, hangs there on its long stalk, held by
    the Spirits.
It shines on that place of the Shade, on the Dugong place, and on
    to the Moonlight clay pan...
The Evening Star is shining, back towards Milingimbi, and over
    the Wulamba people...
Hanging there in the distance, towards the place of the Dugong,
The place of the Eggs, of the Tree-Limbs-Rubbing-Together, and
    of the Moonlight clay pan...
Shining on its short stalk, the Evening Star, always there at the
    clay pan, at the place of the Dugong...

There, far away, the long string hangs at the place of the Evening
    Star, the place of the Lilies.
Away there at Milingimbi... at the place of the Full Moon,
Hanging above the head of that Wonguri tribesman:
The Evening Star goes down across the camp, among the white
    gum trees...
Far away, in these places near Milingimbi...
Goes down among the Ngurulwulu people, towards the camp and
    the gum trees,
At the place of the Crocodiles, and of the Evening Star, away
    towards Milingimbi...
The Evening Star is going down, the Lotus Flower on its stalk...
Going down among all those western clans...
It brushes the heads of the uncircumcised people...
Sinking down in the sky, that Evening Star, the Lotus...
Shining on to the foreheads of all those head-men...
On to the heads of all those Sandfly people...
It sinks there into the place of the white gum trees, at Milingimbi.

Wonguri–Mandjigai People
translated by Ronald M. Berndt

We are Going

For Grannie Coolwell

They came in to the little town
    A semi-naked band subdued and silent,
All that remained of their tribe.
They came here to the place of their old bora ground
Where now the many white men hurry about like ants.
Notice of estate agent reads: 'Rubbish May Be Tipped Here'.
Now it half covers the traces of the old bora ring.
They sit and are confused, they cannot say their thoughts:
'We are as strangers here now, but the white tribe are the strangers.
We belong here, we are of the old ways.
We are the corroboree and the bora ground,
We are the old sacred ceremonies, the laws of the elders.
We are the wonder tales of Dream Time, the tribal legends told.
We are the past, the hunts and the laughing games, the wandering
    camp fires.

We are the lightning-bolt over Gaphembah Hill
Quick and terrible,
And the Thunder after him, that loud fellow.
We are the quiet daybreak paling the dark lagoon.
We are the shadow-ghosts creeping back as the camp fires burn
    low.
We are nature and the past, all the old ways
Gone now and scattered.
The scrubs are gone, the hunting and the laughter.
The eagle is gone, the emu and the kangaroo are gone from this
    place.
The bora ring is gone.
The corroboree is gone.
And we are going.'

Oodgeroo of the tribe Noonuccal,
custodian of the land Minjerribah
(formerly Kath Walker)

'Consultation'

Me, mate?
You'll get no views from me!
Where did I ever go?
Who did I ever meet?
What did I ever see?
Nothin' just the old river, the gumtree
The mission. Me seven kids, four grandkids
Blacks gamblin' drunk, fightin', laughin', cryin'
Mostly gamblin'. Playin' 'pups' wild deuces game
Doin' it, risking their twenty cents to try to win thirty
Price of bread, you know. You know, life ain't too bad here
No runnin' water, no fireplaces, huh, no houses even
Jus the kerosene tin and hessian bag humpies.
They say there's 'welfare' for blacks these days
But the mission looks the same to me. Seven I got
An' another one in the barrel—put there by the 'manager'
'Cause his wife cut him short or somethin'
Nothin' changes. I don't ever see nothin' much
An' no-one asked me my view before.

Kevin Gilbert

Shells

Empty people
Empty Hello
Empty How are you?
You might as well know

We're empty inside
We're looking for shells
Looking for fast rides
My living is hell

Finding a click crowd
A way to fit in
I'm grabbing like real mad
Grabbing nothing but wind

Empty people
Empty Hello
Empty How are you?
You might as well know

Selwyn Hughes

Wanna Be White

My man took off yesterday
with a waagin*
He left me and the kids
To be something in this world
Said he was sick of being
black, poor and laughed at
Said he wanted to be white
have better clothes, a flash car
and eat fancy
He said me and the kids
would give him a bad name
because we are black too
So he left with a waagin

Charmaine Papertalk-Green

---

*East coast word for 'white female', derived from 'white gin'.

NOTES

'Lament for the Drowned Country'
The drowned country is the spirit land of the Mirriwung (or Mirriwong) Aboriginal people on the Durack family's Argyle cattle station in north-western Australia. Much of this tribal land has gone under Lake Argyle, which was created by damming the Ord River. The speaker is an old woman, a real person named Jilligan. Numbajina (or Nambidgina) is her 'skin name' (indicating a section of the tribe). The whites have named her Maggie. She is fishing from the riverbank below the lake that drowned her land. **laugh this old woman:** laugh at this old woman. The grammar of Aboriginal English is different from that of standard English. **Woman belong Mirriwung tribe:** a woman of the Mirriwung tribe. See Bruce Shaw, *My Country*, Australian Institute of Aboriginal Studies, 1981, pp. 140–1, 182, 186–7. **Yakai:** a sound used like *coo-ee* to keep in touch with companions in the bush, pronounced yak-aye. In most languages, including Creole and Pidgin English, the so-called 'long-*I*' diphthong of English is written *AI*. **Djoalung:** the Aborigines generally, or their Dreamtime ancestors. **Moolarli, Bilbilji, Yarralong, Beermum, Gudwirri:** mythical spirit figures or ancestral heroes—'big spirit song men'. Moolarli (or Mulali) is a dreamtime figure who created waterholes and other features of the landscape. He also drained the lake or 'billabong' that has since been re-filled by the dam. See Bruce Shaw, *Countrymen*, AIAS, 1986, pp. 133–4. Bilbilji is the grasshopper spirit. The mountain the whites call Mount Misery is sacred to him. Its top is now an island. **You-eye** or **Yu-ai:** yes. **Jabiroo** or **Jabiru:** the spirit ancestor of the Jabiru stork. **Tuck out:** gobble. **'im:** he. **Talk along:** talk to. **'You can come up now, camp on river':** i.e. the salt-water crocodile, which usually occurs only in rivers that reach the coast, will be able to enter the region. **'You go back up there':** i.e. you (the fish) go back upstream to Lake Argyle. **Only spirit can make him** (= **country**): What does Jilligan mean? **Coolimon** or **coolamon:** a bark cradle for an Aboriginal baby. **She got that dream:** She has that link to the Dreamtime, that sense of responsibility to a place. **Yarralong, that snake fella:** Yarralong is the Rainbow Serpent, an important creation spirit which can turn itself into a rainbow, thus making a bridge between the earth and the sky-world. It also guards the spirits of the unborn in the deepest reaches of the Ord River, and can call up cyclones and thunderstorms. Jilligan's words may seem undignified, but she is speaking a foreign language. **All-about:** everybody. **piccaninny spirit:** the unborn spirits waiting to enter the bodies of women. **dingo dreaming place:** the dam area at Dingo Springs, a sacred site. Jilligan hopes Moolarli will repeat his dreamtime feat. **That water-trap, that bridge close up Bandicoot:** i.e. the Ord River Dam causeway, near ('close up') Bandicoot Bar. **Porcupine:** a white countryfolk's term for the echidna or spiny anteater. **You talk my country:** You (the fish that Jilligan is throwing back) talk to my country.

There is a notable reading of this poem by the author on the audio-cassette 'Ted Egan Presents the Kimberleys,' distributed by ABC Bookshops. Background information on the region can be found in Mary Durack's *Kings in Grass Castles* or Phyllis Kaberry's *Aboriginal Woman*.

'The Evening Star' from 'Song Cycle of the Moon-Bone'
For a full translation of this Aboriginal masterpiece and explanation of its implications, see *Oceania*, vol. XIX, no. 1, 1948. The song was collected in 1946–7. See also the article entitled 'Aboriginal Song and Narrative in Translation' in *The Oxford Companion to Australian Literature*.

In the yirija cycle of the Moon-Bone the Moon lived with his sister Dugong in the ancient Dreamtime. They collected Lily and Lotus Roots, symbolically associated with the Evening Star. The Moon eventually travelled out to sea, cast his bone into the water, and after three days climbed up into the sky. Now every month he repeats this: he throws his bone into the sea, where it becomes a nautilus shell, and is born again. In this song the Evening Star is revealed as a Lotus Bloom and a Lily Root, and the string attached to it is the stalk of these plants.

Ngurulwulu people .. western clans .. the uncircumcised people: other tribes to the west, where the Evening Star sets.

'We are Going'
Bora: a bora ring is a circle, usually of stones, where boys are initiated into manhood.

'Shells'
Selwyn Hughes was born at the notorious Palm Island settlement in Queensland. His poems or guitar songs often explore the emptiness that made him an alcoholic for seven years.

'Wanna be White'
Many Aborigines, both full- and mixed-bloods, are torn between two societies.
Companion Piece: †'Telephone Conversation', Wole Soyinka (Nigeria).

ACTIVITIES

1   In groups, work your way through 'Lament for the Drowned Country' trying to make sense of every line. Make a list of any points you would like to know more about. Then, if possible, listen to the poem on tape.

2   **Project:** Research the background to 'Lament for the Drowned Country'. Present a short report on what you discover.

3   **Discussion:** Should Mary Durack have pruned Jilligan's monologue, or do the repetitions make it more effective? Which lines, if any, would you cut out?

4 As 'The Evening Star' is read aloud, write down or draw whatever it makes you think of. Share this instant reaction with your neighbours.

5 Read aloud a section from the Song of Solomon or the Book of Job, preferably one that has plenty of place-names in it, from the King James version of the Bible. What similarities are there with the style of R. M. Berndt's translation? Or between the world of the Moon-Bone and that of the Old Testament?

6 Starting with the articles in *The Oxford Companion to Australian Literature*, research the world of traditional Aboriginal verse, using whatever texts or reference books you can find. See, for example, R. M. Berndt's *Djanggwul* (Routledge and Kegan Paul, 1952) or *Three Faces of Love* (Nelson, 1976).

7 **Library Project:** Investigate the full text of the 'Song Cycle of the Moon-Bone' or of Bill Neidjie's 'Kakadu Man' (Mybrood Publications, 1985), or the work of Kath Walker, Kevin Gilbert, or Jack Davis. Write a brief report on the style and subject matter.

8 **Discussion or essay:** What qualities of the traditional Aboriginal songs have the more recent Aboriginal poets retained and how? *Or* what links can you find between Aboriginal art and Aboriginal poetry?

9 Write a poem inspired or provoked by one of the poems in this section, for example your own 'wanna be' poem.

Relevant poems from other sections

Most of Section 3.

Poems for further study

*'Song Cycle of the Moon-Bone' (full text); the traditional Aboriginal poems in *The New Oxford Book of Australian Verse*, esp. pp. 1–6, 175–9, 208–9, and 239.

†'Rain', 'Who Tests Today', Hone Tuwhare.

3

WHITE ON BLACK

White settlers developed a variety of attitudes to the Aborigines. Sometimes they were terrified of them, and sometimes, like the 'rednecks' of the southern United States, they found it necessary to be violently prejudiced against the blacks, perceiving them as a lazy inferior race whose land they had a right to take and whose religion and culture were so much nonsense. The whites were also curious about the blacks. One reason was that many of them did not feel truly at home in Australia. Their European religion and culture had no special place for the continent, and made it seem a vast, almost featureless space, without sacred places or religious meaning. Many white poets came to envy the blacks their 'inwardness' with the country.

But the settlers did not understand the world of nomadic hunters and gatherers. Some of them imagined that because the Aborigines did not have fixed addresses they must be vagabonds or failures, like English tramps. White society was based on constant hard work, from school to old age, and on the constant increase of population and possessions. To the whites, the animals and trees of Australia were not the representatives of primal ancestor spirits, but resources to be exploited.

The Aborigines had no system of money. They did not understand the European notion that an individual could buy a part of the world and would then have the right to do with it as he or she liked, and to exploit it to make money. Aboriginal society involved exchanging favours. By contrast, white society was based on the system of free enterprise, or capitalism, in which a person could keep for him or her self whatever he or she had acquired by hard work or good fortune.

Since they did not understand the Aborigines, early white poets tended to sentimentalize them, as in 'The Last of his Tribe'. More recent poets have often idealized the Aborigines as innocent victims or gentle conservationists. None of them has quite solved the problem of using Aboriginal legends and place names in English poetry, but they can nowadays expect their readers to understand at least the basics of Aboriginal history and culture.

The Last of His Tribe

He crouches, and buries his face on his knees,
And hides in the dark of his hair;
For he cannot look up to the storm-smitten trees,
Or think of the loneliness there—
Of the loss and the loneliness there.

The wallaroos grope through the tufts of the grass,
And turn to their coverts for fear;
But he sits in the ashes and lets them pass
Where the boomerangs sleep with the spear—
With the nullah, the sling, and the spear.

Uloola, behold him! The thunder that breaks
On the tops of the rocks with the rain,
And the wind which drives up with the salt of the lakes,
Have made him a hunter again—
A hunter and fisher again.

For his eyes have been full with a smouldering thought;
But he dreams of the hunts of yore,
And of foes that he sought, and of fights that he fought
With those who will battle no more—
Who will go to the battle no more.

It is well that the water which tumbles and fills
Goes moaning and moaning along;
For an echo rolls out from the sides of the hills,
And he starts at a wonderful song—
At the sound of a wonderful song.

And he sees through the rents of the scattering fogs
The corroboree warlike and grim,
And the lubra who sat by the fire on the logs,
To watch, like a mourner, for him—
Like a mother and mourner for him.

Will he go in his sleep from these desolate lands,
Like a chief, to the rest of his race,
With the honey-voiced woman who beckons and stands,
And gleams like a dream in his face—
Like a marvellous dream in his face?

Henry Kendall

At Cooloolah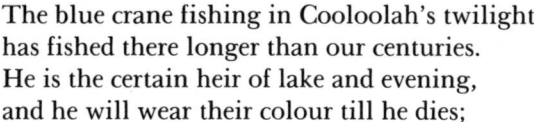

The blue crane fishing in Cooloolah's twilight
has fished there longer than our centuries.
He is the certain heir of lake and evening,
and he will wear their colour till he dies;

but I'm a stranger, come of a conquering people.
I cannot share his calm, who watch his lake,
being unloved by all my eyes delight in
and made uneasy, for an old murder's sake.

Those dark-skinned people who once named Cooloolah
knew that no land is lost or won by wars,
for earth is spirit; the invader's feet will tangle
in nets there and his blood be thinned by fears.

Riding at noon and ninety years ago,
my grandfather was beckoned by a ghost—
a black accoutred warrior armed for fighting,
who sank into bare plain, as now into time past.

White shores of sand, plumed reed and paperbark,
clear heavenly levels frequented by crane and swan—
I know that we are justified only by love,
but oppressed by arrogant guilt, have room for none.

And walking on clean sand among the prints
of bird and animal, I am challenged by a driftwood spear
thrust from the water; and, like my grandfather,
must quiet a heart accused by its own fear.

Judith Wright

Brown, Black and White

Observing that Kanakas pined
For native meats and native sports,
The Cardwell settlers were inclined
To grant a holiday of sorts.

So their brown slaves, in shirts and shorts
Of spotless Sunday cleanness, lined
Up after church, were told the courts
On this occasion wouldn't mind.

Each team was issued with a gun,
Powder and shot—'but don't be lax
And blaze away regardless' (not

Unbiassed counsel!). Off they run
To hunt those unproductive blacks,
The genuine locals, for the pot.

John Manifold

At an Exhibition of Historical Paintings, Hobart

The sadness in the human visage stares
out of these frames, out of these distant eyes;
the static bodies painted without love
that only lack of talent could disguise.

Those bland receding hills are too remote
where the quaint natives squat with awkward calm.
One carries a kangaroo like a worn toy,
his axe alert with emphasized alarm.

Those nearer woollen hills are now all streets;
even the water in the harbour's changed.
Much is alike and yet a slight precise
disparity seems intended and arranged—

as in that late pink terrace's façade.
How neat the houses look. How clean each brick.
One cannot say they look much older now,
but somehow more themselves, less accurate.

And see the pride in this expansive view:
churches, houses, farms, a prison tower;
a grand gesture like wide-open arms
showing the artist's trust, his clumsy power.

And this much later vision, grander still:
the main street, sedate carriages unroll
towards the tentative, uncertain mountain:
a flow of lines the artist can't control—

the foreground nearly breaks out of its frame
the streets end so abruptly in the water...
But how some themes return. A whaling ship.
The last natives. Here that silent slaughter

is really not prefigured or avoided.
One merely sees a profile, a full face,
a body sitting stiffly in a chair:
the soon-forgotten absence of a race...

Album pieces: bowls of brown glazed fruit...
I'm drawn back yet again to those few studies
of native women whose long floral dresses
made them first aware of their own bodies.

History has made artists of all these
painters who lack energy and feature.
But how some gazes cling. Around the hall
the pathos of the past, the human creature.

Vivian Smith

From *The Buladelah-Taree Holiday Song Cycle*

It is the season of the Long Narrow City; it has crossed the Myall.
    It has entered the North Coast,
that big stunning snake; it is looped through the hills, burning all
    night there.
Hitching and flying on the downgrades, processionally balancing
    on the climbs,
it echoes in O'Sullivan's Gap, in the tight coats of the flooded-
    gum trees;
the tops of palms exclaim at it unmoved, there near Wootton.
Glowing all night behind the hills, with a north-shifting glare,
    burning behind the hills;
through Coolongolook, through Wang Wauk, across the
    Wallamba,
the booming tarred pipe of the holiday slows and spurts again;
    Nabiac chokes in glassy wind,
the forests on Kiwarric dwindle in cheap light; Tuncurry and
    Forster swell like cooking oil.
The waiting is buffed, in timber villages off the highway, the
    waiting is buffeted:
the fumes of fun hanging above ferns; crime flashes in strange
    windscreens, in the time of the Holiday.
Parasites weave quickly through the long gut that paddocks shine
    into;
powerful makes surging and pouncing: the police, collecting
    Revenue.
The heavy gut winds over the Manning, filling northward,
    digesting the towns, feeding the towns;
they all become the narrow city, they join it;
girls walking close to murder discard, with excitement, their
    names.
Crossing Australia of the sports, the narrow city, bringing home
    the children.

Les A. Murray

NOTES

See also the article on 'The Aboriginal in Australian Literature', in *The Oxford Companion to Australian Literature.*

'The Last of His Tribe'
like a chief: The whites had a persistent delusion that the senior men of a tribe were chiefs or kings.
Companion Piece: 'Last of His Tribe', Oodgeroo of the tribe Noonuccal, custodian of the land Minjerribah (formerly Kath Walker).

'At Cooloolah'
blue crane: the common Australian white-faced heron. Its main colour is blue-grey.

'Brown, Black and White'
Kanakas: South Sea islanders, imported to work the cane farms. **Cardwell**: a town and port on the tropical east coast of Queesland.

'At an Exhibition of Historical Paintings, Hobart'
absence of a race: Though more Aborigines were killed on the mainland, Tasmania was the only state where full-bloods were exterminated.

From **'The Buladelah-Taree Holiday Song Cycle'**
See the article on this poem in *The Oxford Companion to Australian Literature.* Buladelah and Taree are two towns in hilly forested country a few hours' drive north of Sydney. The Song Cycle is about the annual summer pilgrimage of city people who return 'home' to spend Christmas holidays with their parents and grandparents in the country. As in the 'Song Cycle of the Moon-Bone', each section describes a timeless annual scene. **The Long Narrow City**: the line of cars on the coastal highway. **slows and spurts**: i.e. the holiday traffic causes traffic jams. **Tuncurry, Forster**: larger towns where many people stop for food. **buffed . . . buffeted**: meaning uncertain. **winds over the Manning**: i.e. crosses the Manning River.

ACTIVITIES

1   Compare the extracts from the 'Buladelah-Taree' and the 'Moon-Bone' song cycles. How successfully has Murray imitated the Aboriginal con-cern with place-names and with annual customs? What other features has he imitated?

2   Research the work of early artists like Charles Condor, Eugène von Guérard, Ludwig Becker, Frederick McCubbin and John Glover. Which artist's work comes closest to Vivian Smith's account in 'At an Exhibition of Historical Paintings, Hobart'? A useful book is *White on Black: The Australian Aboriginal Portrayed in Art* by Geoffrey Dutton (Macmillan, 1984).

3 Upon which issues do white poets in this book tend to concentrate, and what do they ignore, when they look at Aborigines? Are there some points they make better than the Aboriginal poets do?

4 Write a poem expressing your own thoughts and feelings about Aborigines. If necessary, use one of the poems in this book as a model.

5 Write your own poem about some timeless event in white society —e.g. Christmas Day, the school concert, speech day, the grand final, the picnic races, election day, Anzac Day.

6 Look up Judith Wright's 'Bora Ring' and compare it with 'At Cooloolah' as two attempts to convey similar thoughts. Which is the better, and why? Write and deliver a short talk (200 words) in defence of your view.

7 **Essay:** Compare 'The Last of his Tribe' with 'Brown, Black and White', and 'At an Exhibition of Historical Paintings, Hobart'. Which makes you feel the most, and how does it do so?

8 Divide into groups, and discuss how the poems you have read have affected the way you think and feel about Aborigines. Prepare a brief group report to present to the class.

Poems for Further Study

*'Garchooka, the Cockatoo', Rex Ingamells; 'Boomerang', William Hart-Smith; 'Deep Well', Roland Robinson

4

BECOMING A NATION

Early British society in Australia was an unstable blend of convicts, ex-convicts, guards, administrators, and free settlers. In many ways it was a crueller version of the British system of upper and lower classes. Once free persons became the majority, a lively debate about democracy and about allegiance to Britain began.

Many of the settlers and ex-convicts were Irish. Their hatred of the British was based on centuries of oppression in Ireland, even though they were now partners with them in the invasion of Aboriginal lands. The Irish looked not to king and country but to Catholicism and Ireland. The Welsh and the Scots, too, had little reason to love the British. Besides, they had the example of the American colonies which had rebelled and become a democracy, and in Europe the nineteenth century was the age of social reforms and movements of national liberation. Such views were strengthened in Australia by popular poets and ballad writers (often anonymous, like the author of 'Jim Jones') whose verse helped people express their sense of human dignity and of solidarity against oppressors. Bit by bit the rule of the governors gave way to democracy; especially after the British authorities were frightened by the Eureka Rebellion in 1854. In 1901 the Australian colonies triumphantly and peacefully achieved both federation and national independence from Britain.

The tradition of popular poems celebrating mateship and the dignity of labour continued well into the twentieth century. This was because the lives of pioneers and settlers remained ones of poverty and hard labour—often in lonely places, as poems like 'Bullocky Bill' and 'The Shearer's Wife' remind us. If A. B. Paterson had idealized bush life in 'Clancy of the Overflow', Henry Lawson reminded his readers of its harsher realities; and, like later poets such as James McAuley, Lawson often criticized the stupidity and spiritual emptiness of many Australians.

Because popular poems of mateship and democratic feeling are well represented in junior-form anthologies, only a sample are included here. One interesting strain is that of poems attacking the British monarchy. For a nineteenth-century democrat like Henry Lawson, one of the most effective ways to attack those with a more British and aristocratic vision of Australia was to ridicule their 'sacred object', the elderly Queen Victoria.

Yet the cult of the British royal family in Australia has survived democracy and national independence. David Campbell's good-humoured 'The Australian Dream,' though it might not please a solemn monarchist, suggests how far some tensions have relaxed.

During the 1960s it seemed to many Australian writers that the old Oedipal relationship to Britain was merely being replaced with a similar one to the United States. However, in the 1970s and 1980s Australia's culture and politics became more independent and multicultural, though perhaps at the same time more dominated by economics and big business, and more like the rest of the world. The national obsession with sport remained a striking feature of popular culture, though even there the commercial media showed an ability to reshape older patterns.

Jim Jones

O, listen for a moment lads, and hear me tell my tale—
How, o'er the sea from England's shore I was compelled to sail.
The jury said, 'He's guilty, sir,' and says the judge, says he—
'For life, Jim Jones, I'm sending you across the stormy sea;
And take my tip before you ship to join the iron-gang.
Don't be too gay at Botany Bay, or else you'll surely hang—
Or else you'll hang,' he says, says he—'and after that, Jim Jones,
High up upon the gallows-tree the crows will pick your bones—
You'll have no chance for mischief then; remember what I say,
They'll flog the poaching out of you, out there at Botany Bay.'
The winds blew high upon the sea, and the pirates came along,
But the soldiers on our convict ship were full five hundred strong,
They opened fire and somehow drove that pirate ship away.
I'd have rather joined that pirate ship than come to Botany Bay.
For night and day, the irons clang, and like poor galley slaves
We toil, and toil, and when we die must fill dishonoured graves.
But by and by I'll break my chains; into the bush I'll go,
And join the brave bushrangers there—Jack Donohoo and Co.:
And some dark night when everything is silent in the town
I'll kill the tyrants, one and all, and shoot the floggers down:
I'll give the law a little shock; remember what I say,
They'll yet regret they sent Jim Jones in chains to Botany Bay.

Anonymous

The Old Prison

The rows of cells are unroofed,
a flute for the wind's mouth,
who comes with a breath of ice
from the blue caves of the south.

O dark and fierce day:
the wind like an angry bee
hunts for the black honey
in the pits of the hollow sea.

Waves of shadow wash
the empty shell bone-bare,
and like a bone it sings
a bitter song of air.

Who built and laboured here?
The wind and the sea say
—Their cold nest is broken
and they are blown away—

They did not breed nor love.
Each in his cell alone
cried as the wind now cries
through this flute of stone.

Judith Wright

Bullocky Bill

As I came down Talbingo Hill
I heard a maiden cry,
'There's goes old Bill the Bullocky—
He's bound for Gundagai.'

A better poor old beggar
Never cracked an honest crust,
A tougher poor old beggar
Never drug a whip through dust.

His team got bogged on the Five-mile Creek,
Bill lashed and swore and cried,
'If Nobbie don't get me out of this
I'll tattoo his bloody hide.'

But Nobbie strained and broke the yoke
And poked out the leader's eye,
Then the dog sat on the tucker-box
Five miles from Gundagai.

Anonymous

Harry Pearce

I sat beside the red stock route
And chewed a blade of bitter grass
And saw in mirage on the plain
A bullock wagon pass.
Old Harry Pearce was with his team.
'The flies are bad,' I said to him.

The leaders felt his whip. It did
Me good to hear old Harry swear,
And in the heat of noon it seemed
His bullocks walked on air.
Suspended in the amber sky
They hauled the wool to Gundagai.

He walked in Time across the plain,
An old man walking in the air;
For years he wandered in my brain,
And now he lodges here.
And he may drive his cattle still
When Time with us has had his will.

David Campbell

The Shearer's Wife

Before the glare o' dawn I rise
To milk the sleepy cows, an' shake
The droving dust from tired eyes,
Look round the rabbit traps, then bake
The children's bread.
There's hay to stook, an' beans to hoe,
An' ferns to cut in the scrub below.
Women must work, when men must go
Shearing from shed to shed.

I patch and darn, now evening comes,
An' tired I am with labour sore,
Tired o' the bush, the cows, the gums,
Tired, but we must dree for long months more
What no tongue tells.
The moon is lonely in the sky,
Lonely is the bush, an' lonely I
Stare down the track no horse draws nigh,
An' start... at the cattle bells.

Louis Esson

Sweeney

It was somewhere in September, and the sun was going down,
When I came, in search of 'copy', to a Darling-River town;
'Come-and-have-a-drink' we'll call it—'tis a fitting name,
    I think—
And 'twas raining, for a wonder, up at Come-and-have-a-drink.

'Neath the public-house verandah I was resting on a bunk
When a stranger rose before me, and he said that he was drunk;
He apologised for speaking; there was no offence, he swore;
But he somehow seemed to fancy that he'd seen my face before.

'No erfence,' he said. I told him that he needn't mention it,
For I might have met him somewhere; I had travelled round a bit,
And I knew a lot of fellows in the bush and in the streets—
But a fellow can't remember all the fellows that he meets.

Very old and thin and dirty were the garments that he wore,
Just a shirt and pair of trousers, and a boot, and nothing more;
He was wringing-wet, and really in a sad and sinful plight,
And his hat was in his left hand, and a bottle in his right.

His brow was broad and roomy, but its lines were somewhat harsh,
And a sensual mouth was hidden by a drooping, fair moustache;
(His hairy chest was open to what poets call the 'wined',
And I would have bet a thousand that his pants were gone behind).

He agreed: 'Yer can't remember all the chaps yer chance to meet,'
And he said his name was Sweeney—people lived in Sussex-street.
He was campin' in a stable, but he swore that he was right,
'Only for the blanky horses walkin' over him all night.'

He'd apparently been fighting, for his face was black-and-blue,
And he looked as though the horses had been treading on him,
    too;
But an honest, genial twinkle in the eye that wasn't hurt
Seemed to hint of something better, spite of drink and rags and
    dirt.

It appeared that he mistook me for a long-lost mate of his—
One of whom I was the image, both in figure and in phiz—
(He'd have had a letter from him if the chap were living still,
For they'd carried swags together from the Gulf to Broken Hill.)

Sweeney yarned awhile and hinted that his folks were doing well,
And he told me that his father kept the Southern Cross Hotel;

And I wondered if his absence was regarded as a loss
When he left the elder Sweeney—landlord of the Southern Cross.

He was born in Parramatta, and he said, with humour grim,
That he'd like to see the city ere the liquor finished him,
But he couldn't raise the money. He was damned if he could think
What the Government was doing. Here he offered me a drink.

I declined—'*twas* self-denial—and I lectured him on booze,
Using all the hackneyed arguments that preachers mostly use;
Things I'd heard in temperance lectures (I was young and rather
      green),
And I ended by referring to the man he might have been.

Then a wise expression struggled with the bruises on his face,
Though his argument had scarcely any bearing on the case:
'What's the good o' keepin' sober? Fellers rise and fellers fall;
What I might have been and wasn't doesn't trouble me at all.'

But he couldn't stay to argue, for his beer was nearly gone.
He was glad, he said, to meet me, and he'd see me later on;
He guessed he'd have to go and get his bottle filled again,
And he gave a lurch and vanished in the darkness and the rain.

And of afternoons in cities, when the rain is on the land,
Visions come to me of Sweeney with his bottle in his hand,
With the stormy night behind him, and the pub verandah-post—
And I wonder why he haunts me more than any other ghost.

Still I see the shearers drinking at the township in the scrub,
And the army praying nightly at the door of every pub,
And the girls who flirt and giggle with the bushmen from the
      west—
But the memory of Sweeney overshadows all the rest.

Well, perhaps, it isn't funny; there were links between us two—
He had memories of cities, he had been a jackeroo;
And, perhaps, his face forewarned me of a face that I might see
From a bitter cup reflected in the wretched days to be.
I suppose he's tramping somewhere where the bushmen carry
      swags,
Cadging round the wretched stations with his empty tucker-bags:
And I fancy that of evenings, when the track is growing dim,
What he 'might have been and wasn't' comes along and troubles
      him.

Henry Lawson

Ned's Delicate Way

Ned knew I was short of tobacco one day,
  And that I was too proud to ask for it;
He hated such pride, but his delicate way
  Forbade him to take me to task for it.

I loathed to be cadging tobacco from Ned,
  But, when I was just on the brink of it:
'I've got a new brand of tobacco,' he said—
  'Try a smoke, and let's know what you think of it.'

Henry Lawson

From *The English Queen*

(A Birthday Ode)

There's an ordinary woman whom the English call 'the Queen':
They keep her in a palace, and they worship her, I ween;
She's served as one to whom is owed a nation's gratitude;
(May angels keep the sainted sire of her angelic brood!)
The people must be blind, I think, or else they're very green,
To keep that dull old woman whom the English call 'the Queen',
            Whom the English call 'the Queen',
            Whom the English call 'the Queen'—
That ordinary woman whom the English call 'the Queen'.

The Queen has reigned for fifty years, for fifty years and five,
And scarcely done a kindly turn to anyone alive;
It can be said, and it is said, and it is said in scorn,
That the poor are starved the same as on the day when she was
    born.
Yet she is praised and worshipped more than God has ever been—
That ordinary woman whom the English call 'the Queen',
            Whom the English call 'the Queen',
            Whom the English call 'the Queen'—
That cold and selfish woman whom the English call 'the
    Queen'...

Henry Lawson

Wine Tasting

The dead-weight of years crushing down, down,
largely destructive, yet has crushed from these barren lives
a wine we'll call Australian, since no tariff has been paid.
Taste it. Not bitter, but with the dust of the outback
prominent. Slide it around the palate. See with what rosy light
the chandelier blazes through this blood you suckle on.
Consider the delicate
bouquet of revolution
it was a good year for martyrs.
Jan Palach lit up half the silent east with his death agonies
taste the ashes you thought were sediment from long storage it is
      hard
to forget. Remember too the vintners whose feet trod flat the
      grapes,
trod flat the barbwire at Lone Pine so the press could sing,
sing of 'significant advances', of selflessness. Taste it at V. C.
      Corner,
how many heroes then trod flat the fields to grow the grapes you
      think you taste.
An amusing little vintage, you call it, vampires of humanity,
from your penthouse the world is beautiful the filth of streets is far
      below
the dead cannot be smelt unless the wind changes bring you
the sound of death of city solitudes of labourers returning home
      exhausted
from factories you control. You suck their lives away, their spirit,
      an amusing little wine.
They toil that you can celebrate your profits, play aristo with some
      amusing friends
drawn from the endless ranks of profiteers, scuttling from Europe
      to get near the cash,
jetting from Texas to pick up the pennies better men would scorn
      to touch.
It was a good year, you say, the auditors agree; inside a wilderness
      a hermit
listens/the change he speaks of to the world will come; dare you
      face it?

Michael Dransfield

The Australian Dream

The doorbell buzzed. It was past three o'clock.
The steeple-of-Saint-Andrew's weathercock
Cried silently to darkness, and my head
Was bronze with claret as I rolled from bed
To ricochet from furniture. Light! Light
Blinded the stairs, the hatstand sprang upright;
I fumbled with the lock, and on the porch
Stood the Royal Family with a wavering torch.

'We hope,' the Queen said, 'we do not intrude.
The pubs were full, most of our subjects rude.
We came before our time. It seems the Queen's
Command brings only, "Tell the dead marines!"
We've come to you.' I must admit I'd half
Expected just this visit. With a laugh
That put them at their ease, I bowed my head.
'Your Majesty is most welcome here,' I said.
'My home is yours. There is a little bed
Downstairs, a boiler-room, might suit the Duke.'
He thanked me gravely for it and he took
Himself off with a wave. 'Then the Queen Mother?
She'd best bed down with you. There is no other
But my wide bed. I'll curl up in a chair.'
The Queen looked thoughtful. She brushed out her hair
And folded up *The Garter* on a pouf.
'Distress was the first commoner, and as proof
That queens bow to the times,' she said, 'we three
Shall share the double bed. Please follow me.'
I waited for the ladies to undress—
A sense of fitness, even in distress,
Is always with me. They had tucked away
Their state robes in the lowboy; gold crowns lay
Upon the bedside tables; ropes of pearls
Lassoed the plastic lampshade; their soft curls
Were spread out on the pillows and they smiled.
'Hop in,' said the Queen Mother. In I piled
Between them to lie like a stick of wood.
I couldn't find a thing to say. My blood
Beat, but like rollers at the ebb of tide.

'I hope your Majesties sleep well,' I lied.
A hand touched mine and the Queen said, 'I am
Most grateful to you, Jock. Please call me Ma'am.'

David Campbell

NOTES

'Jim Jones'
A common style of anonymous ballad that might be sung by convicts, presumably when out of earshot of their guards.
Botany Bay: the Sydney colony. **Jack Donohoo**: Jack Donohue or Donaghue (1806?–1830), a well-known bushranger of the Sydney region. Phonetic spelling rather than 'printers' spelling' is common, even in semi-official documents, till the early nineteenth century. The reference to Donohue suggests that the ballad was written around 1830.

'Bullocky Bill'
A bullocky was the driver of a bullock-dray. **drug**: dragged. **Five-mile Creek**: a creek five miles from town—quite a distance on a bad track. **Nobbie**: a key bullock in the team. **sat on the tucker box**: There are other versions of this line.
Companion Pieces: 'Bill the Bullock Driver', Henry Kendall; 'The Teams', Henry Lawson; 'Bullocky', Judith Wright.

'Harry Pearce'
walked on air: A common mirage in hot weather.

'The Shearer's Wife'
The wife runs the farm alone, because her husband is away shearing to make money—a common example of rural poverty. **o', an'**: Scottish forms of *of, and.* **stook**: gather and stack in bundles. **dree**: endure (Scottish).

'Sweeney'
The basic rhythm is three unstressed to one stressed syllable. **'wined'**: wind. **phiz**: physiognomy, face. **Gulf**: of Carpentaria. **self-denial**: i.e. not easy. **Visions come to me of Sweeney**: cf. 'visions come to me of Clancy' in A. B. Paterson's 'Clancy of the Overflow'. **army**: the Salvation Army often led the fight against drink.
Discussion: Where does Lawson part company with those whose view is simply that drink causes failure?
Companion Piece: 'The Man I might have been', R. G. Hay.

'Ned's Delicate Way'
Note the natural way the rhymes fall into place. The rhythm is basically anapestic, i.e. two unstressed syllables to one stressed. As in 'Sweeney', Lawson keeps the rhythm irregular enough to sound conversational yet still support the rhymes—a skill lesser poets often lacked.

from **'The English Queen'**
This poem parodies the emptiness and repetitions of the complimentary birthday odes addressed to Queen Victoria. **I ween**: I think (a rhyming tag).

Companion Pieces: 'To Myself June 1855', Charles Harpur; 'Much Distressed', Anonymous; 'The Martyred Democrat', C. J. Dennis; 'The Men who made Australia', Henry Lawson; *'Wellington', Charles Harpur; *'Duke of Buccleuch', J. A. Phelp.

'Wine Tasting'
Jan Palach: a Czech student who fatally set fire to himself in Prague in 1969 in protest against the Russian invasion. **Lone Pine, V. C. Corner**: places where Australians heroically accepted casualties in World War I. **vampires of humanity**: presumably those who control the factories. **change...will come**: perhaps a prophecy that the counter-culture of the 1960s and 1970s would replace industrial capitalism in Australia.
Discussion: What would be meant by calling this poem 'immature'?
Companion Pieces: 'Australia', A. D. Hope; 'Melbourne', Chris Wallace-Crabbe; 'Envoi', James McAuley.

'The Australian Dream'
dead marines: empty bottles. **lowboy**: a kind of low wardrobe. **Jock**: perhaps because Campbell is a Scottish name.

ACTIVITIES

1 **Library Project**: Research the ballad tradition in Australia, and write a short report on its usual themes and styles. How typical is 'Jim Jones'? What impression have the terms and details in the poem been selected to give?

2 Write a prose 'translation' of 'The Old Prison', carefully avoiding such poetic imagery as 'flute', 'breath of ice', 'like an angry bee', but trying to keep in all the facts behind the images. How much is lost in the translation? Could the feeling of the place be captured in less imaginative language?

3 Compare 'Bullocky Bill' and 'Harry Pearce'. Which gives you the strongest sense of a bullocky as a real person, and how is that sense conveyed?

4 Examine 'The Shearer's Wife' line by line and work out why each detail in it has been mentioned. Would the poem be better or worse if written in the third person, or without the Scottish words? Why?

5 **Library Project**: Contrast Lawson's view of country life in 'Sweeney' with that in some of A. B. Paterson's poems.

6 Read 'Sweeney' closely, perhaps in groups, making sure you understand every line. Consult with other groups or your teacher if any lines puzzle you. Then, assuming that the poem is based on a real meeting, write the letter that Lawson might have written to a friend that evening. Try to describe Sweeney's personality exactly.

7 Compare 'Wine Tasting' with 'Outback' (section 18). How well does each substantiate its criticisms of Australians?

8 **Library Project**: Investigate some poems by two or three important 'national' poets from other Commonwealth countries, e.g. Wole Soyinka, A. K. Ramanujan, Derek Walcott, Allen Curnow, Nissim Ezekiel, Margaret Atwood, Irving Layton, Iain Crichton Smith.

9 **Library Project**: Discover the work, in translation, of some foreign twentieth century poet who has helped form the literary tradition of his or her nation, for example, Yevtushenko (Russia), Blazhe Koneski (Macedonia), Yannis Ritsos (Greece), Eugenio Montale (Italy), Pablo Neruda (Chile). Or read the work of twentieth century Russian poets like Mandelstam, perhaps in the translations of Rosemary Dobson and David Campbell.

10 'Sweeney'. Could this poem also be scanned as iambic (see section 10)? If so, how is this double scansion possible?

11 'The English Queen'. Compare the attitudes expressed in the contemporary British poems 'Turns' by Tony Harrison and 'Gardeners' by Douglas Dunn (both in the *Penguin Book of Contemporary British Poetry*, 1982), and those of popular magazine articles on British royalty or aristocrats.

12 **Library Project**: Compare the lives and poetry of Dransfield and of the New Zealand poet James Baxter, and the Canadian Leonard Cohen, as examples of instant popularity. Will their reputations last?

Relevant poems from other sections

Most of sections 5 and 6. 'The Conquest,' 'The Convicts' Rum Song'.

Poems for further study

*'Pieta', 'Their Thoughts Cling', Allen Afterman; 'A Bushranger', Kenneth Slessor; 'A Convict's Tour to Hell', Frank MacNamara; 'The Banks of the Condamine', 'The Stringybark Cockatoo', 'John Gilbert was a Bushranger', 'Click go the Shears', Anonymous; 'The Gravy Train', R. R. Davidson; 'Federation', W. T. Goodge; 'The English Queen' (full text), 'When Your Pants Begin to Go', Henry Lawson; 'The Wind at Your Door', R. D. Fitzgerald; 'My Father's Country', Joyce Lee; 'Terra Australis', Douglas Stewart; 'A Finished Gentleman', Geoffrey Dutton; 'Edna's Hymn', Barry Humphries; 'Country Press', Rosemary Dobson.

†'Middleton's Rouseabout', Henry Lawson; 'Casualty', Seamus Heaney; 'The Inheritance', Kamala Das; 'Background, Casually', Nissim Ezekiel; 'next to of course god america', E. E. Cummings; 'England in 1819', Percy Bysshe Shelley, 'Song—for a' that and a' that', Robert Burns.

5

THE AUSTRALIAN VERNACULAR

A vernacular is the ordinary informal language of a particular place or group of people. It can be contrasted with the more formal and more international English we normally use in writing. The English that you normally speak with schoolfriends or workmates or at home with your family is vernacular.

The Australian vernacular is not necessarily a matter of using slang or what some people call 'bad language', or of being exaggeratedly Australian. It is what feels natural. Saying 'chooks' rather than 'fowls', for instance, or 'migrant' instead of 'immigrant'.

Some poets seem unable to write in the vernacular, and in fact many mediocre poets insist on using an outdated English that is full of obsolete words like *forsooth* and *'neath* and *'tis* and *e're* and *olden*. They do this partly because it lets them fall back on particular rhyming phrases and other tricks of style they have learned from the poets of the past, but it is one of the marks of a major poet to be able to write memorable poetry in the language of his or her own time. Good poets keep an ear out for phrases that can be borrowed from the vernacular, and some write in a style that is almost pure vernacular.

In Australia there has sometimes been a 'colonial cringe' that makes people think poetry has to be written in a special 'British' or 'BBC' tone of voice. Poets like Henry Lawson, Bruce Dawe and Geoff Page have proved this is not so: people can write serious and universal poems in the Australian vernacular. In fact it is an important liberating experience for Australians (just as it is for West Indians or Canadians or Scots or any other English-speaking peoples) to discover poetry that is written for their own accent and speaking voice.

Most vernacular poets in Australia write for a recognizable 'Australian accent'. This often differs more in intonation and accent than in vocabulary from the Queen's English. For instance there is less variation in pitch: the voice does not rise and fall as much, so that the tone seems flatter. Sentences tend to be short and understated.

A vernacular poet needs to understand the special effects and tones of Australian speech—for instance its dry pauses when the voice falls away on some flat statement that suggests a world of unstated meaning.

'Yeah, that'd be right...' or 'Besides that there's meatworks and mines...' or 'I reckoned we were glad / To have him on the side'. You will probably spot other recognizably Australian characteristics in the poems in this section.

Of course not everyone speaks like this. There are many different kinds of English in Australia. They include varieties of British, Irish, Asian, American and cosmopolitan accents, as well as the accents of non-English-speaking migrants and of Aborigines. It would be false and unnatural for many people to use something like Bruce Dawe's vernacular. Perhaps the most important thing is for each poet to find his or her own natural 'voice'—that voice in which, as A. D. Hope has put it, 'All things worth saying may be said'.

There is another kind of colloquial English that we might almost call a vernacular, though it is not truly local. This is a kind of folksy intimate 'hip talk' that we hear all the time in the patter of disc jockeys and of radio and TV commercials. Some people think of it as American, but in fact it is universal. We might describe it as the language of the electronic media when they want to be friendly.

Because this is all around us, some poets have tried hard to use forms of it in poetry. John Jenkins, for instance, produces a delightful parody of advertising con-jargon in his 'You're Great'. Other poets like John Forbes have tried to take it more seriously, and have also imitated the way in which film and TV hurl us from one reality to another so breathlessly that vast tragedies like the Second World War become mere entertainments—'and then a terrific Italian raid begins'. Such poems are not always satirical. Sometimes the poet genuinely envies TV and films their popularity, their immediacy, and their contempt for petty questions of logic and grammar. He or she may try to achieve the same qualities in verse.

Folklore

What are the sights of our town?

Well, there is that skeleton they hang
some nights in the bar of the Rest
and everyone laughing in whispers
the barmaid broke down one time, laughing.
The cord goes up through the ceiling
to the undersprings of the big
white bed in the Honeymoon Suite
and when those bones even jiggle
there's cheers (and a donnybrook once)
and when they joggle, there's whooping
and folk stalking out in emotions
and when they dance—hoo, when they dance!
he knows every tune on the honeymoon
flute, does the hollow-hipped fellow.
There are a few, mind, who drink on
straight through it all. Steady drinkers.
Up over the pub there's the sky
full of stars, as I have reflected
outside, while guiding the course of my
thoughts. Some say there's a larger
cord goes on up there, but I doubt it
I mean
but then I'm no dancer.

Besides that, there's meatworks and mines.

Les A. Murray

Life-Cycle

for Big Jim Phelan

When children are born in Victoria
they are wrapped in the club-colours, laid in beribboned cots,
having already begun a lifetime's barracking.

Carn, they cry, Carn... feebly at first
while parents playfully tussle with them
for possession of a rusk: Ah, he's a little Tiger! (And they are...)

Hoisted shoulder-high at their first League game
they are like innocent monsters who have been years swimming
towards the daylight's roaring empyrean

Until, now, hearts shrapnelled with rapture,
they break surface and are forever lost,
their minds rippling out like streamers

In the pure flood of sound, they are scarfed with light, a voice
like the voice of God booms from the stands
Ooohh you bludger and the covenant is sealed.

Hot pies and potato-crisps they will eat,
they will forswear the Demons, cling to the Saints
and behold their team going up the ladder into Heaven,

And the tides of life will be the tides of the home-team's fortunes
—the reckless proposal after the one-point win,
the wedding and honeymoon after the grand-final...

They will not grow old as those from more northern States grow
        old,
for them it will always be three-quarter-time
with the scores level and the wind advantage in the final term,

That passion persisting, like a race-memory, through the welter of
        seasons,
enabling old-timers by boundary-fences to dream of resurgent lions
and centaur-figures from the past to replenish continually the
        present,

So that mythology may be perpetually renewed
and Chicken Smallhorn return like the maize-god
in a thousand shapes, the dancers changing.

But the dance forever the same—the elderly still
loyally crying Carn... Carn... (if feebly) unto the very end,
having seen in the six-foot recruit from Eaglehawk their hope of
    salvation.

Bruce Dawe

The Breach

I am a policeman
it is easier to make me seem an oaf
than to handle the truth

I came from a coaldust town
when I was seventeen, because there was nothing
for a young fellow there

the Force drew me because of a sense I had
and have grown out of

I said to Ware* once, Harry, you're the best
cop of the lot: you only arrest falls
he was amused

I seem to be making an inventory of my life
but in that house opposite, first floor
there is a breach
and me, in this body I am careful with,
I'm going to have to enter that house soon
and stop that breach
it is a bad one people could fall through
we know that three have
and he's got a child poised

I have struck men in back rooms late at night
with faces you could fall a thousand feet down
and I've seen things in bowls

the trick is not to be a breach yourself
and to stop your side from being one
I suppose

*Ware: Special Sgt. Harry Ware (1897–1970) founder and first officer-
    in-charge of N.S.W. Police Cliff Rescue Squad

the sniper Spiteri, when I was just out of cadets—
some far-west cockies' boys straight off the sheep train
came up with their .303s and offered to help
they were sixteen years old

we chased them away, not doubting for a minute
they could do what they said
bury your silver the day we let that start

now I've said my ideals

Snowy cut, snow he cut...
A razor-gang hood my uncle claims he met
is running through my mind
in Woolloomooloo, wet streets, the nineteen twenties
dear kind Snowy Cutmore

Snowy cuts no more
he was a real breach
also, in our town, I
remember the old hand bowsers, that gentle apop-
poplexy of benzine in the big glass heads
twenty years since I saw them

There's a moment with every man who has started a stir
(even this kind, who'd lap up prayer and fasting)

when he tires of it, wants to put it aside
and be back, unguilty, that morning, pouring the milk

that is the time to separate him from it
if I am very good I'll judge that time
just about right

the ideal is to keep the man and stop
the breach
that's the high standard

but the breach must close

if later goes all right
I am going to paint the roof of our house
on my day off.

Les A. Murray

And a Good Friday Was Had by All

You men there, keep those women back
and God Almighty he laid down
on the crossed timber and old Silenus
my offsider looked at me as if to say
nice work for soldiers, your mind's not your own
once you sign that dotted line Ave Caesar
and all that malarkey Imperator Rex

well this Nazarene
didn't make it any easier
really—not like the ones
who kick up a fuss so you can
do your block and take it out on them
                                        Silenus

held the spikes steady and I let fly
with the sledge-hammer, not looking
on the downswing trying hard not to hear
over the women's wailing the bones give way
the iron shocking the dumb wood.

Orders is orders, I said after it was over
nothing personal you understand—we had a
drill-sergeant once thought he was God but he wasn't
a patch on you

then we hauled on the ropes
and he rose in the hot air
like a diver just leaving the springboard, arms spread
so it seemed
over the whole damned creation
over the big men who must have had it in for him
and the curious ones who'll watch anything if it's free
with only the usual women caring anywhere
and a blind man in tears.

Bruce Dawe

Reverie of a Mum

Here let me rest me feet!
The boys have gone to try
The shooting gallery, the girls
Are off to prospect for boys.
Here let me drop me bundle
Of bulging sample bags,
I was lucky to find this seat
In the shade, away from the noise.
We come on an early bus,
We seen the fruit and the jams,
The handicrafts and the flowers,
Bacon like marble, hams
Big as the side of a palace,
Wheels of golden cheese
Like off one of them olden chariots
From them spectacle films. And Jeez
The cakes done in royal icing!
There was one great galleon—clever!
All icing: sails, decks, ropes,
You could hardly credit. I never
Seen such a cake. It took me
Back to that Spanish Gob
Off the Yankee ship in the war years
And a lying, promising slob
He turned out. Now my eldest, Marie,
Her eyes are funny but,
As hot and black as that little goat's feet
And she's a stuck-up slut.
She's got ideas of the stage now
Since we let her stay on at school
And they chose her for Cleopatra
In that play they done by the pool
In Hyde Park there. It's queer,
You marry and you settle down
Like they say, and you never think
Of the boys who done you brown.
Jeez! When I think of me hair
With frangipanis, and a high
Pompadour style—I used to swing
As if I'd of owned the sky.

There was that night in the Dom.
(I'd tan my kids if they went
Where we used... War-time, but,)
And all around was the scent
Of gabardine coats and hair-oil
And frangipani in the night—
Whispers, rustling, and the giggles
When one Yank shinned up the light
And took out the bulb.... My God
But those boys knew what they wanted.
The whole world turned on velvet.
The sky came down and panted
Like a dog that's been running. Them fig-trees
Rattled that sky in their leaves.
Well, it isn't like that when you settle.
If my hubby knew! Funny though, I grieves
For them boys. Just sometimes. And the Vice Squad
Out on their surf-boat boots
Treading the Moreton Bay fig-leaves....
Fig-leaves! We up and we scoots
With my Spanish Yank having zip trouble,
It was funny giving coppers the slip,
The frangipani night laughed with us
As we dodged through the 'Loo to their ship.
We all took a sickie from the factory
When they sailed—'See youse again'....
Then the grey boys in jungle green come home.
And *that* was my castle in Spain.

Nancy Keesing

You're Great!

From *Read This!*

Welcome to this poem. Why you? Because
you're one of us, and belong here. You
have the right credentials: the taste,
sensibility and above all intelligence
to appreciate and enjoy poetry. Now,
imagine a breast. A shapely, tanned breast.
The sun and beach background is optional,
but I know you'll want it too. You are
driving in your open-necked way, enjoying
the ocean view. You've always recognized
fine Scotch, and mix one in the cocktail
bar of your sedan. It's good and mellow,
like sunlight through an amber windshield.
Very good, you're doing fine. The girl strides
her slim, long-legged way to the beautiful
and easy shoreline. You admire her, the shape
of her tanned breasts beneath her sheer, silky
bikini. Then you smile again in your terrific
way, sure and cool above a new white cravat.
The girl's golden undulations merge into the
smooth dunes rippling in a heat haze,
fading out into the middle distance: a beautiful
shot! Then you throw your car into gear,
accelerating under tremendous power, thinking
of the clear certainty and amazing devices of
the poem. The highway is like a soft rubber
band stretching into sunset. You know just
how good poetry feels now and disappear into the
future; assured, impressed, another great reader!

John Jenkins

NOTES

See also the article on 'Australian English' in *The Oxford Companion to Australian Literature*.

'Folklore'
Rest: perhaps the Travellers Rest, a hotel. **donnybrook:** an all-in fight. Note the dry yet confident way the speaker builds up the comedy, yet how he becomes tongue-tied when he strays onto more serious thoughts at the end.

'Life-Cycle'
Carn: Come on. **League:** Victorian Football League, the 'big league' for Australian Rules in Victoria. **they will not grow old:** a parody of Laurence Binyon's 'For the Fallen'. **Chicken Smallhorn:** a football personality. **like the maize god:** a reference to corn-god mythology as discussed in Sir James Frazer's *The Golden Bough*. **Eaglehawk:** a country town in Victoria.
Discussion: How much of Dawe's poem might apply to any sport, in any state?

'The Breach'
The poem is a dramatic monologue by a policeman who is awaiting orders to join in ending a siege. As he waits, his mind wanders back over his years in the Police Force.
breach: literally, a gap. Hence a breach of the peace; extended to mean a person or situation requiring police intervention. **and have grown out of:** Note the vernacular brevity. **you only arrest falls:** 1. easy victims 2. persons falling from cliffs etc. **fall through:** i.e. die? **silver:** medals, police badge. **said my ideals:** vernacular for 'stated my ideals'. **Snowy cut etc.:** free-associations with the name Snowy Cutmore. **I remember the old hand bowsers** etc.: Does this memory deserve its place in the poem?
Discussion: Contrast this policeman with the stereotypes of the honest cop and of the corrupt cop in recent films. What ideals and standards does he state for police work? What is his attitude to the siege?

'And a Good Friday Was Had by All'
Silenus: the name suggests the fat drunken jovial old man, friend of Bacchus in Greek mythology. **Ave Caesar...Imperator Rex:** Hail Caesar... Emperor King.
Discussion: How does Dawe create a foot-slogger's view of the crucifixion? How does the speaker's view differ from that of the 'big men' who ordered the execution? Do Australian vernacular terms like 'offsider' help or hinder the effect? How specifically Australian is the vernacular?

'Reverie of a Mum'
Gob: a sailor in the US navy (US slang). **done you brown**: fooled, cheated, bested, took you for a ride. **hair/With frangipanis**: The extravagant hairstyles of the time compensated for war-time restrictions on clothing. **The Dom**: During World War II the Sydney Domain was sparsely lit parkland. It was much used by love-making couples, though they were harassed by the Vice Squad. **'Loo**: Woolloomooloo, the dockside suburb. Its streets and pubs, Keesing has written, were full of hopeful girls sporting pompadour hairstyles, often decorated with frangipani flowers. **in jungle green**: the Australian troops on leave. Their faces were yellow-grey from the antimalarial atebrin with which they were dosed.

'You're Great'
Discussion: By what stages does the opening address ('Welcome to this poem') turn into a fantasy that is almost a film script ('...a beautiful shot!' etc.)? Do many advertisements work this way? How interesting do you find the idea of a poem that consists of an advertisement for itself?

ACTIVITIES

1 When starting on this section divide into groups, each of which takes one poem and works out the most effective way to read it aloud. Try not to look at the other poems. Then each group reads its poem to the others who have not yet met it on the page.

2 Make your own list of poems in other sections or other anthologies that are written in vernacular styles.

3 Compare Page's 'The Landing of Christ at Gallipoli' with Dawe's 'And a Good Friday Was Had by All'. Which do you prefer, and why?

4 Rehearse and tape-record your own readings of one or more poems from your list or from this section. How do they sound when played back? Do some poems seem written for a broader Australian tone or accent than others? What differences do you notice between vernacular and standard (or London, or New York) English? Are there some things that cannot be expressed well in the vernacular?

5 If possible listen to recordings of any of these poets reading their own poems. Compare their reading style with that of less vernacular poets.

6 Compare the different vernaculars of Dawe, Lawson and Murray. Would it be true to say that Dawe and Lawson see the vernacular as partly comic, whereas Murray treats it as a matter of course?

7 Compare the woman in 'Reverie of a Mum' and the policeman in 'The Breach'. Which character's history and present personality is best established? Could either have been created without using the vernacular?

How does the woman's vernacular differ from the policeman's? How did she get 'done brown' and made into what she is today?

8 Listen to any other poets you have on tape or record. Would you agree that every poet, even those who write more formally, has a certain 'voice' in which they feel most at home? Write a poem (for your eyes only) in what you take to be your natural 'voice'.

9 A foreign poetry-lover who speaks perfect 'standard' English writes to you, 'I think I understand almost every word in these poems, yet I still can't get the overall feel of them.' Write back, explaining what he or she might be missing in one or more poems.

10 **Library Project:** Compare Lawson, Dawe or Murray with the American poets Whitman and Frost or with the contemporary vernacular and regional poets represented in the *Penguin Book of Contemporary British Poetry* (1982)—Tony Harrison, Seamus Heaney and Douglas Dunn— or with any of the 'Mersey poets'.

11 **Research Project:** Investigate Geoff Goodfellow, Richard Tipping or other 'performance-poets', using sound tapes, videos, or memories of live performances. Is 'performance-poetry' really a separate category from ordinary poetry?

Relevant poems from other sections

Most of Murray, Dawe and Page. 'Consultation', 'Sweeney', 'Mute Conversations', 'Couples', 'Going Down. With no permanence', 'The Shearer's Wife'.

6

ACCEPTING A LANDSCAPE

For at least a hundred years white Australians have found it easier to talk accurately about each other than about the strange continent they had seized. Part of their problem was that they did not yet have words for many things they found here. They had only a migrant language called English, which had evolved over the centuries to describe the realities of a north-west European island. It took a long while for unsuitable British terms like *meadow, brook, native bear* and *New Holland jay* to be replaced by the more Australian-flavoured *paddock, creek, koala* and *kookaburra*. In the tropical north, and especially in the coral regions, this change of language is only beginning. A fish or bird far more beautiful than a minnow, stickleback, lark or chaffinch may still have no common name in Australian English.

Even more importantly, European Australians had no body of traditional knowledge, such as the Aborigines had, about the country. They had no myths or beliefs to help them make sense of it. If most of Europe could be described as the planet Earth disguised as a human possession, most of Australia was the thing itself—the vast semi-desert surface that showed little sign of being put there for human use.

Nineteenth-century Australian writers rarely mention the distinctions between different types of eucalypt forest, or even between rainforests, mangrove estuaries, and open savannah or heathland which we now take for granted. All too often they saw everything as just 'bush'—that is, country that was featureless and even meaningless. Even so, there were differences between those writers (and painters) who, with European eyes, saw the country as harsh and forbidding, and those who found beauty and richness beneath its harshness. Dorothea Mackellar's hackneyed 'I Love a Sunburnt Country' was in its day an important statement. So too was the work of painters like Tom Roberts, Arthur Streeton, and Hans Heysen, and more recently Russell Drysdale and Clifton Pugh.

In the 1930s there was a group of poets, including Roland Robinson, Ian Mudie and Rex Ingamells, who were determined to abandon out-of-date British poeticisms and attach their poetic language more closely to the country they lived in. They called themselves 'Jindyworobaks' from an Aboriginal word meaning 'to annexe, or join'. Though they wrote as white persons, they sometimes tried to introduce Aboriginal words and legends into Australian poetry. Their experiments were not very successful, partly because there is no single 'Aboriginal' culture or language to use, and perhaps because none of these poets had the metrical genius to solve the problem of making Aboriginal names work well in English verse. In any case, the Aborigines' understanding of the land was no longer enough for modern Australians. It needed to be combined with modern science.

Judith Wright showed the way with a poem called 'The Cycads'. Cycads are common Australian plants that look like small palm trees. They had no literary or mythological associations for European Australians, and were easily passed over as just part of the meaningless 'bush'. What Judith Wright did was to look at them in terms of modern ecology.

She recognized that these plants were from an older age of the earth, half way in their evolution between ferns and flowering plants. They had survived from the vast swamp vegetation that had laid down the coal-seams in which we still find cycads preserved. She knew that they grow more slowly than modern plants, perhaps because they come from a time when the metabolic competition was less intense. This was a time when the world was warmer, and when, scientists believe, the moon stood closer to the earth than it does today. She also noticed an interesting point about the fossil record: that there was a long age when birds of relatively modern type and plumage whistled and flew through forests in which our own ancestors, the mammals, were few and small. To a cycad a bird must seem a very impermanent creature. She put all these thoughts into the poem, and combined them with a certain human romanticism.

Other poets soon realized that it was possible to interpret the once meaningless details of Australia's landscapes in terms of modern geology and ecology. Ecology in particular gives to every species its own unique place and story. No longer was the land just bush. Even poets like James McAuley, who had seemed more interested in making the landscape a symbol for human or religious meanings, began, like the painters, to show an eye for the details and subtleties of the landscape. Australian poets today have much less trouble in getting the landscape to 'talk back' to them; yet no two do it in quite the same way.

A Dedication

They are rhymes rudely strung with intent less
   Of sound than of words,
In lands where bright blossoms are scentless,
   And songless bright birds;
Where, with fire and fierce drought on her tresses,
Insatiable Summer oppresses
Sere woodlands and sad wildernesses
   And faint flocks and herds.

Where in dreariest days, when all dews end,
   And all winds are warm,
Wild Winter's large flood-gates are loosened,
   And floods, freed by storm,
From broken-up fountain-heads, dash on
Dry deserts with long pent-up passion—
Here rhyme was first framed without fashion,
   Song shaped without form.

Whence gathered?—The locust's glad chirrup
   May furnish a stave;
The ring of a rowel and stirrup,
   The wash of a wave;
The chant of the marsh-frog in rushes,
That chimes through the pauses and hushes
Of nightfall, the torrent that gushes,
   The tempests that rave.

In the deepening of dawn, when it dapples
   The dusk of the sky,
With streaks like the reddening of apples,
   The ripening of rye,
To eastward, when cluster by cluster,
Dim stars and dull planets that muster,
Wax wan in a world of white lustre
   That spreads far and high;

In the gathering of night-gloom o'erhead, in
   The still silent change,
All fire-flushed when forest trees redden
   On slopes of the range;
When the gnarled, knotted trunks Eucalyptian
Seem carved like weird columns Egyptian,

With curious device, quaint inscription,
   And hieroglyph strange;

In the Spring, when the wattle-gold trembles
   'Twixt shadow and shine,
When each dew-laden air-draught resembles
   A long draught of wine;
When the sky-line's blue burnished resistance
Makes deeper the dreamiest distance
Some song in all hearts hath existence—
   Such songs have been mine.

             Adam Lindsay Gordon

Fire in the Heavens, and Fire along the Hills

From *The Quest of Silence*

Fire in the heavens, and fire along the hills,
and fire made solid in the flinty stone,
thick-mass'd or scatter'd pebble, fire that fills
the breathless hour that lives in fire alone.

This valley, long ago the patient bed
of floods that carv'd its antient amplitude,
in stillness of the Egyptian crypt outspread,
endures to drown in noon-day's tyrant mood.

Behind the veil of burning silence bound,
vast life's innumerous busy littleness
is hush'd in vague-conjectured blur of sound
that dulls the brain with slumbrous weight, unless
some dazzling puncture let the stridence throng
in the cicada's torture-point of song.

             Christopher Brennan

Crow Country

Gutted of station, noise alone,
The crow's voice trembles down the sky
As if this nitrous flange of stone
Wept suddenly with such a cry;

As if the rock found lips to sigh,
The riven earth a mouth to moan;
But we that hear them, stumbling by,
Confuse their torments with our own.

Over the huge abraded rind,
Crow-countries graped with dung, we go,
Past gullies that no longer flow
And wells that nobody can find,
Lashed by the screaming of the crow,
Stabbed by the needles of the mind.

Kenneth Slessor

South of My Days

South of my days' circle, part of my blood's country,
rises that tableland, high delicate outline
of bony slopes wincing under the winter,
low trees blue-leaved and olive, outcropping granite—
clean, lean, hungry country. The creek's leaf-silenced,
willow-choked, the slope a tangle of medlar and crabapple
branching over and under, blotched with a green lichen;
and the old cottage lurches in for shelter.

O cold the black-frost night. The walls draw in to the warmth
and the old roof cracks its joints; the slung kettle
hisses a leak on the fire. Hardly to be believed that summer
will turn up again some day in a wave of rambler roses,
thrust its hot face in here to tell another yarn—
a story old Dan can spin into a blanket against the winter.
Seventy years of stories he clutches round his bones.
Seventy summers are hived in him like old honey.

Droving that year, Charleville to the Hunter,
nineteen-one it was, and the drought beginning;
sixty head left at the McIntyre, the mud round them
hardened like iron; and the yellow boy died
in the sulky ahead with the gear, but the horse went on,
stopped at the Sandy Camp and waited in the evening.
It was the flies we seen first, swarming like bees.
Came to the Hunter, three hundred head of a thousand—
cruel to keep them alive—and the river was dust.

Or mustering up in the Bogongs in the autumn
when the blizzards came early. Brought them down; we brought
    them
down, what aren't there yet. Or driving for Cobb's on the run
up from Tamworth—Thunderbolt at the top of Hungry Hill,
and I give him a wink. I wouldn't wait long, Fred,
not if I was you; the troopers are just behind,
coming for that job at the Hillgrove. He went like a luny,
him on his big black horse.
                      Oh, they slide and they vanish
as he shuffles the years like a pack of conjuror's cards.
True or not, it's all the same; and the frost on the roof
cracks like a whip, and the back-log breaks into ash.
Wake, old man. This is winter, and the yarns are over.
No one is listening.
              South of my days' circle
I know it dark against the stars, the high lean country
full of old stories that still go walking in my sleep.

                             Judith Wright

Mangrove

I saw its periscope in the tide;
its torpedo-seed seeking the soft side
of the island, the grey mud-bank.
And, where it touched, it seemed the land sank
with its trees exploding from water; the green
mangroves' fountainhead of leaves bursting, seen
like a mushroom-top of detritus and spray.
Today, in my boat, at the close end of the bay,
I saw its dark devastations; islet and spit
sunk in the flat high tide. Where these war-seeds hit,
gaps of horizon and sea; then trees... gaps... trees
... like men on a flushed foredeck. No ease:
the drab olive-green swarming everywhere;
troops of the mangroves, uniform, everywhere.

                             John Blight

Terra Australis

Voyage within you, on the fabled ocean,
And you will find that Southern Continent,
Quiros' vision—his hidalgo heart
And mythical Australia, where reside
All things in their imagined counterpart.

It is your land of similes: the wattle
Scatters its pollen on the doubting heart;
The flowers are wide-awake; the air gives ease.
There you come home; the magpies call you Jack
And whistle like larrikins at you from the trees.

There too the angophora preaches on the hillsides
With the gestures of Moses; and the white cockatoo,
Perched on his limbs, screams with demoniac pain;
And who shall say on what errand the insolent emu
Walks between morning and night on the edge of the plain?

But northward in valleys of the fiery Goat
Where the sun like a centaur vertically shoots
His raging arrows with unerring aim,
Stand the ecstatic solitary pyres
Of unknown lovers, featureless with flame.

James McAuley

Egrets

Once as I travelled through a quiet evening,
I saw a pool, jet-black and mirror-still.
Beyond, the slender paperbarks stood crowding;
each on its own white image looked its fill,
and nothing moved but thirty egrets wading—
thirty egrets in a quiet evening.

Once in a lifetime, lovely past believing,
your lucky eyes may light on such a pool.
As though for many years I had been waiting,
I watched in silence, till my heart was full
of clear dark water, and white trees unmoving,
and, whiter yet, those thirty egrets wading.

Judith Wright

Drought in the Mallee, 1940

The dunes slide to swallow
a house like a child's toy
forgotten in sand play.

Thirty miles south they're hopeful still,
plant money each year
burying wheat to see it shoot and die.

Dry follows dry.
'I selected here. I rolled the Mallee,
put the first crops in.

I've grown wheat all my life.
There'll be good years again.'
Sand spreads from naked roadsides

across sown land, all parched
and blowing. The red dust
reaches the city three hundred miles away.

Mick's gone before good years. His sons
breed pigs, grow barley and diversify
and saved in the nick of time

sell out and move away.

Barbara Giles

The Cycads

Their smooth dark flames flicker at time's own root.
Round them the rising forests of the years
alter the climates of forgotten earth
and silt with leaves the strata of first birth.

Only the antique cycads sullenly
keep the old bargain life has long since broken:
and, cursed by age, through each chill century
they watch the shrunken moon, but never die,

for time forgets the promise he once made,
and change forgets that they are left alone.
Among the complicated birds and flowers
they seem a generation carved in stone.

Leaning together, down those gulfs they stare
over whose darkness dance the brilliant birds
that cry in air one moment, and are gone;
and with their countless suns the years spin on.

Take their cold seed and set it in the mind,
and its slow root will lengthen deep and deep
till, following, you cling on the last ledge
over the unthinkable, unfathomed edge
beyond which man remembers only sleep.

Judith Wright

A Kangaroo

That hungry face
moves on grass
the way an artist's pencil
retouches
shadows.

Then, when he's bounding,
the head's borne
refined as a deer's, relaxed,
before
a powerful tight basketball attack.

And the toe-nail, in the forefront,
a stevedore's claw
(tears with it, cantilevered on his tail);
the forepaws
are a housedog's, begging.

So that here,
sitting up and simply, is the unknown
energy, which is nature,
that's able to spawn, as one,
every extreme thing.

Robert Gray

The Beginning

God himself
having that day planted a garden
walked through it at evening and knew
that Eden was not nearly complex enough.
And he said:
'Let species swarm like solutes in a colloid.
Let there be ten thousand species of plankton
and to eat them a thousand zooplankton.
Let there be ten phyla of siphoning animals,
one phylum of finned vertebrates, from
white-tipped reef shark to long-beaked coralfish,
and to each his proper niche,
and—no Raphael, I'm not quite finished yet—
you can add seals and sea-turtles & cone-shells & penguins
(if they care) and all the good seabirds your team can devise—
oh yes, and I nearly forgot it, I want a special place
for the crabs! And now for parasites to hold
the whole system in balance, let...'

'...well, anyway, I want,' he said
'ten thousand mixed chains of predation—
none of your simple rabbit and coyote stuff!
This ocean shall have many mouths, many palates,
many means of ingestion. I want
a hundred ways of death, three thousand regenerations—
all in technicolor naturally. And oh yes, I nearly forgot,
we can use Eden again for the small coral cay in the center.

'So now Raphael, if you please,
just draw out and marshall these species,
and we'll plant them all out in a twelve-hectare patch.'

So for five and a half days God labored
and on the seventh he donned mask and snorkel
and a pair of bright yellow flippers.

And, later, the host all peered wistfully down
through the high safety fence around Heaven
and saw God with his favorites finning slowly over the coral
in the eternal shape of a grey nurse shark,
and they saw that it was very good indeed.

Mark O'Connor

NOTES

'A Dedication'
This dedication is from Gordon's last book, *Bush Ballads and Galloping Rhymes* (1870). The basic rhythm is anapestic, two unstressed syllables followed by a stressed syllable. Double and single rhymes and alliteration also create striking effects.
less of sound than of words: Is this true of this poem? **stave**: set of verses.
trunks Eucalyptian: eucalypt trunks. This licence of putting words the wrong way round in order to create a rhyme is usually avoided today.
resistance: opaqueness?
Discussion: 'Gordon's ornate style is like a prancing horse, not easily brought to any precise point of meaning. Yet he always knows what he means to say.' Do you agree?
Companion Piece: 'A Midsummer Noon', Charles Harpur.

'Fire in the Heavens, and Fire along the Hills'
in stillness of the Egyptian crypt: perhaps, 'as quiet as a pharaoh's tomb'.

'South of my Days'
Charleville... the Hunter: Charleville is a town in southern Queensland, about 800 kilometres west of Brisbane. The Hunter River flows down to the coast of New South Wales, entering the sea at Newcastle. **the McIntyre**: part of the Darling River system. **the Bogongs**: a high mountain range in north-eastern Victoria. **Tamworth**: a city in the New England district. **that tableland**: the New England tableland in NSW, where Judith Wright grew up. **Thunderbolt**: (1835–70) a famous bushranger, a.k.a. Frederick Ward.
Companion Piece: 'South Country', Kenneth Slessor.

'Mangrove'
torpedo-seed: Some mangroves drop seeds over 30 cms long, which can stick in a mud-bank and begin growing. **it seemed the land sank**: Perhaps because the mangrove trees raised the horizon-line. **gaps** etc.: i.e. exposed mud-flats.

'Terra Australis'
The title means 'South Land'. **Quiros**: The Spanish explorer Fernandez de Quiros (1563–1614) dreamed of a holy southern continent. **hidalgo**: a minor nobleman. **Angophora**: a genus of trees related to the eucalypts—perhaps *Angophora costata* which has gnarled pink branches.
the fiery Goat: i.e. the Tropic of Capricorn. **ecstatic solitary pyres**: perhaps Ayer's Rock and the Olgas? or trunks left burning after a bushfire?
Note how McAuley alternates between liking Australia for itself and wanting to make it a symbol of something else.
Companion Pieces: *'Terra Australis', Douglas Stewart; 'Terra Australis', Chris Wallace-Crabbe; 'Australia', A. D. Hope.

'**Drought in the Mallee, 1940**'
I rolled the Mallee: cleared the scrub with rollers. **the city**: Melbourne.
Companion Piece: 'My Father's Anger', John Griffin.

'**The Beginning**'
like solutes in a colloid: i.e. like the chemical components inside a living
cell. **Raphael**: the archangel.
Could you take seriously the notion of God as a mad ecologist? If not,
how would a believer explain the perfection of, say, a grey nurse shark?

ACTIVITIES

1 Rank the poems in this section according to how 'positively' they view
the country. Then re-rank them according to whether they see it in
detail and with an adequate vocabulary. Are these necessarily the better
poems? Are there any important differences between the earlier ones
and those written later?

2 Examine also the poems 'Brindabella', 'Garrakeen', 'Bringing the Cattle',
'The Fishermen at South Head', 'To Kill an Olive', and 'Natural Increase'
from other sections. How many of them use the modern scientific and
evolutionary understanding of the planet's landscapes? Do you prefer
this evolutionary approach to the Aboriginal myths of section 2?

3 Which of these poems come closest to your own vision of Australian
landscapes? Write a reply to one of them, or your own poem called
'Australia'.

4 Research the biology, geography, appearance and ecological effects of
mangroves. Are they 'uniform'? Do they deserve Blight's rather negative
vision of them as a devouring army? Find some different image of
mangroves (for example, as peaceful colonists) and try to construct an
alternative poem around that image.

5 Research the creation story in the Book of Genesis, and compare it
with other creation myths or stories, and with the theory of evolution.
Write your own creation-myth poem, in which the Garden of Eden
or its equivalent is set up in a part of the world that you know well.

6 **Library Project**: Investigate the art work and/or texts of the early scientific
investigators in Australia, for example Joseph Banks, John Gould,
Ludwig Becker. Can you find evidence that scientifically-minded people
were less troubled by the 'strangeness' of Australian landscapes than
those who were more inclined to be literary or artistic? Some useful
books include *Scientists in Nineteenth Century Australia*, Anne Mozley
Moyal (Cassell, 1976), *Eugène von Guérard's Australian Landscapes*,
Marjorie Tipping (Landsdown, 1975) and *Ludwig Becker: Artist and
Naturalist with the Burke and Wills Expedition*, Marjorie Tipping
(Melbourne University Press, 1978).

Poems for further study

*'Bell-Birds', Henry Kendall; 'West of Alice', W. E. Harney; 'The Bush Speaks', E. G. Moll; 'This Land', Ian Mudie; 'The Sun-Hunters', Mark O'Connor; 'Making Hay', Philip Hodgins; 'A Hot Day in Sydney', Anonymous.

†'The Broad Bean Sermon', Les A. Murray; 'Ravens', Ted Hughes; 'Train Journey', Judith Wright; 'The Travelling Post Office', A. B. Paterson; 'The Magpies', Denis Glover; 'Snake', D. H. Lawrence; 'The Snow Man', Wallace Stevens; 'God's Grandeur', Gerard Manley Hopkins; 'To Autumn', John Keats; 'Ode to The West Wind', Percy Bysshe Shelley; 'Frost at Midnight', Samuel Taylor Coleridge; 'Lines', 'Nutting', William Wordsworth; 'The Garden', Andrew Marvell.

7

MIGRANT EXPERIENCE

People who were born in Australia are often surprised that poetry by migrants is so often about the sadness of living in a foreign land. Perhaps they would understand this better if they'd ever had to leave their home and language behind and become stammering foreigners in someone else's country.

Yet the stress involved in migration varies enormously. An adult who migrates to Australia from another English-speaking country in order to further his or her career may well suffer no more stress than an Australian who moves from Tasmania to Darwin or vice versa. At the other extreme are refugees who have lost all their possessions, and even the right to speak their own language, and now find themselves isolated and discriminated against in a bewildering land at the end of the world. In between are a great mass of 'economic refugees', people from overpopulated or troubled countries with faltering economies, who have had to leave behind their language and culture. To many, Australia seems a material paradise but a spiritual and cultural desert. Sometimes they come only for the sake of the future of their children. Often they come from hundreds of years of agricultural background, yet find themselves trapped in Australian cities, with no chance to use their skills.

In time, most migrants adapt, and some very happily. In fact all non-Aboriginal communities in Australia, including the English and Irish, have gone through the painful process of losing their homeland and adapting to a new one. For most migrants the 'other country' remains a persistent reality. For some it is part of childhood; for others it is part of a lost world that their parents inhabit, but which they can only dimly grasp.

Officially sponsored migration into Australia has gone on for nearly two centuries. Originally it was overwhelmingly English, Irish, Scottish, and Welsh. The main reason for it, once Australia had an established economy, was military security. The country needed more people to reduce the risk of invasion. The early immigration policies were frankly racist, and were intended to keep Australia 'white' and as British as possible. Extreme measures were taken to discourage the Chinese immigration which came with the goldrushes; and Australians were paranoid about being 'swamped' by 'coloured' peoples. This led to the infamous 'Dictation Test' and the White Australia Policy.

After the Second World War, in which the Japanese came close to invading Australia, the guidelines for immigration were relaxed. Non-communist migrants were welcomed from all parts of Europe, and later from other countries. Eventually the preference for 'white' immigrants was dropped altogether, and for the first time Australia began to welcome migrants from South-east Asia.

In the 1970s Australia introduced an enlightened multi-cultural policy. Migrants were no longer supposed to be simply assimilated or digested but were encouraged to retain their own languages and customs. Belatedly Australians were recognizing the cultural riches many migrants bring with them. Sadly, many migrant children still lose their native language—usually because they give up speaking it after being teased in the primary school playground by jealous or narrow-minded Australian children who have only one language.

During the first half of the twentieth century, emigration to Australia and North America was the salvation of people in desperately poor and crowded areas of Britain, Yugoslavia, Greece and Italy. Migration brought rapid population growth to Australia. Even though much of Australia is desert, its politicians believed they would never have too many people. More people brought development, and prosperity, especially to business-men and to those who owned land in or around the cities. More people also brought urban and traffic problems, polluted air, steep rents and land prices, and destruction of the natural environment. By the 1980s some demographers were beginning to suggest that Australia needed to limit its population. At the same time the arrival of permanent unemployment made unions wary of bringing in migrant workers. By the 1980s the days of mass migration from a handful of European countries were over; but Australia still takes in tens of thousands of migrants a year from around the world, including a large number of refugees.

Migrants often want desperately to talk or write about their experiences. Yet many face a huge obstacle: the English language. English is one of the world's harder languages to learn to speak well, because (unlike most migrant languages) it is not written as it is pronounced, and it distinguishes two or three times as many vowel sounds as languages like Greek or Spanish. Often it is left to the children of migrants to express in English what they and their parents went through.

Smugglers

We were met
By brisk efficiency.
> Passport. Landing Permit.
> Vaccination. Chest X-Ray.
> Name. Nationality.
> And yes,—
> Anything to declare?

> Hands shuffled,
> Fingers lifted,
> Eyes looked
> Scanned.

Nothing was confiscated.
We were free to go.
> Our bodies bent
> Under the heavy cargo
> Of our past.
> We smuggled in
> Values and slanted opinions.

> We failed to declare
> Ever-lasting nostalgia,
> Memories of distant people,
> Already fading cities
> And lost sunsets.

Nobody asked, nobody cared.
We were left alone.
> And wherever we go,
> We leave a trail
> Of unsuspected contraband,
> Sometimes polluting, sometimes enriching
> Our adopted Home.

Maria Lewitt

The Exile

From *East Timor Poems*

The lights in strange houses,
Like fireflies in trees,
Are the silent symbols
Of my apartheid.
Chilled, enisled,
I lift the collar of my coat
Up under my ears
And pretend I am a family.
I address myself
Father, Mother, Son—
A play in three parts.
And life goes on.

J. J. Encarnação

From *Prague, 1968*

As if the entire population but you
slipped off the globe during the night: you wake
to find the house empty, the sort of silence
that hunts around abandoned aerodromes,
and quicken outside hoping to find someone
but feel a carbine thrust into your back,
a burst of knuckled consonants from behind...
It must have happened while you dreamed. He leads
you off, across the city, past mounds of things
still burning, tanks blundering down the street
much faster than you'd think, until the distant
thunder of orders, tanks and guns, contracts
to a crowded Square where soldiers raise their flag,
divide those captured into groups, open trucks,
slowly collect your first row, then your second...

Kevin Hart

Freedom Fighter

A freedom fighter, she said
lighting the gas stove.
In the mountains we fought...
great days...
the words stubborn
weary in the shabby kitchen
with the yellowed fridge
and the tinted photograph
of the dead husband.
The house full of morose
rooms suffocated with rugs.

We came out on the low verandah
her heavy stockings pitch black
the rough spun dress the
indigo blue of some wild flower
the Sunday neighbourhood still asleep.
Come again, she said indifferently
watching the windy street
and the Town Hall squatting
on its elephant legs,
come again.

Antigone Kefala

Bonegilla 1961

the heat of burnt grass,
impotent anger
at an english class,
men getting younger
by each disciplined day,
till they are school-boys
again, told to pay
attention, roll-calls
into another
life, how to translate
the humid weather,
the shame and the hate—
at night, the huts throb
with desperate love-
making, young men sob
in darkness, dreams of
childhood call them home,
twilight rains set in,
morning builds its dome,
the snake sheds its skin.

Manfred Jurgensen

Migrant Woman on a Melbourne Tram

Impossibly black
Amid the impudence of summer thighs
Long arms and painted toenails
And the voices
Impossibly obscure
She hunches sweltering
Twists in sweating hands
A scrap of paper—address, destination,
Clue to the labyrinth
Where voices not understood
Echo
Confusing directions.

> (There was a time
> They sent them out of Greece
> In black-sailed ships
> To feed the minotaur.
> Whose is the blind beast now
> Laired in Collingwood,
> Abbotsford, Richmond,
> Eating up men?)

Street-names in the glare
Leap ungraspably from sight
Formless collisions of letters
Impossibly dark
She is forlorn in foreign words and voices,
Remembering a village
Where poverty was white as bone
And the great silences of sea and sky
Parted at dusk for voices coming home
Calling names
Impossibly departed.

Jennifer Strauss

Post Card

1
A post card sent by a friend
haunts me—
Warsaw: Panorama of the Old Town.
He requests I show it
to my parents.

Red buses on a bridge
emerging from a corner,
highrise flats and something
like a park borders
the river with its concrete pylons.
The sky's the brightest shade.

2
Warsaw, Old Town.
I never knew you
except in the third person—
great city
that bombs destroyed,
its people massacred
or exiled—You survived
in the minds
of a dying generation
half a world away.
They shelter you
and defend the patterns
of your remaking,
condemn your politics,
cherish your old religion
and drink to freedom
under the White Eagle's flag.

For the moment,
I repeat, I never knew you,
let me be.
I've seen red buses
elsewhere
and all rivers have
an obstinate glare.

My father
will be proud
of your domes and towers,
my mother
will speak of her
beloved Ukraine.
What's my choice
to be?

I can give you
the recognition
of eyesight and praise.
What more
do you want
besides
the gift of despair?

3
I stare
at the photograph
and refuse to answer
the voices
of red gables
and a cloudless sky.

On the river's bank
a lone tree
whispers:
'We will meet
before you die.'

Peter Skrzynecki

Mute Conversations: Conversazioni Mute

1   *The lie*

Halfshadowed hospital room
whitish light: a neapolitan noon.
But for an occasional moan
as he slumbers to and from,
but for his brow
which is furrowed and drawn,
you wouldn't know his pain
since surgery at dawn.
He was cut and quickly sewn
back: nothing could be done:
'His pain will grow and grow.
There are no guidelines,
it may come or go
it may burn or ice.'
The son was told it all:
'The old man is at the ropes.'

Days before, an intercontinental call,
a frankly sad voice:
'Catch the first plane.
You are needed at once.'
In the faraway place
which the son calls home,
the moment ever since dreaded
had now truly come.

The mother's stunted body
clutches her son. Despair and a trace
of joy: *'Figlio mio, ma che tiene?'*   *'My son, but what has he got?'*
Oh white gentleness of lies:
'Mamma he will be well again.
Vedrai. Will see. The purple space   *You will see*
and the birds red blue green
of Pittwater. Paoletta. Riccardo
sailing for him on that strange sea ...
Shall book a flight. Back with me.
Back, back with me.'
No moment of truth for the ill man
and his wife. They are so frail
and old. Here, you tell only those
who should be told.

2 ***Primo notturno: le voci di dentro***
    Night signals:
    nightnurses' noises
      muffled,
and the inner ear's. Wave
upon wave, other voices,
thinner than air. They belong
to the dying man and his son.

    'I had to go. To migrate
    was fugue and revolt.
    Against you? Maybe so;
we always fought. A tug of love.
Remember in jest I once said:
    my first resistance
    as an oppressed minority
was against father's hegemony!
Pater patria potestas oh father
    your time has come
    and you cannot be told.
    Here it is not done
    you are so tired and old.'

Slow caresses along greyspent hair
searching, bent, halfclosed eyes
    as you do with a baby
    if you want his smiles.

3   ***Secondo notturno: food***
    'Don't you eat, *babbino*?
Just this morsel, will you please?'

      '*No, non posso.*
      Il sapore.
      Mi delude.'

He remembers taste, smells
of his once upon a time
    in a village.
        '*Pane, acqua,*
un poco d'aglio.'

        Any effort
to relive his appetite
    dies with him.

    '*Mi dispiace.*'

First night scene or nocturne: the voices within.

father, paternal authority (Latin words)

little father, dear father

'No, I can't. The taste disappoints me.'

'Bread, water, a little (a whiff of) garlic.'

'I'm sorry'

4   ***Terzo notturno: shelters***

  Unreachably tall
  he lifted the child,
  his arms and chest
  a fort and a cradle.
 Hell on earth, airshelters:
  they ran most nights
  and the sky was alight
 with *mitraille* and groundfire.   *machine-gun fire*
  'Were you scared, *babbo*?'   *Dad*
  'For you only. To die
was matter of fact. Four years.
Hell on earth. Airshelters.
The war was your childhood
   companion.'

 'I remember: till now,
 a siren, or the rumble
of the pistons of a slow aircargo
  arouse that scream
 you taught me not to voice.'

Now as then he tries to shelter
 others. His pain his own
 to bear. His care is quiet.
 Open, stabs the side;
 a blade his back *piagato*,   *wounded, plagued.*
  the mouth a cave of fire,
  yet he says subdued:
   '*Mi dispiace*'.

  Gli dispiace.   *He is sorry.*
 When they clean that waste
  which was his body
 he just says with his eyes:
  'Don't tire.'

  And the screams
 all the screams of a life
time of war, of love, of patient
  toil do remain
 as unvoiced now as then
 when he sheltered his son
from *mitraille* and groundfire.

    Paolo Totaro

ΑΝΑΒΟΛΗ
Anavolee

Μὲ *ρωτᾶζ ποῦ σπούδαξα νὰ δτείλειζ τό παιδί σου.*
Μὲ rotas̀ poò spoòthaxa nà steèlees tò petheè soo.
Τὸ *οχέφτηχα χαί θὰ σοῦ πῶ*
Τὸ skèfteeka kyè thà soò pò
ἀλλὰ *νὰ πάει πρῶτα σὲ σξολειὸ μὲ δασχάλουζ.*
allà nà pàee pròta sè scholeeò mè thaskàloos.

Postponement

Where did I study, you ask—to send your son there too.
I've thought about it and I'll tell you,
but first let him go to a school with teachers.

Dimitris Tsaloumas

Be Good, Little Migrants

Be good, little migrants
We've saved you from starvation
war, landlessness, oppression
Just display your gratitude
but don't be heard, don't be seen

Be good, little migrants
Give us your faithful service
sweep factories, clean mansions
prepare cheap exotic food
pay taxes, feed the mainstream

Be good, little migrants
use leisure with prudence
sew costumes, paint murals
write music, and dance to our tune
Our culture must not be dull

Be good, little migrants
we've given you opportunity
for family reunion
equality, and status, though
your colour could be wrong

Be good, little migrants
Learn English to distinguish
ESL from RSL
avoid unions, and teach children
respect for institutions

Be good, little migrants
you may fight one another, but
attend Sunday School, learn manners
keep violence within your culture
save industry from criminals

Be good, little migrants
Intelligence means obedience
just follow ASIO, CIA
spy on your fellow countrymen
hunt commies for Americans

Be good, little migrants
Museums are built for your low arts
for your multiculturalism
In time, you'll reach excellence
Just waste few generations

Uyen Loewald

NOTES

From '**Prague, 1968**'
Hart migrated from Britain, not Czechoslovakia; but his poem reflects the sort of nightmare experiences many refugees have had.

'**Bonegilla 1961**'
Bonegilla: an ex-army camp near Albury, used to house recently-arrived migrants after World War II.

'**Migrant Woman on a Melbourne Tram:**'
What is the connection between the Minotaur story and the way young people emigrate from Greece?

'**Post Card**'
Companion Pieces: '10 Mary Street', Peter Skrzynecki; 'Summer Pogrom', Fay Zwicky.

'**Mute Conversations: Conversazioni Mute**'
Many migrants think and feel in two languages. Totaro wrote the poem when he was called back to his father's deathbed in Naples in 1985. He wrote in English so his father would not know that he was dying. **neapolitan**: the adjective from Naples. **at the ropes**: on the ropes. **che tiene?/what has he got?** The mother doesn't know that the father is dying of cancer. **birds red blue green of Pittwater**: the rosella parrots of Pittwater. (He pretends that his father will recover and visit Australia to go sailing with the grandchildren on Sydney Harbour.) **the voices within**: The son imagines a voiceless, mute conversation. **fugue**: (derived from Italian *fuga*, flight or escape). **don't tire**: i.e. don't give up.

'**Postponement (Anavolee)**'
Dimitris Tsaloumas is a Greek Australian who sometimes works with the translator Philip Grundy and sometimes on his own to produce English versions of his poems. The Greek version is also presented in the English alphabet to show what it sounds like. The accents mark which syllables to stress. This poem is from a book of epigrams, and like most of Tsaloumas's work it is not specifically about being a migrant.
a school with teachers: As opposed to the school of hard knocks? or, a school with real teachers? What do you think?

'**Be Good, Little Migrants**'
ESL: English as a Second Language. **RSL**: Returned Services League.

ACTIVITIES

1 Compare the poems in this section. Which seem to you to make the most important statements about migration? Are they also the best poems?

2 Make your own artistic comment on any of these poems. You could do a sketch or painting, write a poem of your own, reply to the author in either prose or verse (or perhaps a letter), or write a few paragraphs from a novel or short story about migration.

3 Research Warsaw and its fate in World War II, and see what this adds to your reading of 'Post Card'.

4 Work out the story of 'Mute Conversations: Conversazioni Mute' in detail. Then retell it in the form of your choice (e.g. letter, short story, application requesting leave to visit a sick parent, poem or playlet). Perhaps start the story years earlier, or adapt it to a different country (e.g. Vietnam, Cambodia, Lebanon, Turkey). You can tell it from the point of view of the father, or of the mother, or of a brother or sister who never migrated, or of the grand-children Paoletta and Riccardo (who perhaps prefer to be called Paula and Rick at school).
Discussion: Does the strength of this poem lie more in individual lines, or in its cumulative effect?

5 Invent the full story behind the poem 'Freedom Fighter', and tell it from the heroine's point of view. End with the day when she realizes it is impossible to explain her past to Australian friends. Perhaps include an account of her first Australian barbecue.

6 **Discussion**: Write a poem about your own experience of migration, or about a migrant whom you now think you understand better than when you first met him or her.

7 **Project**: Write down what you know about when and from where your various ancestors came to Australia. If you wish, share this information with your classmates.

8 **Library Project**: Make a special study of the work of Peter Skrzynecki, Dimitris Tsaloumas, Antigone Kefala, or some other migrant poet of your choice.

9 **Activity**: 'Having only one language is like having only one eye in your head.' If you know, or have studied, another language make a list of words or phrases in it that cannot be translated exactly into English. Conversely, what English words has that language found it convenient to borrow?

10 **Social Research Project**: Identify one or more writers in your region who write in a community language other than English. Try to find out what their writing means to their communities. Is it true that poetry in one's own language is more important to migrant communities than it is to most native-born monolingual Australians? If so, is this a peculiarity of English-speaking culture, or is it due merely to the fact that migrants are deprived of their homelands? Do you think English benefits or suffers as a literary language because it is no longer the language of a single nation?

11 **Multicultural Exercise**: More than half of the Greek capital letters are the same shape as ones in the Roman alphabet; and each Greek letter (except Chi and Gamma) corresponds to some common English sound. Find out from a good encyclopaedia what sounds the Greek letters stand for, and use Greek capitals to write simple sentences in English. Then find out how the Roman, Arabic and Cyrillic alphabets came to diverge from the Greek; or research how the Roman alphabet was expanded and adapted to suit different languages like English, Turkish, French, German, Vietnamese, etc. Find out if other languages are written unphonetically, as English and French partly are. Which alphabets, other than the Roman, are important in South-east Asia?

Relevant poems from other sections

'Jim Jones', 'The Shearer's Wife', 'The Conquest'.

Poems for further study

*'Van Diemen's Land', Allen Afterman; 'The Female Transport', Anonymous; 'Dreams in German', David Martin, 'The Jews Speak in Heaven', 'Australia', Gary Catalano.

†'House and Land', Allen Curnow; 'To the Virginian Voyage', Michael Drayton.

8

WAR

For most of its history Australian society has had a certain military flavour. The early colonies had military garrisons, and their governors were usually army or navy officers. The settlers stood ready to defend Australia against invasion by foreign powers. At different times France, Russia, America, Japan, and communist China were feared as possible aggressors.

The skirmishes with the Aborigines and the long 'war' against the bush were interrupted by a series of foreign wars. The most important were the Boer War of 1899-1902, the First World War (1914-18), the Second World War (1939-45), the Korean War (1950-53) and the Vietnam War (1962-72). It seemed that each generation of Australian men must expect to go to war.

Australian males often attempted to leave the softer and more humane emotions to women, while they pursued a cult of toughness and male prowess because they were afraid that admitting their feelings might make them 'soft'. In peace time, as the film *Gallipoli* suggests, they often channelled their toughness into sport. Foreign visitors sometimes noticed that at parties Australian men and women seemed to have nothing to say to each other.

The First World War (and its unsuccessful conscription referendum) left deep marks on Australia. The struggles and sufferings of Gallipoli brought a new dimension to mateship and a stronger sense of national identity; but, especially in the trenches of France, the discovery of mass-produced mechanized death weakened people's belief in the value of human courage and strength, and also in the might of the British Empire. Over the years the impact of the vast casualty lists sank in. Yet the poets of the day were often inhibited by a need to keep up morale and by their habit of seeing poetry as a kind of ornamental language that had no way to describe such horrors.

It has been left to younger Australian poets, like Roger Macdonald and Geoff Page who were born long after the war but have continued to brood on the tragedy of the First World War, to write some of the most direct and moving poems about it.

The Second World War, in which Australia for the first time was nearly invaded, was widely accepted as a necessary war. It has received less attention from the poets, perhaps partly because it brought fewer casualties.

In the 1950s Australia had compulsory 'national service'. Later, in the 1960s, there was two years conscription for a percentage of young men selected at random. The Vietnam War, in which Australia played a minor part, aroused the concern of many young people in the 1960s and 1970s. Eventually the Labor government of 1972 took Australia out of the Vietnam War and ended conscription. Since then a generation of young men has grown up to whom compulsory military service seems only a distant possibility. This in turn has led to demands for a readjustment in the roles and responsibilities of the sexes.

Epitaph, World War I

You who shall come, exalt these childless dead
To be your fathers, from whose life you are bred.
The dead beget you now: for now they give
Their hope of sons that you their sons may live.

C. R. Jury

Adieu...

From the diary of an Australian soldier, September 1917

Adieu, the years are a broken song,
And the right grows weak in the strife with wrong,
The lilies of love have a crimson stain
And the old days never will come again.

Anonymous

Inscription for a War

*Stranger, go tell the Spartans
we died here obedient to their commands.*
Inscription at Thermopylae

Linger not, stranger; shed no tear;
Go back to those who sent us here.

We are the young they drafted out
To wars their folly brought about.

Go tell those old men, safe in bed,
We took their orders and are dead.

A. D. Hope

The Regulars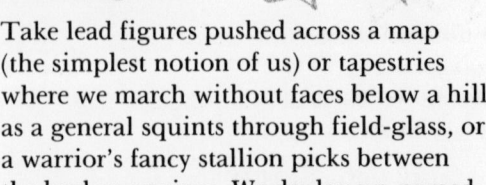

Take lead figures pushed across a map
(the simplest notion of us) or tapestries
where we march without faces below a hill
as a general squints through field-glass, or
a warrior's fancy stallion picks between
the broken engines. We deploy un-named

through these reputations, bridge the gap
where rhetoric juts toward the blackened countries.
We're known as Wall, Fist, and later The Bill;
idealists call us 'coin' or 'guarantor';
stabs in the dark. We are where we've been
and what we've used—Plataea's missiles aimed

at ancient envies and half-men bent on the rape
of sister. It's a blink or twenty centuries
on from Hellas; the seconds tick still
toward that constant zero when the procedure
that women have called odd, that boys of sixteen
have lied to join, that's paid many, shamed

more into reticence, will reopen to the clap
and cheer of the bored in the bannered, rainy cities
that spring from kinder soil than ours. Our skill
is keeping the lowest profile. Let the warrior
and recruit posture on the marksman's skyline.
We will turn shadow, insect, be tamed

to a field of wheat to outwit the sudden trap
entailed in our luck. The risk, the cruelties
are nutrient, as my friend Curly L ———
is now to earth; I missed his ancient humour,
and should have said, if I got through this clean,
if I married, then my son would be named

after him. But 'ifs' are not my calling. The map
and its frontier changes are; the rest for tapestries
and archives. More on me? In the fold of a hill
I see men resting. Some are smiling or
without malice gesturing at the camera. Between
their smiles and memories I'm lying, un-named.

Alan Gould

Beach Burial

Softly and humbly to the Gulf of Arabs
The convoys of dead sailors come;
At night they sway and wander in the waters far under,
But morning rolls them in the foam.

Between the sob and clubbing of the gunfire
Someone, it seems, has time for this,
To pluck them from the shallows and bury them in burrows
And tread the sand upon their nakedness;

And each cross, the driven stake of tidewood,
Bears the last signature of men,
Written with such perplexity, with such bewildered pity,
The words choke as they begin—

'Unknown seaman'—the ghostly pencil
Wavers and fades, the purple drips,
The breath of the wet season has washed their inscriptions
As blue as drowned men's lips,

Dead seamen, gone in search of the same landfall,
Whether as enemies they fought,
Or fought with us, or neither; the sand joins them together,
Enlisted on the other front.

El Alamein.

Kenneth Slessor

Christat Gallipoli

*This synod is convinced that the forces of the Allies are being used of God to
vindicate the rights of the weak and to maintain the moral order of the world.*

Anglican Synod, Melbourne, 1916

Bit weird at first,
That starey look in the eyes,
The hair down past his shoulders,
But after a go with the ship's barber,
A sea-water shower and the old slouch hat
Across his ears, he started to look the part.
Took him a while to get the way
A bayonet fits the old Lee-Enfield,
But going in on the boats
He looked calmer than any of us,
Just gazing in over the swell
Where the cliffs looked black against the sky.
When we hit he fairly raced in through the waves,
Then up the beach, swerving like a full-back at the end
When the Turks'd really got on to us.
Time we all caught up,
He was off like a flash, up the cliffs,
After his first machine gun.
He'd done for three Turks when we got there,
The fourth was a gibbering mess.
Seeing him wave that blood-red bayonet,
I reckoned we were glad
To have him on the side.

Geoff Page

Pozières Cemetery

A graveyard grows re-cycling myths;
but the green is greedy, must be cropped
or it transmutes friends beyond remembrance.
The scuffed-up lawn today is raw
as a mis-shaved skull on a winter's day.

Elegant-spaced palisades
hammered in the turf's bare crown,
whose soft indifference sucks them down
a quarter inch a year, report
the tight-jammed *grinners* underground
that dance like angry sperm

in a horizontal frieze, two feet
below ground water. The earth
for centuries will show dark greasiness.

They had enough of mud in life.
Now it surrounds them, ambers them,
like ammonites in shale, pressing
the bones on every side, until it might,
if grass relaxed its sullen hold,
buoy them aloft, as clean
as bubbled gnats from muddy streams.
Rest on lads! Like Caesar's men
These knew that all wars worth the game
are won in lousy weather.

Known unto God
their name liveth forever—Johnson, Hagan,
Brown-Jones, Brentley, Symons, Bright
and Worth. To X-ray eyes
they pack in oddly. Fingers a clinking heap
below wry ribs; the haunch-bones
disconnected; curve of the buttock, beef
of the biceps, jowl-slack gone. Scarce weeping-room
between one's toe-bones and the next row's crowns.

In France's tranquil evening light the gray phantoms rise
—a thrush-like clink of plate and mug, a laugh, a whistle;
nasal orders start the toil. Great-coated bodies tumbling
others into holes. The coat that kept the mammal warmth within
is snatched back as they fall, lie crumpled like shot grouse.

—Our fathers: did they dream as yabbying boys on
their farms in Deniliquin, Horsham, Scotshead, Yass,
of so deep a subsoil waiting for their bones?
So many lads they planted in those weeks—
if men could turn to hazels, as in myth,
these fields would copse impenetrable with boughs
that sob and shed black tears on breaking.

Instead two old men hobble down the rows
dreaming of young men whom they knew; while
honour and folly hold the ground
under the gently piddling skies of France.

Mark O'Connor

1915

Up they go, yawning,
the crack of knuckles dropped
to smooth the heaving
in their legs, while some,
ashamed, split bile
between their teeth,
and hum to drown their stomachs.

Others touch their lips
on splintered wood
to reach for home—
'a bloke's a mug'
thinks one (who sees
a ringbarked hill)
another hisses drily
(leaping burrs).

All dreaming,
when the whistle
splits the pea, as up
they scramble, pockets fat
with Champion Flake
in battered tins,
and letters wadded thick
from Mum (who says
'always keep
some warm clothes on...')

Up from slits in dirt
they rise, and here they stop.
A cold long light swings over.

Hard like ice
it cracks their shins—
they feel a drill and mallet
climb their bones, then cold
then warmth as blood spills out from pockets,
chests, and mouths.
No mother comes to help, although
a metal voice is whining
'boys, relax', as one
by one they totter to their knees.

Roger McDonald

Brothers

Two days beyond the Last Post dawn
The khaki streets and brass at ten
These plastic wreaths survive,
Apex, Lions and Rotary, courtesy the florist—
Also a bunch of dahlias
Dilute-yellow and a shoebox card
Filled carefully in biro.

In loving memory of my brothers
*   Pte. K. L. McK—, Lone Pine 1915*
*   Pte. T. K. McK—, France 1917*
*   Pte. P. L. McK—, France 1918*
*   Gnr. S. L. McK—, 1st A.I.F.*

Old man in a kitchen. 4 a.m.
One bare bulb above his head.
Scissors, string, a mug with steam
And flowers dew-wet across the table.
He finds the words again

And somewhere just beyond them still
Four boys run in a steel-grey paddock
Headlong for the wire.

Geoff Page

Weapons Training

And when I say eyes right I want to hear
those eyeballs click and the gentle pitter-patter
of falling dandruff   you there what's the matter
why are you looking at me   are you a queer?
look to your front   if you had one more brain
it'd be lonely   what are you laughing at
you in the back row with the unsightly fat
between your elephant ears - open that drain
you call a mind and listen - remember first
the cockpit drill when you go down   be sure
the old crown-jewels are safely tucked away   what could be more
distressing than to hold off with a burst
from your trusty weapon a mob of the little yellows
only to find back home because of your position
your chances of turning the key in the ignition
considerably reduced?   allright now suppose
for the sake of argument you've got
a number-one blockage and a brand-new pack
of Charlies are coming at you   you can smell their rotten fish-
        sauce breath hot on the back
of your stupid neck allright now what
are you going to do about it?   that's right grab and check
the magazine man it's not a woman's tit
worse luck or you'd be set   too late you nit
they're on you and your tripes are round your neck
you've copped the bloody lot just like I said
and you know what you are?   you're dead dead dead

Bruce Dawe

Homecoming

All day, day after day, they're bringing them home,
they're picking them up, those they can find, and bringing them
    home,
they're bringing them in, piled on the hulls of Grants, in trucks, in
    convoys,
they're zipping them up in green plastic bags,
they're tagging them now in Saigon, in the mortuary coolness
they're giving them names, they're rolling them out of
the deep-freeze lockers—on the tarmac at Tan Son Nhut
the noble jets are whining like hounds,
they are bringing them home
—curly-heads, kinky-hairs, crew-cuts, balding non-coms
—they're high, now, high and higher, over the land, the steaming
    chow mein,
their shadows are tracing the blue curve of the Pacific
with sorrowful quick fingers, heading south, heading east,
home, home, home—and the coasts swing upward, the old
    ridiculous curvatures
of earth, the knuckled hills, the mangrove-swamps, the desert
    emptiness...
in their sterile housing they tilt towards these like skiers
—taxiing in, on the long runways, the howl of their homecoming
    rises
surrounding them like their last moments (the mash, the
    splendour)
then fading at length as they move
on to small towns where dogs in the frozen sunset
raise muzzles in mute salute,
and on to cities in whose wide web of suburbs
telegrams tremble like leaves from a wintering tree
and the spider grief swings in his bitter geometry
—they're bringing them home, now, too late, too early.

Bruce Dawe

NOTES

'Inscription for a War'
Thermopylae: a mountain pass in eastern Greece where in 480 BC the Spartan army under Leonidas was overcome by the Persians.

'The Regulars'
Regulars: professional soldiers of the permanent army. **The Bill**: a medieval weapon with hook-shaped blade. **Plataea**: a city north-west of Athens where the Greeks defeated a Persian invasion in 479 BC. **Hellas**: ancient Greece.
How true is it that the common soldiers pass 'unnamed' (line 6) while historians concentrate on how the generals used them? Find some examples of this.

'Beach Burial'
El Alamein: the famous battle which ended the Axis advance in North Africa. El Alamein is in northern Egypt, on the Gulf of Arabs.

'Christ at Gallipoli'
Lee-Enfield: a rifle.

'Pozières Cemetery'
Pozières: a town in flat country in northern France which the British and Australians took with appalling casualties in World War I. **ammonites**: extinct molluscs whose shells are found in vast numbers in sedimentary rocks. **hazels**: hazelnut trees. **as in myth**: e.g. Virgil's *Aeneid*, III, 19–68.

'1915'
1915 was the year of Gallipoli. **Champion Flake**: tobacco.

'Weapons Training'
crown-jewels: genitals. **Charlies**: probably Viet Cong.

'Homecoming'
green plastic bags: Body bags were used as temporary coffins for American dead in the Vietnam War.

ACTIVITIES

1   Compare the differing attitudes to war in these poems. Is there a consensus?

2   Military training traditionally begins by depriving the recruit of his existing self-esteem and replacing it with a different self-image better suited to military life. How does the dramatic monologue from the sergeant in Dawe's 'Weapons Training' illustrate this process? What more positive sides to military life emerge in Gould's 'The Regulars'? What is Gould's main objection to the way armies have been run? Compare and contrast 'The Regulars' with Donovan's song 'The Universal Soldier'.

3 Which poem do you think makes the most effective protest against war? How does it avoid 'preaching' or stating the obvious?

4 Try reading several of these poems aloud, to see which are the most effective.

5 Make your own artistic or literary response to one of these poems: sketch, poem in reply, parody or imitation, etc. Or write a poem or short story titled 'My War' or 'The War I Missed'.

6 Compare the poems about World War I in this section with those of British poets like Siegfried Sassoon, Ted Hughes (e.g. 'Out'), and Michael Longley ('Wounds'). In the long run does the war seem to have been more a unifying or a divisive experience for Britain? for Australia?

7 Compare any of these poems with the texts of songs such as Eric Bogle's 'No Man's Land' or 'And The Band Played Waltzing Matilda'. What are the differences?

Relevant poems from other sections

'The Conquest', 'Prague, 1968', 'Goya Paints a Portrait of a Child', 'The Electors', 'Your Attention Please', 'Living Dangerously'.

Poems for further study

*'The Year of The Foxes', David Malouf; 'The Enemy', Randolph Stow; 'Inscription at Villers-Bretonneux', Geoff Page; 'Soliloquy at Potsdam', Peter Porter; 'Homage to Ferd. Holthausen', Gwen Harwood; 'Grotesque', Mary Finnin; 'The Trenches', Frederic Manning; 'On the Death of Ludwig Erhard', 'One Tourist's Cologne', Hal Colebatch; 'The Bus-stop on the Somme', David Rowbotham; 'Dog Fight', Eric Rolls; 'Women are not Gentlemen', Harley Matthews; 'The Farmer Remembers the Somme', Vance Palmer.

†'Casualty', Seamus Heaney; 'Civilian and Soldier', Wole Soyinka; 'The Inheritance', Kamala Das; 'my sweet old etcetera', E. E. Cummings; 'Dulce et Decorum Est', 'Strange Meeting', 'Futility', Wilfred Owen; 'Easter 1916', W. B. Yeats; 'Channel Firing', Thomas Hardy.

9

URBAN LIFE AND WORKPLACES

Australia is one of the world's most urbanized countries. Much of its interior is sparse 'station country' or semi-arid wheatlands whose flat expanses are worked by vast machines and a tiny labour force. The agricultural machines have left the rural population free to migrate, over the last fifty years, to the coast and the major cities.

A city like Melbourne or Sydney covers a greater area than Paris or Rome, because most Australians live not in multi-storey apartments but on suburban blocks with both front and back garden. European visitors have been known to remark that Australia's suburbs with their private gardens are not so much cities as sprawling poems in praise of the country.

The suburban block satisfies many human needs; but it tends to isolate families from each other, and the huge area covered forces people to depend on private cars for transport. As a result, traffic is often funnelled through the inner city where it causes noise and annoyance, endangers pedestrians, and tends to destroy the city's human scale, making it less convenient for people to walk about and meet each other. Throw in the common problems of break-ins, violence and drug addiction, or of people having to choose between unemployment, crime, and tedious repetitive jobs, and it is not hard to see why Australians tend to think firstly of their cities as places with problems. Yet most of them choose to live there rather than anywhere else.

Late Ferry

The late ferry is leaving now;
I stay to watch
from the balcony, as it goes up onto
the huge dark harbour,

out beyond that narrow wood jetty;
the palm tree tops
make a sound like touches
of the brush on a snare drum

in the windy night. Going beyond
street lights' fluorescence
over the dark water, a ceaseless
activity, like chromosomes

uniting and dividing. And out beyond
the tomato stake patch
of the yachts, with their orange
lights; leaving this tuberous

small bay, for the city
across an empty dark. There, neon
redness trembles down in the water
as if into ice, and

the longer white lights
feel nervously about in the blackness,
towards here, like hands
after the light switch.

The ferry wades now into the broad
open harbour, to be lost soon
amongst a silver blizzard of light
swarming below the Bridge:

a Busby Berkeley spectacular
with thousands in frenzied, far-off
choreography, in their silver lamé,
the Bridge like a giant prop.

One does seem in a movie theatre:
that boat is small as a moth
wandering through the projector's beam,
seeing it float beneath the city.

I'll lose sight of the ferry soon—
I can see it while it's on darkness,
and it looks like a honeycomb,
filled as it is with its yellow light.

Robert Gray

Prosperity

monday to friday at the plant
concrete yards are busy with
vehicles and movement altho most of what
moves is machinery
now and then a human figure crosses the open
space looking small & helpless
in the sky above the plant not much is blue
behind the buildings in a grey channel something
oozes past seeming to have been a river

on friday night when the machines are silent
& the watchman finishes his rounds
walking away with gun and torch like some
mistaken supplicant then only the dark
finds its way through wire fences
and sometimes due to atmospheric conditions (for which
the management is not responsible) the wind will rise
or in the wasteland hours of industrial sunday
rain might start falling inadvertently as if
still thinking of a plant as some kind of
flower

Michael Dransfield

The Meat Works

Most of them worked around the slaughtering
out the back, where concrete gutters
crawled off
heavily, and the hot, fertilizer-thick,
sticky stench of blood
sent flies mad,
but I settled for one of the low-paid jobs, making mince
right the furthest end from those bellowing,
sloppy yards. There, the pigs' fear
made them mount one another
at the last minute. I stood all day
by a shaking metal box
that had a chute in, and a spout,
snatching steaks from a bin they kept refilling
pushing them through
arm-thick corkscrews, grinding around inside it, meat or not—
chomping, bloody mouth—
using a greasy stick
shaped into a penis.
When I grabbed it first time
it slipped, slippery as soap, out of my hand
in the machine
that gnawed it hysterically a few moments
louder and louder, then, shuddering, stopped;
fused every light in the shop.
Too soon to sack me—
it was the first thing I'd done.
I had to lug gutted pigs
white as swedes
and with straight stick tails
to the ice rooms, hang them by their heads
on hooks. Or fill a long intestine
with sausage meat.
You got meat to take home—
bags of blood;
red plastic with the fat showing through.
We'd wash, then
on the blue metal
towards town; but after sticking your hands all day
in snail-sheened flesh,
you found, around the nails, there was still blood.

I didn't usually take the meat.
I'd walk home on
the shiny, white-bruising beach, in mauve light,
past the town.
The beach, and those startling, storm-cloud mountains, high
beyond furthest fibro houses, I'd come
to be with. (The only work
was at this Works.)—My wife
carried her sandals, in the sand and beach grass,
to meet me. I'd scoop up shell-grit
and scrub my hands,
treading about
through the icy ledges of the surf
as she came along. We said that working with meat was like
burning-off the live bush
and fertilizing with rottenness,
for this frail green money.
There was a flaw to the analogy
you felt, but one
I didn't look at, then—
the way those pigs stuck there, clinging onto each other.

Robert Gray

Lines from a Factory

Iris has her hands full
of dead chickens
and her face full of thick make-up
the colour of her name.

It cracks as the day wears on,
wearing off under stress:
the wagging arms and tongues
of overhead machines.

Her cheeks sag
so like the skin
flapped over chicken torsos
ready for the bag.

A vulnerable tower above the others
she doesn't join their conversation;

her riled hands decimate
the corps of birds

dead and denuded.
Iris listens to the radio.
I stand beside her on the line;
we wear protective clothing.

At night I have no arms.
I cannot turn.
By morning they are back. All day they work
exposed from elbow down, forcing chickens into bags.

Fast and rhythmically
you pucker up the bag (like a stocking)
and drawing the chicken's body into yours you squeeze
one into the other.

My mound of bodies never slackens;
I cannot keep up.
I cannot compare with those other arms,
red and violent, tense and always cold.
From where I stand I can see the rabbits being killed.
Not on a roundabout upside down,
but by two men in a side room.
With chickens there is a lot of blood

borne from the slashes by open gullies.
The rabbits die quick:
against a wall
then a scalpel down the length of their bodies.

Sometimes the men wave them at us for fun.
There are no windows here
nor secrets.
Sentience ends.

Marion Alexopoulos

Doctor to Patient

Please sit down. I'm afraid I have some
rather bad news for you: you are now seventeen
and you have contracted an occupational disease called
unemployment. Like others similarly afflicted
you will experience feelings of
shock, disbelief, injustice, guilt, apathy, and aggression
(although not necessarily in that order)
and you'll no doubt be urged to try the various
recommended anodynes: editorials in newspapers,
voluntary unpaid work for local charities, booze,
other compulsive mind-destroyers, prayer, comforting
talks with increasingly less-interested friends.
It is small comfort to know that the disease
is universal and can accommodate
the middle-aged and thirtyish and strikes down
those in camps in Kompong Sam and Warsaw.
However, you will discover, as time passes,
that your presence in itself will make others
obviously uncomfortable. Try not to let
your shadow, at this stage,
fall across your neighbour's plate; eat
with the right hand only; do not touch
others in public (this can be easily
misconstrued); keep always
down-wind, if possible. Please remember
you have now become our common vulnerability
personified. Oh yes, and, by the way,
you will be relieved to know the disease
is only in a minority of cases terminal.

Most, that is, survive. Next, please.

Bruce Dawe

Living Dangerously

O to live dangerously again,
meeting clandestinely in Moore Park
the underground funds tucked up between our bras,
the baby's pram stuffed with illegal lit.
We hung head down for slogans on The Bridge,
the flatbed in the shed ran ink at midnight.

Parked in the driveway, elaborately smoking,
the telltale cars, the cameras, shorthand writers.
Plans for TAKING OVER. .3YRS. THE REVOLUTION.
The counter revs. out gunning for the cadres.
ESCAPE along the sea shelf, wading through
        warm waters soft with blood.
WOW! WHAT A STORY!... guerrilla fighters
wear cardigans and watch it on The Box,
lapsed Party cards, and Labor's in again.
Retired, Comrade X fishes Nambucca Heads,
& Mrs. Petrov, shorthand typist,
                    hiding from reporters
                    brings home the weekly bacon.

But   O   O   O   to live
                so dangerously again,
their stamina trousers pulling at the crutch.

Dorothy Hewett

That Which We Call a Rose

(For George Alexandrov and for Rick)

Black greyed into white a nightmare of bicycling
over childhood roads harried peaceless
tomorrow came a mirage packed in hypodermic
the city we lived in then was not of your making
it was built by sculptors in the narcotic rooms of Stanley Street
we solved time an error in judgement
it was stolen by the bosses and marketed as the eight hour day

Waking under a bridge in Canberra to chill scrawl
seeing the designs we had painted on its concrete like gnawed
        fresco
Venice with merchants feasting while Cimabue sank deeper into
        cobweb
as the huns approached in skin boats
back in the world Rick and George on the morgue-lists of morning
one dead of hunger the other of overdose their ethics precluded
        them
from the Great Society they are with the angels now

I dremt of satori a sudden crystal wherein civilisation was seen
more truly than with cameras but it was your world not this
yours is a glut of silent martyrs money and carbon monoxide
I dremt of next week perhaps then we would eat again sleep in a
        house again
perhaps we would wake to find humanity where at present
freedom is obsolete and honour a heresy. Innocently
I dremt that madness passes like a dream.

Michael Dransfield

NOTES

'Late Ferry'
The setting is Sydney Harbour.

'The Meat Works'
it slipped, slippery as soap: note the sound effects. **The beach etc.**: What do the lines about the beach add to the poem? **fertilizing with rottenness**: perhaps a reference to blood-and-bone fertilizer.
What is the analogy between this and burning the bush to make it grow green again? or with earning money at a meat-works so as to live in a pretty area?
Discussion: Does it (or should it) change your response to Gray's poem to know that he has become a vegetarian?

'Lines from a Factory'
the colour of her name: Iris means rainbow. **Iris listens to the radio**: What does this detail suggest? **corps of birds**: Does this metaphor work? **sentience**: i.e. capacity for feeling.

'Living Dangerously'
3 Yrs. The Revolution: Dorothy Hewett recalls that when she joined the Australian Communist Party after World War II many members believed there would be a revolution in Australia within three years. **Mrs. Petrov**: Evdokia Petrov and her husband Vladimir were Russian spies who had to be given new identities after they defected to Australia in 1954. Their revelations at the subsequent Royal Commission strengthened anti-communist feeling in Australia.

'That Which We Call a Rose'
Cimabue: Italian painter, 1240?–1302?. **skin boats**: i.e. made of animal hides stretched over wooden frames. Venice was built on islands for protection from invaders like the Huns. **satori**: in Zen Buddhism, the state of sudden indescribable intuitive enlightenment.

ACTIVITIES

1   List the criticisms the poets make of city life. Which poem gives the most positive view of a city?

2   **Discussion**: Why is it that though most of us live in cities, poets seem to find so little good to say about them?

3   Compare Gray's factory poem with Alexopoulos's. Does she gain or lose by describing more than one person's reactions to the factory? What is the point of describing Iris's make-up? Do you get a sense of the speaking voices of both poets?

4   **Discussion**: Does factory work have to be as deadening as Gray and Alexopoulos's accounts of meat-works suggest? What kinds of work are more satisfying?

5   **Discussion**: What does the notion of unemployment as a disease enable Dawe to suggest in 'Doctor and Patient'?

6   Make your own artistic comment on one of these poems (sketch, painting, short story, letter, song etc.).

7   Write a poem giving a more positive view of a city, or of your street or suburb.

8   Write a revised version of 'Living Dangerously', describing a more up-to-date struggle, and perhaps with a different ending.

Relevant poems from other sections

'Life-Cycle', 'The Breach', 'Post Card', 'The Bulldozer', 'Play Group',

Poems for further study

*'Men at Work', Richard Tipping; 'Act Six', Peter Goldsworthy; 'Puritan Poet Reel', Vincent Buckley; 'The Fire Station's Delight', Susan Hampton.

†'Divisions (I)', Tony Harrison; 'Lines Composed upon Westminster Bridge, September 3 1802', William Wordsworth; 'London', William Blake; 'A Satyr in Imitation of The Third of Juvenal', John Oldham.

Relevant poems from other sections

10

TRADITIONAL VERSE

'If it rhymes, it's poetry.' Much of our dreariest verse is produced by people who think poetry is simply commonplace statements with extra words or phrases dropped in at intervals to create rhymes and rhythm. Poetry is much more than this; and yet, other things being equal, a poem is the better for having a metre.

A metre or verse-form is any fairly regular pattern of sound-effects that a poet sets out to create. In English, metre is usually a pattern of rhythm and rhymes. (Rhythmic pattern without rhyme is acceptable, but rhyme without rhythmic pattern usually is not.) In other languages metre can mean something different. French words, for instance, do not have a strong stress accent, so our type of English rhythm, which is based on alternating stressed and unstressed syllables, would be impossible. French metre is based instead on having a regular number of syllables per line. Japanese haiku is another form that depends on counting syllables. Classical Latin and Greek had metres that depended not on stress, but on patterns of long and short syllables—which made it easier to set poems to music. Old English or Anglo-Saxon poetry worked mainly on alliteration, having usually three words per line that began with the same sound.

So there are many possible kinds of metre, but a given language at a particular time often has one dominant metre which the reader tends to look for. The poet can then either gratify, or partly gratify and partly tease this expectation.

In English verse the best-known metre has long been the iambic pentameter. We can describe it as a line of about ten syllables in which the stress tends to fall on the second, fourth, sixth, eighth and tenth syllables. For example:

Ĭtăliăn bŏys ăre nŏt, ănd nĕvĕr wĕre.

However this is such a simple pattern that a series of perfectly regular pentameter lines would sound artificial and boring. The great English poets from Shakespeare onwards have allowed themselves a number of irregularities or 'licences'. One very common licence is to invert the first 'foot', so that the line starts off with a strong stress:

Dŏwn thĕ ăssĕmblў lĭne thĕy rŏll ănd păss.

Another common licence is to pretend that an unstressed even-numbered syllable is stressed, provided the syllables on either side of it are unstressed: for example, the *with* in

That evening I had dinner with a man.

This tends to lighten and speed up a line.

Conversely a quite strongly-stressed syllable can be regarded as 'unstressed' provided the syllable after it is at least as strongly stressed, for example, the *our* in Shakespeare's

Now is the winter of our discontent.

In fact this line uses all three licences.

Of course good poets do not use irregularities entirely at random. They use them to slow or speed up a line, and to capture the particular tone or emphasis they want: for example,

Now slowly through the show-room's flattering glare

or

He ordered coffee. She did not refuse.

or

Once on a silver and green day, rich to remember.

For about three centuries, from 1570 to 1870, the iambic pentameter was the main metre of English poetry. It was both the work-horse and the show-pony, and was used for everything from light verse to the most serious tragedies. It sometimes occurred, as in Shakespeare's plays, without rhymes on the end. (In this case it is called 'blank verse', not to be confused with 'free verse' which is verse with no regular rhythm.) It also worked very well in rhymed stanzas and sonnets. In fact the combination of regular rhyme and rhythm produced heady effects that are still essential to bush ballads and to many types of popular verse.

However, by the late nineteenth century, poets like Whitman had begun to feel that the iambic pentameter no longer fitted the English language so well. They began to loosen it towards various kinds of verse in which it is more difficult to find a regular rhythm; and by the 1920s many British and American poets had abandoned traditional verse-forms altogether for 'free verse'. Rhyme too tended to disappear, because the combination of regular rhymes with an irregular rhythm often gives a faltering or doggerel effect. Traditional rhyme and rhythm came to be seen as artificial. Many poets reserved them mainly for comic verse, perhaps because in a comic poem we don't mind twisting the language into artificial patterns. This can be part of the fun, as in a limerick.

In Australia, poets like James McAuley, Douglas Stewart and A. D. Hope resisted this change, and considered free verse to be the easy way out. They found at least three ways to update the traditional metres.

First, since it was still possible to write comic verse in regular metre, they sometimes used a half-comic tone to write of serious subjects. A. D. Hope in 'Louise and Alessandro' can even rhyme 'over coffee' with 'to finish off, he'. Evan Jones's 'Generations' carries this technique to what may be its limit.

Second, they found that rhymes could still be used with lines whose rhythm was irregular, provided the rhymes were not too predictable or emphatic. David Campbell is one of the masters of this technique. Like the Irish poet W. B. Yeats, he often prefers half-rhymes to full-rhymes, and uses them to achieve a haunting lyric effect. Les Murray is another who tends to 'bury' his rhymes. How many readers of his poem 'The Bulldozer' would even notice that it rhymes?

Third, some poets have found ways to loosen the iambic metre still further. For instance they may vary the length of the lines at will, or they may give themselves the licence to put two unstressed syllables in place of an unstressed one at any point in the line. For example:

In the garden, pausing to sniff at the flowers, I said

In practice this sort of verse is hard to distinguish from a traditional English ballad metre, in which the poet creates a given number of stresses per line, without worrying how many unstressed syllables there are. An additional licence is that after a pause in the middle of a line the poet may seem to lose count, and start with, for instance, a stressed syllable when in fact an unstressed one was due. When all these licences are heavily used, as in much of Murray or Beaver, we get a verse that is almost 'free' but still has the ghost of the old iambic pentameter behind it.

The Convicts' Rum Song

Cut yer name across me backbone,
　Stretch me skin across a drum,
Iron me up on Pinchgut Island
　From to-day till Kingdom Come!

I will eat yer Norfolk dumpling
　Like a juicy Spanish plum,
Even dance the Newgate Hornpipe
　If ye'll only gimme RUM!

Anonymous

The Bystander

I am the one who looks the other way,
In any painting you may see me stand
Rapt at the sky, a bird, an angel's wing,
While others kneel, present the myrrh, receive
The benediction from the radiant hand.

I hold the horses while the knights dismount
And draw their swords to fight the battle out;
Or else in dim perspective you may see
My distant figure on the mountain road
When in the plains the hosts are put to rout.

I am the silly soul who looks too late,
The dullard dreaming, second from the right.
I hang upon the crowd, but do not mark
(Cap over eyes) the slaughtered Innocents,
Or Icarus, his downward-plunging flight.

Once in a Garden—back view only there—
How well the painter placed me, stroke on stroke,
Yet scarcely seen among the flowers and grass—
I heard a voice say, 'Eat', and would have turned—
I often wonder who it was that spoke.

Rosemary Dobson

The Brides

Down the assembly line they roll and pass
Complete at last, a miracle of design;
Their chromium fenders, the unbreakable glass,
The fashionable curve, the air-flow line.

Grease to the elbows Mum and Dad enthuse,
Pocket their spanners and survey the bride;
Murmur: 'A sweet job! All she needs is juice!
Built for a life-time—sleek as a fish. Inside

'He will find every comfort: the full set
Of gadgets; knobs that answer to the touch
For light or music; a place for his cigarette;
Room for his knees; a honey of a clutch.'

Now slowly through the show-room's flattering glare
See her wheeled in to love, console, obey,
Shining and silent! Parson with a prayer
Blesses the number-plate, she rolls away

To write her numerals in his book of life;
And now, at last, stands on the open road,
Triumphant, perfect, every inch a wife,
While the corks pop, the flash-light bulbs explode.

Her heavenly bowser-boy assumes his seat;
She prints the soft dust with her brand-new treads,
Swings towards the future, purring with a sweet
Concatenation of the poppet heads.

A. D. Hope

Louise and Alessandro

From *Letter From Rome*

That evening I had dinner with a man
Who has lived forty years in Italy,
Half English, more than half Italian
With all the latter's gift of irony;
And while we drank our wine my host began
To talk of Florence and her history,
Her life, her people, and to finish off he
Told me the following story over coffee:

'In Florence there is a well-known foundation,
Richly endowed from the United States,
Trimmed to the latest trends in education,
It "finishes" young women graduates
And gives them poise and polish for the station
Their family's bank-balance indicates,
The sort of thing entitled, as a rule,
A Continental Summer Graduate School.

'Its aims are serious, its methods sound,
Its courses academically respectable,
Fine Arts for those who like to shop around,
Western Philosophy for the directable,
And Poetry from Poe to Ezra Pound,
With, just to stiffen subjects so delectable,
A weekly seminar, a monthly test,
And Love is on the course with all the rest.

'Of course it is not on their syllabus,
As best confined to individual choice;
But hints are dropped in sessions to discuss
How to attain maturity and poise
That, if arranged discreetly, without fuss,
Brief love-affairs with nice Italian boys
May well repay the trouble and expense
Since nothing broadens like experience.

'Italian boys are not, and never were,
Averse to girls when rich, well-dressed and pretty.
The summer school created quite a stir
Among the young Lotharios of the city;
The alleys throbbed with an expectant purr;

The streets were filled with amorous banditti.
The girls of Florence, it may be, were less
Well-pleased, but that is anybody's guess.

'But how to set about it? How to find
A lover? That's quite simple in a town
Where every girl gets pinched on the behind
In shops, trams, church, or walking up and down.
It's half an invitation, half a kind
Of compliment. If she should turn and frown
That's that; but if she smiles, he'll raise his hat
And ask her to take coffee, and that's that!

'Louise, though very beautiful, was what I'm
Inclined to call a serious girl at heart,
And, though endowed with an attractive bottom,
Thought pinching it no proper way to start;
And Alessandro was well-bred; if not I'm
Sure he knew just how to act the part.
He met her at a concert, did not pinch,
But said the *pizzicati* made him flinch.

'She smiled and said: "How's that?" The ice was broken.
He ordered coffee. She did not refuse.
They talked on various topics which betoken
The parties each have cultivated views.
And, as they talked their eyes said things unspoken.
The world was all before them, where to choose.
He saw her home and on the doorstep they
Arranged to meet again the following day.

'Louise went in and calmly jotted down
Some notes on her emotional reactions,
Removed her make-up, donned her dressing gown
And nicely planned her conduct and her actions;
While Alessandro wandered through the town
Enraptured by her charms and her attractions.
His plans were just the usual well-bred
Young man's to get the girl to go to bed.

'To his surprise, and more to his chagrin,
She went to bed without the least demur.
Passion expects resistance, and to win
Without it, on his passion cast a slur.

He loved her voice, her eyes, her shape, her skin,
But found no answering response in her.
She loved him, not for love however fiery,
But for providing data for her diary.

'They went to bed; they took a trip to Pisa;
They "did" the Pitti; and they went to bed;
She told him all about herself; to please her
He talked about Etruscan tombs; she read
Her diary to him and that day to ease a
Sense of strain they took a walk instead;
They walked, they talked, she reasoned and he swore,
But in the end they went to bed once more.

'And at the close of a divine semester
She annotated and revised her notes,
Wrote "Field-Work" on the cover and repressed a
Less serious urge to label it: "Wild Oats".
She can't say Europe very much impressed her,
Though Sandro is a name on which she dotes.
She thinks that Kinsey overrates the male.'
And here my host broke off his merry tale.

A Merry Tale? Boccaccio might have written:
'How Messer Sandro wooed a learnèd dame,
But found his labour lost, the biter bitten
And half a thesis cooked upon his flame.'
Yet I am sad to see so many smitten
By the same view of art and much the same
Approach as this poor girl's who thought her fee
Made Love one more post-graduate degree...

A. D. Hope

The Scarecrow

Beneath the moon in the standing corn at midnight,
Thus was the scene set for our latest meeting,
And I addressed the Devil in this fashion:
'Sir, our next subject is this scarecrow person;
He's stood here long enough to merit freedom,
Day after day with empty arms extended,
A lolling head and a sad hat to crown it;
Your turn to ask him, as is customary,
Whether he goes with you the rollicking, treacherous
Way to damnation; or with me to Heaven,
There to be solaced with the psalm and psalter,
Ringed round with angels, garlanded with lilies.'

I give the fellow praise for oratory.
He minded, perhaps, his failure and my triumph
Over the recent business of the statue—
Some mid-Victorian statesman—I forget now—
Who chose the better way and winged to Heaven
Only on Thursday last.
Briefly, I say, he made it most impressive.
At his conclusion I addressed the scarecrow
Who all this while lolled back, and, half attending
Rolled one bright eye from out his thatch of straw;
Then we stood silent waiting his decision.
'Heaven,' he said. 'Hell,' he said. 'Give me a field of sunshine
And the birds,' he said, 'and their rude remarks in passing;
And a bit of a banter with hares in the corn at evening,
And the farmer taking a swig from his bottle at noonday,
And a slip of a girl with his lunch tied up in a napkin;
Don't talk to me,' he said.
                              I confess to discomfort,
And I stole away; but remarked, looking over my shoulder,
That the Devil was stealing away in the other direction.

Rosemary Dobson

An Art of Poetry

To Vincent Buckley

Since all our keys are lost or broken,
Shall it be thought absurd
If for an art of words I turn
Discreetly to the Word?

Drawn inward by his love, we trace
Art to its secret springs:
What, are we masters in Israel
And do not know these things?

Lord Christ from out his treasury
Brings forth things new and old:
We have those treasures in earthen vessels,
In parables he told,

And in the single images
Of seed, and fish, and stone,
Or, shaped in deed and miracle,
To living poems grown.

Scorn then to darken and contract
The landscape of the heart
By individual, arbitrary
And self-expressive art.

Let your speech be ordered wholly
By an intellectual love;
Elucidate the carnal maze
With clear light from above.

Give every image space and air
To grow, or as bird to fly;
So shall one grain of mustard-seed
Quite overspread the sky.

Let your literal figures shine
With pure transparency:
Not in opaque but limpid wells
Lie truth and mystery.

And universal meanings spring
From what the proud pass by:
Only the simplest forms can hold
A vast complexity.

We know, where Christ has set his hand
Only the real remains:
I am impatient for that loss
By which the spirit gains.

James McAuley

Brindabella

Once on a silver and green day, rich to remember,
When thick over sky and gully rolled winter's grey wave
And one lost magpie was straying on Brindabella
I heard the mountain talking in a tall green cave
Between the pillars of the trees and the moss below:
It made no sound but talked to itself in snow.

All the white words were falling through the timber
Down from the old grey thought to the flesh of rock
And some were of silence and patience, and spring after winter,
Tidings for leaves to catch and roots to soak,
And most were of being the earth and floating in space
Alone with its weather through all the time there is.

Then it was, struck with wonder at this soliloquy,
The magpie lifting his beak by the frozen fern
Sent out one ray of a carol, softened and silvery,
Strange through the trees as sunlight's pale return,
Then cocked his black head and listened, hunched from the cold,
Watching that white whisper fill his green world.

Douglas Stewart

Lament

SIGH, wind in the pine;
River, weep as you flow;
Terrible things were done
Long, long ago.

In daylight golden and mild
After the night of Glencoe
They found the hand of a child
Lying upon the snow.

Lopped by the sword to the ground
Or torn by wolf or fox,
That was the snowdrop they found
Among the granite rocks.

Oh, life is fierce and wild
And the heart of the earth is stone,
And the hand of a murdered child
Will not bear thinking on.

Sigh, wind in the pine,
Cover it over with snow;
But terrible things were done
Long, long ago.

Douglas Stewart

The Bulldozer
From *Machine Portraits with Pendant Spaceman*

The bulldozer stands short as a boot on its heel-high ripple soles;
it has toecapped stumps aside all day, scuffed earth and trampled
    rocks
making a hobnailed dyke downstream of raw clay shoals.
Its work will hold water. The man who bounced high on the box
seat, exercising levers, would swear a full frontal orthodox
oath to that. First he shaved off the grizzled scrub
with that front-end safety razor supplied by the school of hard
    knocks
then he knuckled down and ground his irons properly; they
    copped many a harsh rub.
At knock-off time, spilling thunder, he surfaced like a sub.

Les A. Murray

The Big Web

I've a good nose for perfumes but no head
For the names of flowers, therefore when I walked
In the garden, pausing to sniff at the flowers, I said
To myself no more than 'Nice'. I sometimes talked
At the big fat spider with the small round head
And his (or her) innumerable offspring (or assistants)
Who tinily skittered about while their daily bread
Was packaged and stacked for them by the big boss (or mistress);
Meaning all those insects who flew or crawled to the aforesaid
Garden, no doubt like myself merely to say 'Nice',
Only being more concerned with the taste of the air and the
        fountainhead
Of the flowers' sweet selves (their perfume, that is) than twice
As careful as usual, wound up in the web, mere bread
For those of and by whom 'Nice' has never been said.

Bruce Beaver

Generations

I go to see my parents,
we chew the rag a bit;
I turn the telly on
and sit and look at it.

Not much gets said:
there doesn't seem much point.
But still they like to have
me hanging round the joint.

I go to see my son,
I'm like a Santa Claus:
he couldn't like me more;
mad about him, of course.

Still years before he learns
to judge, condemn, dismiss.
I stand against the light
and bleed for both of us.

Evan Jones

NOTES

'The Convicts' Rum Song'
The rhythm is a regular alternation of stressed and unstressed syllables. Note that it continues on over line-endings. Since the stressed syllable comes first in each pair, this is technically trochaic, not iambic rhythm. The ABCB rhyme-pattern, like the regular alternation of lines with four and three stressed syllables, is typical of popular ballads.
Pinchgut Island: now Fort Denison in Sydney Harbour. Convicts were sometimes marooned there without food as punishment. **Norfolk:** Norfolk Island, considered as a harsh and primitive penal settlement. **dance the Newgate hornpipe:** be hanged? Newgate was a famous prison in London. **RUM!:** Rum, not beer, was the favoured drink of the early convicts and settlers.

'The Bystander'
a garden: perhaps the Garden of Eden.
Companion Piece: 'Painter of Antwerp'.

'The Brides'
The metre is iambic pentameter with ABAB rhyme.
How many similarities does Hope find between a wedding and a new car show? What do they enable him to suggest about weddings? Do you find phrases like 'room for his knees' or 'a place for his cigarette' sexist? If so, do you blame the poem, or the attitudes it describes? Have attitudes to weddings changed since this poem was published in 1951?

'Louise and Alessandro'
How does Hope manage to combine rhyme and rhythm with such a conversational tone? What licences does he use here that he does not use in 'The Brides'?

Lotharios: rakes, seducers. **banditti:** bandits. **raised his hat:** This poem was drafted in 1958. **pizzicati:** 'pinched' notes, made by plucking a stringed instrument with the fingers. **all before them, where to choose:** quoted from Milton's concluding lines about Adam and Eve in 'Paradise Lost'. **the Pitti:** the Pitti Palace in Florence. **Sandro:** short for Alessandro. **Kinsey:** (1894–1956) American zoologist, author of a famous report on human sexuality. **Boccaccio:** (1313–75) Italian author who wrote *The Decameron*. **Messer:** old form of Mister.
Should Hope have omitted the last stanza and left readers to draw their own moral?

'The Scarecrow'
This is from a series of poems in which an angel and a devil release figures from paintings and offer them the choice of heaven or hell. Note how Dobson frequently uses two unstressed syllables where in strict blank verse there would be only one. **minded:** remembered, took to heart.

'An Art of Poetry'

McAuley argued that the truest freedom in verse occurs when poets create their own expressive variations on an underlying regular metre. Note the alternation of four-stress and three-stress lines, the latter ending with falling intonations as in ballad metres.

Word: i.e. Christ. See the opening of St John's Gospel. **Israel**: perhaps the ancient sacred kingdom rather than the modern state. *Masters in Israel* is the title of a book by Buckley. **living poems**: the episodes of Christ's life. **self-expressive**: expressing the writer's private self, rather than general human truths.

Does McAuley's poem achieve the artistic virtues he preaches?

Companion Piece: 'Because'.

'Brindabella'

Brindabella: a mountain range in southern NSW.

'Lament'

The metre is three stresses to the line, with an unfixed number of unstressed syllables.

Glencoe: a glen in the highlands of West Scotland where, with the help of English troops, the Campbells massacred the Macdonalds in 1692.

'The Bulldozer'

Does Murray succeed in finding words and rhythms that match his subject without making it comic?

'The Big Web'

Emphatic rhymes with irregular rhythm can be a mistake. Does Beaver make it work here? How irregular is his rhythm?

'Generations'

Not much gets said: If Jones had written 'Not very much gets said' the line would be regular. Would it be better?

Do the half-rhymes (**Claus/course, dismiss/us**) make any difference?

ACTIVITIES

1 What is the cost of rhyme? Examine the words used to create rhymes in each poem in this section, and in three other poems of your own choice. Can you find cases where the poet has had to use a misleading word to get the rhyme, or has had to waste words or use odd or confusing expressions? Select one poem where you think the rhymes may have done more harm than good, and another where you feel they are a definite advantage. Which poet is most skilful in having rhymes seem to fall naturally into place?

2 Make a complete table of the rhyme-schemes of each poem in this section. Also note which licences each poet allows him or her self with the

iambic rhythm. Do any of these poems strike you as formal, in the sense of stiff and inflexible? If so, are there others where the metre makes the poem more lively? Is any poem perfectly regular?

3 Mark all the stressed and unstressed syllables in one poem to show the underlying iambic rhythm. Now scan it a second time (with a different coloured pen) marking the syllables you would actually stress when reading the poem in a normal voice. For example, you wouldn't really say:

Wĕstérn phĭlosŏphỳ fŏr thĕ dĭrectăble.

Are there more or less stressed syllables when you scan it the second way?

4 Compare the metres of 'The Bystander' and 'The Scarecrow'. Which poem, and which metre do you prefer?

5 **Project**: Investigate the metres of Lawson, A. B. Paterson and C. J. Dennis. Which writer do you find most skilful, or most varied?

6 Memorize a rhymed poem from this section. Do the rhymes make it easier or harder for the words to stick in your memory? Now memorize an unrhymed poem that interests you. When there is no rhyme, what things help you remember which lines come after which?

Relevant poems from other sections

Most poems by Hope, McAuley, Stewart, Lawson, Gordon, Campbell, Dobson.

Poems for further study

*'The Search', Charles Shaw; 'A Convict's Tour to Hell', Francis Macnamara.

†'A Song for St Cecilia's Day 1687', John Dryden; 'On The Late Massacher in Piemont', John Milton; 'A Song', Thomas Carew; 'Song', John Donne; 'Sonnets', William Shakespeare; 'The Wife of Usher's Well', Anonymous; 'Piers Plowman', William Langland.

11

FREE VERSE

Free verse is now the single most common metrical pattern in Australia, as in most English-speaking countries. Yet it is almost impossible to find a simple explanation of what it is. In fact many people have given up reading modern poetry partly because they can't see the point of 'lines of chopped-up prose'.

Let us take this objection first. Even if a poem were just a piece of prose, it would still be altered by dividing it into lines. A line-ending creates a break which is at least the equivalent of a comma's pause. Some poets omit a comma at the end of a line for this reason. Broken up into lines, a passage takes up at least twice as much space on the page, and so calls on us to read it much more slowly.

By contrast, we normally read prose at a steady rate, rarely pausing or turning back. Good prose writers know this, and make sure that everything is clearly set out and signposted for us. That is why if you chop a piece of good prose up into lines it will seem very ponderous and obvious. It simply does not need that kind of slow reading.

In comparison, a short-line free verse poem like Lilian Tait's 'After the "Ball"' can progress in bold jumps. Each line is a unit, and deserves a moment's pause. Each line emerges logically out of the previous line, yet adds something you could not have predicted. If you read it aloud, pausing after each line, you will find that it is a perfect example of T. S. Eliot's remark about good poetry always containing a perpetual slight surprise. Yet if you were to read it as prose its ninety words would flash past before there was time to take them in.

To write this kind of short-line free verse a poet has to be very economical with words. A poem, like a sports car, needs a good power-to-weight ratio. When each line is only two or three words long, those two or three words must have punch and precision. Geoff Page is one of the masters of this style. It seems that without the advantage of a metre, the poet has to be briefer and bolder, and cannot afford to be as chatty and conversational as A. D. Hope can in a poem like 'Louise and Alessandro'.

But what about those free verse poems that use much longer lines? How do they avoid dissolving into prose? And why do they insist on doing without the obvious pleasures of regular rhythm?

Those who defend free verse emphasize the advantage of being free to express exactly what they feel, without the hobbles of metre. But traditional poets reply that with sufficient skill it is possible to write about anything in metre—'Look at Shakespeare'. The argument is further confused because free verse was associated earlier this century with Modernism. This is a movement which different people define very differently; but it certainly had something to do with breaking away from traditional kinds of metre, grammar and logic, and with freeing the subconscious, and with getting into the darker recesses of the psyche or soul. Traditional metres were felt to be too restrictive for Modernism.

Why is free verse still gaining ground today? I suggest a linguistic explanation which may cover the facts.

The iambic metre depended on two assumptions about the English language: first, that any English word could be divided into a precise number of syllables; and second that the language offered roughly equal numbers of stressed and unstressed syllables. Over the centuries English borrowed so many long words from the Latin languages and from Greek that it was forced to slur many syllables and to have far more unstressed than stressed syllables. (For example, how would you normally pronounce *generally, usually, comfortable, biodegradable, January, speedometer*?) This made the iambic rhythm seem artificial.

The obvious solution, if this is the case, would be to abandon the iambic rhythm and use the *anapestic* one in which there are *two* unstressed syllables to each stressed one. Unfortunately, regular anapestics create a sing-song rhythm that is best suited to comic verse or to poems about galloping horses ('I sprang to the stirrup and Joris and he. / I galloped, Dirk galloped, we galloped all three...')

In practice, what good free verse poets often do is to mix iambic feet into a fairly regular anapestic rhythm. This slows it down and gives a more measured and variable pace, like that which the Spaniards describe as 'the rhythm of a horse walking'. The result is a rhythm in which there is certainly a pattern and a recurrence, but not one that can be specified by any simple *de dum, de dum* or *de de dum, de de dum* formula.[*]

In fact there can be great skill in alternating the lighter anapestic feet and the heavier iambic ones according to meaning. With this clue, some poems that seem to be free verse will turn out to scan quite regularly. Not that the poet need have thought it out like that. Most free verse poets simply have an ear for what sounds right.

There may be other hidden regularities in so-called free verse. Some poets work, consciously or unconsciously, on counting a certain number of syllables to the line. Others, as we have already seen do not count all syllables but tend to keep a fixed number of stresses to the line. Others regard a line as a breath-unit—the amount that can be said on a single

---

[*] For a fuller discussion of these issues see Mark O'Connor, *Modern Australian Styles*, ch. 2 (James Cook University, 1982).

breath-impulse. (Apparently some poets are more short-breathed than others.) Other poets rely on repetitions, as in Tipping's delightful 'Mangoes', to create a structure. Some, like Murray, often use a quite regular or striking rhythm for a line or two, and then replace it with a different one.

So if the term 'free verse' sometimes seems vague, one reason may be that it is being used for several different types of verses. All that most of these have in common is that the poet is creating a pattern by 'feel' rather than by any principle that he or she can state in so many words. No wonder that literary critics sometimes give up, and talk vaguely about a poet's 'sensitive rhythms' or 'subtle sense of rhythm'! Yet if you can find time to analyse these poems closely, you will uncover many of the poets' secrets.

One thing you will probably notice is that free verse depends more than traditional verse upon the poet's personal 'voice'. The great free verse poets like Ted Hughes or Bruce Dawe stamp their personal tone on their work. Yet this can make free verse less international. A reader in New York or London might miss all sorts of subtleties in Bruce Dawe or Les Murray.

If you want to try your hand at free verse, try to make each line-ending fall at a point where there is some reason to pause. And as you reveal the subject matter, try to keep far enough ahead of the readers so that they won't have already guessed what comes next—no one likes to read predictable writing—but do not get so far ahead of them that they give up trying to follow you. It is rather like walking a tightrope. If you ask your friends to comment frankly on what you have written you should be able to find out whether you have got the balance right.

After the 'Ball'

After the fingernails
are cleaned
and the debris examined
microscopically
After the pubic hair
is sponged and tweezed
vagina scraped for
contents
to be specified
After the bruise
of a throat is measured
and photographs
of other welts
are checked
for abnormalities
in the bite
After the p.m.,
After the forms are filed
and the mortician
restores with art
spaces underneath
minus teeth
to create
a little smile
on a small face
After the final
farewell celebration
After dark
After light
After all
It might have been me
After the ball . . .

Lilian Tait

Note on Rhyme

Likeness of sound,
With just enough of difference
To make a change of sense;
So we have contrast,
A piquancy,
And a certain victory of contrivance.
But Heaven keep us from an inevitable rhyme,
Or from a rhyme prepared!

Rhymed verse is a wide net
Through which many subtleties escape.
Nor would I take it to capture a strong thing,
Such as a whale.

Anna Wickham

Mangoes

mangoes are not cigarettes
mangoes are fleshy skinful passionate fruits
mangoes are hungry to be sucked
mangoes are glad to be stuck in the teeth
mangoes like slush & kissing

mangoes are not filter tipped
mangoes are idiosyncratic seasonal seducers
mangoes are worse than adams apple
mangoes are what parents & parliaments warn against
mangoes like making rude noises

mangoes are not extra mild
mangoes are greedy delicious tongueteasers
mangoes are violently soft
mangoes are fibrous intestinal lovebites
mangoes like beginning once again

mangoes are not cigarettes
mangoes are tangible sensual intelligence
mangoes are debauched antisocialites
mangoes are a positive good in the world
mangoes like poetry

Richard Tipping

Mort aux Chats

There will be no more cats.
Cats spread infection,
cats pollute the air,
cats consume seven times
their own weight in food a week,
cats were worshipped in
decadent societies (Egypt
and Ancient Rome), the Greeks
had no use for cats. Cats
sit down to pee (our scientists
have proved it.) The copulation
of cats is harrowing; they
are unbearably fond of the moon.
Perhaps they are all right in
their own country but their
traditions are alien to ours.
Cats smell, they can't help it,
you notice it going upstairs.
Cats watch too much television,
they can sleep through storms,
they stabbed us in the back
last time. There have never been
any great artists who were cats.
They don't deserve a capital C
except at the beginning of a sentence.
I blame my headache and my
plants dying on to cats.
Our district is full of them,
property values are falling.
When I dream of God I see
a Massacre of Cats. Why
should they insist on their own
language and religion, who
needs to purr to make his point?
Death to all cats! The Rule
of Dogs shall last a thousand years!

Peter Porter

The Gull's Flight

    The gull's flight
is low
           flat
  & hard

    they go
to sea
        to the edge
where the day's fire
        is lit

    they go
as shiftworkers
        to the dawn.

Nigel Roberts

The Night-Ride

Gas flaring on the yellow platform; voices running up and down;
Milk-tins in cold dented silver; half-awake I stare,
Pull up the blind, blink out—all sounds are drugged;
The slow blowing of passengers asleep;
Engines yawning; water in heavy drips;
Black, sinister travellers, lumbering up the station,
One moment in the window, hooked over bags;
Hurrying, unknown faces—boxes with strange labels—
All groping clumsily to mysterious ends,

Out of the gaslight, dragged by private Fates.
Their echoes die. The dark train shakes and plunges;
Bells cry out; the night-ride starts again.
Soon I shall look out into nothing but blackness,
Pale, windy fields. The old roar and knock of the rails
Melts in dull fury. Pull down the blind. Sleep. Sleep.
Nothing but grey, rushing rivers of bush outside.
Gaslight and milk-cans. Of Rapptown I recall nothing else.

Kenneth Slessor

A Victorian Hangman Tells his Love

Dear one, forgive my appearing before you like this,
in a two-piece track-suit, welder's goggles
and a green cloth cap like some gross bee—this is the State's
    idea...
I would have come
arrayed like a bridegroom for these nuptials
knowing how often you have dreamed about this
moment of consummation in your cell.
If I must bind your arms now to your sides
with a leather strap and ask if you have anything to say
—these too are formalities I would dispense with:
I know your heart is too full at this moment
to say much and that the tranquilliser which I trust
you did not reject out of a stubborn pride
should by this have eased your ache for speech, breath
and the other incidentals which distract us from our end.
Let us now walk a step. This noose
with which we're wed is something of an heirloom, the last three
members of our holy family were wed with it, the softwood beam
it hangs from like a lovers' tree notched with their weight.
See now I slip it over your neck, the knot
under the left jaw, with a slip ring
to hold the knot in place... There. Perfect.
Allow me to adjust the canvas hood
which will enable you to anticipate the officially prescribed
    darkness
by some seconds.
The journalists are ready with the flash-bulbs of their eyes
raised to the simple altar, the doctor twitches like a stethoscope
—you have been given a clean bill of health, like any
modern bride.
          With this spring of mine
from the trap, hitting the door lever, you will go forth
into a new life which I, alas, am not yet fit to share.
Be assured, you will sink into the generous pool of public feeling
as gently as a leaf—accept your role, feel chosen.
You are this evening's headlines. Come, my love.

Bruce Dawe

Garrakeen

Garrakeen, the parakeet, is slim and swift.
Like a spear of green and red he flashes through
the cumbered branches by the river-bank.
Watch him, brighter than the clouds, before the day is done;
watch him in the morning, when the gums are bathed with dew,
rivalling the spears of the sun.

When dawn flamed on the Murray I watched for Garrakeen...
Opaline purple and crimson was the river...
He came from the west with blood on his breast,
and the colours of the water were sluggish in sheen
compared with his fire in the air;

the voice of the water was shattered by one
shrill from the spear-bird hurrying there,
flying with the light of the east in his sight,
rivalling the spears of the sun.

Rex Ingamells

Petit Testament

In the twenty-fifth year of my age
I find myself to be a dromedary
That has run short of water between
One oasis and the next mirage
And having despaired of ever
Making my obsessions intelligible
I am content at last to be
The sole clerk of my metamorphoses.
Begin here:

In the year 1943
I resigned to the living all collateral images
Reserving to myself a man's
Inalienable right to be sad
At his own funeral.
(Here the peacock blinks the eyes
of his multipennate tail.)

In the same year
I said to my love (who is living)
Dear we shall never be that bird
Perched on the sole Arabian Tree
Not having learnt in our green age to forget
The sins that flow between the hands and feet
(Here the Tree weeps gum tears
Which are also real: I tell you
These things are real)
So, I forced a parting
Scrubbing my few dingy words to brightness.

Where I have lived
The bed-bug sleeps in the seam, the cockroach
Inhabits the crack and the careful spider
Spins his aphorisms in the corner.
I have heard them shout in the streets
The chiliasms of the Socialist Reich
And in the magazines I have read
The Popular Front-to-Back.
But where I have lived
Spain weeps in the gutters of Footscray
Guernica is the ticking of the clock
The nightmare has become real, not as belief
But in the scrub-typhus of Mubo.

Ern Malley (James McAuley and Harold Stewart)

Bringing the Cattle

All afternoon I've lain about in this illuminated country, on one of the round hillsides, and have heard the squeak of cropped grass, and smelt the cow smell, like a warm convalescence, the cows close and oblivious, or with a sun-drugged interest.

A hare stopped in the heat, and shivered, folding back its ears— the same way as the butterfly did its wings, on a plaited head of grass that hung above the ripe valley.

But now the farmer, who all year wears shorts and rubber boots, and wades through the running shallows of paddock grass, who cracks his cattle with a stick across their bony outcrops, makes his voice float here.

And the cattle jolt down with everything swinging—the bellies rounded as hammocks stretched full, the four long tits, and the udders that are grooved and furry like a peach.

Their foreheads, between the big eyeballs' slow permanent surprise, make a wide, hollow-sounding target for the crowbar-wielding farmer when they've something broken or a germ.

The hips, draped sharp Henry Moore shapes. And the splayed feet are placed with mincing care, as if they've high heels on.

Now a last cow is flouncing along the top of the slope, its spider-web fine thread of slobber blown out long in the final brightness of the sun.

The air is staining quickly with moisture, and the paddocks fill with vacancy.

These corridors laid across the beaten grass are alight and chill. The river, willow-shouldered, that was silk in the distance, now at twilight is ice panels.

And the mist that will lie, kerosene-blue and thick as smoke, all night a succubus on the creeks and dams, and that will drag among the raided, fluttering cornstalks, and stick the turned earth thickly, is already starting to seep from every dark socket of the ground.

So, following the cattle, and at their pace, I am also going down.

Robert Gray

Snake

The tiger snake moves
Like slow lightning. Like
A yard of creek water
It flows over rocks
Carving the grass.

Where have you gone,
Long fellow, cold brother,
Like a lopped limb or
Truth that we shy from
Leaving a cast skin?

Snakes are like a line
Of poetry: a chill
Wind in the noon,
A slalom in the spine
Setting ears back, hair on end.

'Some people will not live
With a snake in the house.'
Mice make off. Look
Under your chair; worse
Take down a book:

A line like an icicle!

David Campbell

NOTES

'After the "Ball" '
Note that line endings replace punctuation. **p.m.**: post mortem.
Read the poem line by line. By what stages does it become clear that the person described is a corpse, and how she died?
Companion Pieces: 'Punishment', 'Strange Fruit', Seamus Heaney; 'In the Mortuary', Craig Raine. All are in the *Penguin Book of Contemporary British Poetry*.

'Mangoes'
Would this poem be better without its last stanza?
Contrast Poem: 'Smokers for Celibacy', Fleur Adcock (N.Z.)

'Mort aux Chats'
The title is French for 'Death to Cats'.

'The Night-Ride'
Scan this poem, marking the stresses as you would normally pronounce them. Is there any regularity? Does the poem's rhythm adapt, from line to line, to what is being described?

'A Victorian Hangman Tells his Love'
Following a public outcry over the hanging of Ronald Ryan, hanging has been abolished in Victoria.
What does Dawe achieve by describing the hanging as if it were a wedding?

'Garrakeen'
Read the poem aloud. Would it be fair to say that Ingamells has excellent ideas but a poor ear for verse? Might his second sentence be better as prose? Do the traces of rhyme help?

'Petit Testament'
This is one of the famous Ern Malley poems, written as a hoax by James McAuley and Harold Stewart. The aim was to ridicule the fashion for free verse poems that seemed richly evocative but did not say anything very precise. There was a similar hoax by Gwen Harwood in 1970 in the anthology *Australian Poetry Now* (Sun Books) using the pen-name T. F. Kline. Some victims of the hoax claimed later that the Ern Malley poems were actually McAuley's best work. Compare this one with a serious poem by McAuley and see what you feel. For an excellent argument about how to tell good from bad in modern verse see Chapter 1 of James Dickie's *Babel to Byzantium*, Ecco Press (U.S.A.), 1981.

'Bringing the Cattle'
This is a prose poem, so the unit is the sentence rather than the line. A prose poem should presumably be more complete, and also more compressed, musical, and rich in images, than a passage from a novel. **Henry Moore**: British sculptor, b. 1898. **So, following**, etc.: Note how the three

commas, each requiring an upward inflection of the voice (rising pitch) prepare us for the downward inflection, which carries the note of finality, on 'down'.

Is this poem complete in itself?

ACTIVITIES

1 Devise some additional lines for Peter Porter's 'Mort aux Chats'. Then divide into groups, and write a poem about race prejudice similar to 'Mort aux Chats', but using a different pair of animals—a cat talking about sparrows, a tree's view of dogs, or a mouse's view of people. Throw in everything you can think of; later prune back to the strongest lines. Then read the poems aloud. If two groups have used the same two animals, see if the best lines can be combined into a single poem. Try to get a striking opening and a strong closing line, and to get the lines between into the best order.

2 Do your own version of Tipping's 'Mangoes', but using a different fruit or vegetable. Or use any other object whose name has interesting associations, or even use a made-up name. For example, Dingoes are... Flies are... Quonks are...

3 Choose your favourite free verse poem from any other section of this anthology, and write either a parody or your own poem inspired by its example.

4 **Project**: Investigate the Ern Malley hoax, starting with the article in *The Oxford Companion to Australian Literature* (under 'Ern').

5 Check through the Notes of any one section of this book. In how many cases could the poet have made a note unnecessary by writing more clearly or more skilfully? Do free verse poets on average write more or less obscurely than users of traditional verse?

6 Select three free verse poems from any *other* section of this anthology and write two or three sentences about how the authors use free verse. Do they use short lines, or long, or variable? vernacular tone? variations of tone? any special effects?

7 Investigate those free verse poets whose work seems closest to prose— R. G. Hay, Bruce Beaver, Barbara Giles are possibilities. How does their verse differ from that of Lilian Tait or Geoff Page? What would it lose if written out as prose?

8 Make a special study of Bruce Dawe's free verse. How does he vary it from poem to poem, and from line to line? Do its changes of rhythm match what is being said? Is there the ghost of regular rhythm behind it?

9 Library Project: Compare the personal 'voice' of any Australian poet who writes in free verse with that of either Ted Hughes, Sylvia Plath, T. S. Eliot, Robert Lowell, Allen Ginsberg or Seamus Heaney.

10 'A line like an icicle'. Would the last line of 'The Electors' be an example? Select, copy out and read to the class your own mini-anthology of such lines. Do some lines actually send a physical shiver down your spine?

11 Have someone write up the lines of an unknown free verse poem, one by one, on a blackboard. After each new line is added, try to guess how the poem will develop next. What do you learn about the poem's structure?

Relevant poems from other sections

Almost anything by Bruce Dawe, Kate Llewellyn, Geoff Page, and most of the younger poets.

†'Shame', Richard Wilbur; 'Journey of The Magi', T. S. Eliot; 'I Saw in Louisiana a Live-Oak Growing', 'This Compost', Walt Whitman.

12

YOUNG AND OLD

We may like to think of ourselves as people of a particular age, playing a particular role in society, but time is always moving us on, out of that age group, until one day we find ourselves in the opposing team. As Shakespeare remarked, 'One man in his time plays many parts'. This thought may lead to melancholy reflections on the inevitability of old age and death. To understand the stages of human life is also a powerful and positive key to understanding who we are. Many aspects of our personalities are decided in childhood, and especially by our interaction with our parents. It is important to discover both how we are changing and why our parents behave as they do, and even what sort of parents we might be. Some of the wisest and most poignant of twentieth-century Australian poems deal with a poet's memories of childhood and of parents, and with a consequent understanding of how time has altered him or her.

The Old

You cannot forget the old.
They become part of you.
They take you for themselves.

I have watched them in the city.
They stack themselves up
against the walls like chairs.

They always seem to be waiting
for something to happen.
It never does.

Or if it does I'm never there.
I do not trust them.
They aren't satisfied with death.

They keep on coming back.
Someone old will be inside your flesh
not long from now—

taking you over completely
going about your business
sleeping with your wife.

I know the one who wants me.
Sometimes I think I know his thoughts.
He will know me very well.

But still we won't get on.
He will walk for miles
just thinking of me.

It will be very much like love.
He will leaf through old books
where I have written silly things.

He will search out photograph albums
and stare at pictures of me—
adjusting old white corners

smelling the gum.

Kevin Hart

Parents

My father asks me how I stand it all,
The work, the debts, the spite. My mother talks
As though I were a famous man and yet
Unguarded somehow, too fragile to touch.
It's their needs, not mine, that flutter here
In the questions and the anecdotes. I stare
At the rust encroaching on the walnut-branches
Or the pile of litter where the biggest pinetree
Used to stand, before my absence killed it.
Their door has a vine over it; they murmur
Endearments to the animals, and cry
At small wrongs. Which is the oldest of us three?

Facts sound like charges. The least important man
Is a legend in his neighbour's living-room,
Menacing and remarkable as the lightning
That ran from tree to tree about the house
So recently, like the shining of its ghosts.
I nod, but the names, perils, dates mean nothing;
And where that's true, the deepest bonds are lost.
How will the vine bear this year? I feel
My heart growing till my thoughts are hoarse
And the old branches pick at the heap of leavings.
There is so much I don't recall. They stand,
Timid, waving to watch me go, barely
Visible in the window's copper sheen.

Vincent Buckley

Weights

In memory of my mother, Miriam Murray née Arnall

Not owning a cart, my father
in the drought years was a bowing
green hut of cattle feed, moving,
or gasping under cream cans. No weight
would he let my mother carry.

Instead, she wielded handles
in the kitchen and dairy, singing often,

gave saucepan-boiled injections
with her ward-sister skill, nursed neighbours,
scorned gossips, ran committees.

She gave me her factual tone,
her facial bones, her will,
not her beautiful voice
but her straightness and her clarity.

I did not know back then
nor for many years what it was,
after me, she could not carry.

Les A. Murray

Father and Child

I *Barn Owl*

Daybreak: the household slept.
I rose, blessed by the sun.
A horny fiend, I crept
out with my father's gun.
Let him dream of a child
obedient, angel-mild—

old No-Sayer, robbed of power
by sleep. I knew my prize
who swooped home at this hour
with daylight-riddled eyes
to his place on a high beam
in our old stables, to dream

light's useless time away.
I stood, holding my breath,
in urine-scented hay,
master of life and death,
a wisp-haired judge whose law
would punish beak and claw.

My first shot struck. He swayed,
ruined, beating his only
wing, as I watched, afraid
by the fallen gun, a lonely
child who believed death clean
and final, not this obscene

bundle of stuff that dropped,
and dribbled through loose straw
tangling in bowels, and hopped
blindly closer. I saw
those eyes that did not see
mirror my cruelty

while the wrecked thing that could
not bear the light nor hide
hobbled in its own blood.
My father reached my side,
gave me the fallen gun.
'End what you have begun.'

I fired. The blank eyes shone
once into mine, and slept.
I leaned my head upon
my father's arm, and wept,
owl-blind in early sun
for what I had begun.

II Nightfall

Forty years, lived or dreamed:
what memories pack them home.
Now the season that seemed
incredible is come.
Father and child, we stand
in time's long-promised land.

Since there's no more to taste
ripeness is plainly all.
Father, we pick our last
fruits of the temporal.
Eighty years old, you take
this late walk for my sake.

Who can be what you were?
Link your dry hand in mine,
my stick-thin comforter.
Far distant suburbs shine
with great simplicities.
Birds crowd in flowering trees,

sunset exalts its known
symbols of transience.
Your passionate face is grown
to ancient innocence.
Let us walk for this hour
as if death had no power

or were no more than sleep.
Things truly named can never
vanish from earth. You keep
a child's delight for ever
in birds, flowers, shivery-grass—
I name them as we pass.

'*Be your tears wet?*' You speak
as if air touched a string
near breaking-point. Your cheek
brushes on mine. Old king,
your marvellous journey's done.
Your night and day are one

as you find with your white stick
the path on which you turn
home with the child once quick
to mischief, grown to learn
what sorrows, in the end,
no words, no tears can mend.

Gwen Harwood

Because

My father and my mother never quarrelled.
They were united in a kind of love
As daily as the *Sydney Morning Herald*,
Rather than like the eagle or the dove.

I never saw them casually touch,
Or show a moment's joy in one another.
Why should this matter to me now so much?
I think it bore more hardly on my mother,

Who had more generous feeling to express.
My father had dammed up his Irish blood
Against all drinking praying fecklessness,
And stiffened into stone and creaking wood.

His lips would make a switching sound, as though
Spontaneous impulse must be kept at bay.
That it was mainly weakness I see now,
But then my feelings curled back in dismay.

Small things can pit the memory like a cyst:
Having seen other fathers greet their sons,
I put my childish face up to be kissed
After an absence. The rebuff still stuns

My blood. The poor man's curt embarrassment
At such a delicate proffer of affection
Cut like a saw. But home the lesson went:
My tenderness thenceforth escaped detection.

My mother sang *Because*, and *Annie Laurie*,
White Wings, and other songs; her voice was sweet.
I never gave enough, and I am sorry;
But we were all closed in the same defeat.

People do what they can; they were good people,
They cared for us and loved us. Once they stood
Tall in my childhood as the school, the steeple.
How can I judge without ingratitude?

Judgment is simply trying to reject
A part of what we are because it hurts.
The living cannot call the dead collect:
They won't accept the charge, and it reverts.

It's my own judgment day that I draw near,
Descending in the past, without a clue,
Down to that central deadness: the despair
Older than any hope I ever knew.

James McAuley

Naked Girl and Mirror

This is not I. I had no body once—
only what served my need to laugh and run
and stare at stars and tentatively dance
on the fringe of foam and wave and sand and sun.
Eyes loved, hands reached for me, but I was gone
on my own currents, quicksilver, thistledown.
Can I be trapped at last in that soft face?

I stare at you in fear, dark brimming eyes.
Why do you watch me with that immoderate plea—
'Look under these curled lashes, recognize
that you were always here; know me—be me.'
Smooth once-hermaphrodite shoulders, too tenderly
your long slope runs, above those sudden shy
curves furred with light that spring below your space.

No, I have been betrayed. If I had known
that this girl waited between a year and a year,
I'd not have chosen her bough to dance upon.
Betrayed, by that little darkness here, and here
this swelling softness and that frightened stare
from eyes I will not answer; shut out here
from my own self, by its new body's grace—

for I am betrayed by someone lovely. Yes,
I see you are lovely, hateful naked girl.
Your lips in the mirror tremble as I refuse
to know or claim you. Let me go—let me be gone.
You are half of some other who may never come.
Why should I tend you? You are not my own;
you seek that other—he will be your home.

Yet I pity your eyes in the mirror, misted with tears;
I lean to your kiss. I must serve you; I will obey.
Some day we may love. I may miss your going, some day,
though I shall always resent your dumb and fruitful years.
Your lovers shall learn better, and bitterly too,
if their arrogance dares to think I am part of you.

Judith Wright

Lake in Spring

The shallow reaches of the lake
on welcome-swallow days, lie still,
holding within a waveless blue
whatever comes, whatever goes
on path or hill.

So he and I not long ago
were there received and echoed back;
our living looks met eye to eye,
from calm and perfect surfaces
reflected to a perfect sky.

But now we move, we shift, we pass.
The images are overlaid.
The lake is driven by the wind
and stills again, and others cross
its mirror, and the world's remade.

Now when I bend to it again
another spring, another year
have changed and greyed the images,
and the face that lay beside
my own, no longer answers there.

There's little change in lake and sky,
they watch each other steadily;
but years took him and altered me.
Two look me back in this calm weather,
but who is this, and who am I?

A ripple goes across the glass.
The faces break and blur and pass
as love and time are blurred together.

Judith Wright

NOTES

'The Old'
Companion Pieces: 'The Invaders', 'Hay Fever', A. D. Hope; 'Sex and the Over Forties', Peter Porter. Also 'The Old Fools', 'Posterity', 'This be the Verse', 'Annus Mirabilis', Philip Larkin (All in *High Windows*, Faber, 1974).

'Parents'
Companion Pieces: 'Book Ends', 'Long Distance', Tony Harrison (UK).

'Weights'
Not owning a cart...: Murray grew up on a small farm north of Taree in NSW.

'Father and Child'
horny: callous and tough; like a horned devil. **daylight-riddled**: perhaps 'dazzled by daylight'. **owl-blind in early sun**: What are the implications of this phrase? **ripeness is... all**: cf. **Be your tears wet?** and **Old King**: references to *King Lear*. **transience**: being transient, passing away with time. **your night and day are one**: Why?
How could you best describe the rhythm in this poem: iambic with some feet reversed? three stresses to a line? a near-equal number of stressed and unstressed syllables in no fixed order? other?

'Because'
The rhythm is iambic pentameter, but it would be pedantic to read the poem with a stress on every second syllable. Note how the poet's conversational tone creates variations from the regular iambic pentameter, and puts the emphasis where he wants it. The rhymes are a mixture of exact and inexact (e.g. blood/wood).

'Naked Girl and Mirror'
hermaphrodite: in the sense that a child's body before puberty is not fully assigned to either sex.
Why does the girl wish to refuse her new sexual identity at puberty?
Companion Pieces: 'Andromeda', 'Breasts'.

ACTIVITIES

1   One of these poems is selected and read aloud at the start of class each day for a week by a different member of the class. The others jot down an 'instant reaction' each time. At the end of the week general discussion of the poem may follow.

2 Divide into groups for initial discussion of one of these poems. If they are willing, one group's discussion may be tape-recorded and played back to the others.

3 It is said that the hardest thing in the world to get into perspective is one's own family. Which of the poets here do you think has been most successful, and why? Perhaps divide into groups according to which poem you favour, and together produce a short written argument for your view.

4 Which poem in this section do you like best? Divide into groups according to your choice, and then produce your own artistic response to the poem or to various sections and aspects of it. A response may include sketches, cartoons, calligraphy of part of the text, original verse, or prose comments by different members of the group. Final result might be a compound poster, or a loose-leaf folder. If your ideas don't fit with a group, make your own minority report.

5 Imagine that you are the author of 'Lake in Spring'. Write a letter to a close friend expressing the same thoughts as you put in the poem.

6 Write a poem or part of a short story inspired by Buckley's 'Parents', in which someone visits a relative, teacher or friend whom they had worshipped as a small child. To their dismay the person seems shrunken, elderly, and somehow silly.

7 Do the same for a person who returns to live with their parents after three or four years in a foreign country.

8 **Library Project**: Compare 'Father and Child' with another Gwen Harwood poem, 'Mother Who Gave Me Life'. Which do you think shows the warmer feelings towards a parent, and which do you prefer? Should the two halves of 'Father and Child' be separate poems, or do they gain by being joined?

9 Write a poem, perhaps for your eyes only, about your family's situation. Would you ever want to make it public? Why? Or why not? Would it hurt your family if you published it?

Relevant poems from other sections

'The Apparition', 'Sea Children,' 'Ulinda' 'Starting from Central Station', 'Hay Fever', 'Woman to Child', 'In the Park, Looking', 'Post Card', 'Reverie of a Mum', 'Goya Paints a Portait of a Child', 'Theatre'.

Poems for further study

*'Puritan Poet Reel', Vincent Buckley; 'One Day', Ray Mathew; 'The Smell of Coal Smoke', Les A. Murray; 'Pope Alexander VI', Geoffrey Lehmann; 'June Fugue', Thomas W. Shapcott; 'The Year of the Foxes', David Malouf; 'Parabola', A. D. Hope.

†'Book Ends (I)', Tony Harrison; 'Love Poem for a Wife', A. K. Ramanujan; 'Pain for a Daughter', Anne Sexton; 'Five Days Old', Francis Webb; 'Lines on a Young Lady's Photograph Album', Philip Larkin; 'Fern Hill', Dylan Thomas; 'Ecce Puer', James Joyce; 'Sailing to Byzantium', W. B. Yeats.

13

PEOPLE

To say that 'people are people the world over' is not quite true. Different countries and cultures do make a difference, but it is true that people everywhere are remarkably different both from each other, and from the official or average notions of 'the citizen', 'the school child', 'the teacher', 'the sportsperson' and so on. Idealistic science fiction writers have designed many perfect worlds for perfect people (Utopias), but no one has yet designed a perfect world for real people. The varieties of human personality continue to fascinate, delight, and frighten.

Cricket

Thud of leather on willow—and the ball
Streaks by the incompetent outfielders
To hit the wall for 2. A bright Sunday.
My discontent squirms at the guffawing

Good-humour of my fellows. A Sunday
To consign to the past like a package
Mailed to an unknown address; the waste
Will be an agony to remember.

Thud of leather on willow—the batsmen
Blunder back and forth. Flocks of birds drift high
Over the lake. The trees glisten with light
Like a Monet painting, still as canvas.

Frankie sits cross-legged in the long grass;
George heaves rocks at the wall; Tom rolls a smoke;
And I hang about waiting for a catch,
Full of the sap... my twenty-first summer.

Peter Kocan

Ladies and Gentlemen

You are such a gentleman
that when you showed me round your house
you didn't point your bedroom
and showed me rows of whips and guns and saddles
but I can't act the lady
when you're turning my soul over
and I'm calling to the lava
in the centre of the earth
you gazed amazed
as if you'd bought a horse
which was wilder than you thought
and until the day you break me
you'll try bit and boots and saddle
to make a lady for the ring of me
and on the day I break
as every horse has done
you'll sell me at the show
and get another wild one

Kate Llewellyn

The Fishermen at South Head

They have walked out as far as they can go on the prow of the
    continent,
on the undercut white sandstone, the bowsprits of the towering
    headland.
They project their long light canes
or raise them up to check and string, like quiet archers.
Between casts they hold them couched,
a finger on the line, two fingers on a cigarette, the reel cocked.

They watch the junction of smooth blue with far matt-shining
    blue,
the join where clouds enter,
or they watch the wind-shape of their nylon
bend like a sail's outline
south towards, a mile away, the city's floating gruel
of gull-blown effluent.

Sometimes they glance north, at the people on that calf-coloured
    edge
lower than theirs, where the suicides come by taxi
and stretchers are winched up
later, under raining lights
but mostly their eyes stay level with the land-and-ocean glitter.

Where they stand, atop the centuries
of strata, they don't look down much
but feel through their tackle the talus-eddying
and tidal detail of that huge simple pulse
in the rock and in their bones.

Through their horizontal poles they divine the creatures of ocean:
a touch, a dip, and a busy winding death gets started;
hands will turn for minutes, rapidly,
before, still opening its pitiful doors, the victim
dawns above the rim, and is hoisted in a flash above the suburbs
—or before the rod flips, to stand
trailing sworn-at gossamer.

On that highest dreadnought scarp, where the terracotta
waves of bungalows stop, suspended at sky,
the hunters stand apart.
They encourage one another, at a distance, not by talk

but by being there, by unhooking now and then
a twist of silver for the creel, by a vaguely mutual
zodiac of cars TV windcheaters.
Braced, casual normality. Anything unshared,
a harlequin mask, a painted wand flourished at the sun
would anger them. It is serious to be with humans.

Les A. Murray

Painter of Antwerp

Plod homeward, peasant, north-bound from Italy
With head full of slow wonder, pondering
On frescoes at Venice and all the odd adventures—
The bear in the way, the painter at Padua
In a great plumed hat, full of queer notions,
Ships in the harbour at Naples with a new rigging—
Strangeness enough to empty many tankards.

Plod homeward, Brueghel, Painter of Antwerp.

At the top of the Alps he paused perhaps, looked backwards,
Rejecting the fanciful, and took for a painting
Ploughman, fisherman, and moon-faced shepherd,
The furrow cut cleanly, the sheep contented;
Put thumb to nose with neither pride nor envy
At soaring wings—a Southerner's invention—
Icarus sprawling, two feet out of the sea.

Rosemary Dobson

For David Campbell ⚝⚝⚝⚝

And, lo, they were very dry
Ezekiel, XXXVII.2.

At the Last Judgement, as the final batch
Is sorted out: 'Goats, seventeen; sheep, three!'
God may permit himself at last to snatch
A yawn or two; then, looking at his watch:
'TIME, Gentlemen, please! Henceforth Eternity!'

At which, well pleased with a decisive clap
Recording Angel will shut up his book,
And Devil's Advocate, dog-tired poor chap,
Take off his horns, put on his halo, wrap
His nimbus round, when someone bawls: 'Hey, look!

'Hold it! There's someone coming up the street!'
And sure enough, far down that dusty slope
Trod by so many million shuffling feet
A straggler comes in view. God takes his seat
Saying: 'I might have known it: Alec Hope!

'Always the tail-end of the bloody mob;
Always too feckless even to cut it fine.
The Foolish Virgins did a proper job
Compared with him, well, when that loafing slob
Arrives, we'll really lay it on the line!'

'Wait, Lord! He does not come alone, though,' cries
The D.A. putting back his horns and tail.
'One in, all in's the rule!' The Lord replies,
'Contempt of court will fit them all for size,
And just don't let me hear you ask for bail!'

And round the last bend weaving up the straight,
Glorious, hilarious, erratically slow,
The company of the incorrigibly late,
Campbell and Hope approach the Pearly Gate,
Passing a long-necked bottle to and fro.

God bends his ireful brows upon the pair;
Singles me out: 'Well, Alec Hope, you have
Ten seconds flat, I say, ten seconds bare,
If either of you have anything to declare
Against the bottomless pit, the fiery grave.'

'Well, Lord, there's little enough that I can say;
We met this morning after the final crunch,
(The Resurrection, I mean) and thought the way
To celebrate Damnation and the Last Day
Would be to give ourselves a splendid lunch.'

'Lunch!' says the Lord, 'You poets beat the band!
Lunch on a day like this? My Day of Doom!
You keep ME waiting, and you turn up canned:
What excuse can you possibly...?' 'Lord, you understand,
We poets develop a grand thirst in the tomb

'We've been a long time dead; our bones were dry
As those Ezekiel in his vision raised up.
And there were these new tongues of ours to try
For wine and song—Well, David Campbell and I
Resolved to make a halt for bite and sup.

'We met outside the Bacchus too. In short
He said: "Look, Alec, this seems the finger of Fate;
Why don't we...?" "Dave," I said, "the selfsame thought
Occurred to me. My turn to shout though, sport;
I've owed you a lunch since nineteen sixty-eight."

'"Ten centuries?" he said: "Well, what d'you know?
That's quite a time for building up a thirst.
We mustn't forget, of course, there's a big show
At Heaven's Gate today—we've got to go,
But what I always say is: First things first!

'"Besides, there's something more: I think I've got
A poem coming on." "For that a fine
Pokolbin, David, would be just the shot;
And Heaven will be dry as like as not."
Well that's our story, Lord, Campbell's and mine.'

'Campbell?' the Lord will say, 'Now let me see;
He's a good poet and always dead on time.
I'd put this lapse down to bad company.
We're short of poets in Heaven too... Dear me,
He wouldn't, by any chance, have finished that rhyme?'

'Just what he did, Lord! You should hear it, you should!'
And Dave will speak those lines at Heaven's Gate
And God will say: 'Well done, Campbell, jolly good!
Let's hear more, Campbell, while we're in the mood
Let Time continue: Eternity can wait!'

There in a listening silence the world will end
With poetry as with poetry it began
And, when it is done, the Lord will smile and bend
His eyes on me and say: 'Well, Hope, your friend
Has saved your bacon; at least I think I can

'Just stretch the rules a little—So, on your way!
Get along, both of you; and don't forget:
There'll be no lunching in Heaven from today;
Pick up your harps from Peter, and learn to play;
We'll expect some heavenly music from you yet.'

A. D. Hope

Near the school for handicapped children

His hat is rammed on.
His shirt jerks at his body
his feet cannot hold in
      the sway, he cannot keep still.
When I see his face it is freckled
to remind me of nephews.
His limbs remind me of how straight
is my own spine and that I take my fingers
for granted.
He is waiting for the Green Light.

      My fingers clench
      I am hurt by my wholeness
      I cannot take my eyes from him.
      I fear my daughter may be watching.

He has been dressed carefully
    I'm here I'm here I'm here
his whole struggle rasps me like a whisper

and when the lights do change
he skips across the road he
skips he skips he dances and skips
leaving us all behind like a skimming tambourine
brittle with music.

Thomas W. Shapcott

NOTES

'Cricket'
Peter Kocan spent years in a psychiatric prison after attempting to assassinate the then Leader of the Opposition, Arthur Calwell.
for 2: not 4, because the boundary is so near.

'Ladies and Gentlemen'
Discussion: How unusual is the gentleman?

'The Fishermen at South Head'
South Head is the southern entrance to Sydney Harbour. Because the cliffs are so high and undercut, a person standing near the edge often has to fish 'blind', without looking down.
junction: of sea and sky. **talus:** broken blocks where an earlier cliff has fallen down. **its pitiful doors:** mouth and gill-covers. **hunters:** fishers.
zodiac: What senses of *zodiac* are relevant here? Is the word strained?

'Painter of Antwerp'
Peter Brueghel the Elder (1525–69) visited Renaissance Italy, the home of advanced 'modern art' in his day. Dobson admires him for keeping his feet on the ground.
Icarus: In classical mythology Icarus rashly flew too near the sun. The heat melted the wax with which his artificial wings were held together, and he fell into the sea. Brueghel painted this mythological story, but with a wealth of realistic detail. See W. H. Auden's poem 'Musée de Beaux Arts'† and Dobson's 'The Bystander'. **Southerner's:** Brueghel came from the 'less advanced' north of Europe.
Companion Pieces: 'Marble Gods', Mark O'Connor; and from *The Penguin Anthology of Contemporary British Verse:* 'St Kilda's Parliament', Douglas Dunn; 'Mossbawn (Part 2)', Seamus Heaney; 'The Ballad of Babelabour', Tony Harrison.

'For David Campbell'
Hope writes in *A Book of Answers* (Angus and Robertson, 1978): 'I have admired and enjoyed David Campbell's work for so many years and have been gratified by a growing friendship with the man himself. In November 1968 he invited me to lunch at the Lobby Restaurant in Canberra where he discovered from the head waiter that they had stocks of Pokolbin wines from the recently destroyed vineyards which had been devastated by bushfires. The lunch was an epic celebration; I chiefly recall the head waiter approaching David and saying: "Mr Campbell, it is now nearly half-past six and we are about to begin the next meal: would you and your friend care to go on to dinner?" '
nimbus: cloud or aura surrounding a heavenly personage. **the bloody mob:** Hope makes God speak broad Australian. **the Bacchus:** a restaurant in Canberra.

'Near the school for handicapped children'
he/skips he skips he: Note the effect of the line-break (creating suspense) and the repetition.

ACTIVITIES

1   Which of the poems in this section do you think best captures a personality? Defend your choice by quoting its most effective phrases, and comparing them with those of two other poems you find less impressive.

2   **Discussion:** Is it possible to describe someone's personality without showing it in action?

3   Write your own version of Hope's 'For David Campbell', describing the scene at the Pearly Gates on the arrival of one of your fellow scholars or teachers. Try, like Hope, to keep the persons true-to-life, even though the story is a fantasy.

4   David Campbell was obviously an unusual character: farmer, writer, international rugby player and war pilot. Compare all the poems by and about him in this book, and see what aspects of his personality emerge.

5   Read 'The Fishermen at South Head' through twice in class, trying to sort out any difficulties. Then, using it as a model, try to write a similarly vivid description (in prose or verse) of any place and group of people you know well.

6   Research the life of Brueghel, his historical background, painting style, and subject matter. Also investigate the Icarus myth in art and poetry (for example, Roger McGough's poem 'Icarus Allsorts'). Perhaps write a poem or a piece of descriptive prose about one of Brueghel's other paintings.

7   **Library Project:** Investigate R. D., Fitzgerald's techniques for describing characters in 'Fifth Day' or A. D. Hope's in 'Clover Honey' or *The Age of Reason* and compare them with those of any contemporary prose-fiction writer.

Relevant poems from other sections

Most of Section 12, and 'Five Visions of Captain Cook', 'Wanna be White', 'Sweeney', 'The Shearer's Wife', 'The Breach', 'Reverie of a Mum', 'Freedom Fighter', 'The Regulars', 'Brothers', 'Louise and Alessandro', 'Generations', 'The Big Web', 'Emily Brontë', 'Theatre', 'In the Park', 'A Simple Story', 'Mark', 'Brother and Sisters', 'So Quietly', 'Semi-Conductors', 'Living Dangerously'.

Poems for further study

*'Grit', 'Country Nun', Geoff Page; 'A Poem for Maurice O'Shea', Geoffrey Lehmann; 'Galaxies', Alan Gould; 'Mutton Bird Man', Rhyll McMaster; 'A Queer Thing', Nancy Keesing; 'The Execution of Madame Du Barry', J. J. Bray; 'Country Press', Rosemary Dobson.

†'Casualty', Seamus Heaney; 'Return the Bridewealth', Okot p'Bitek; 'Ogun', Edward Kamau Brathwaite; 'Lament for Barney Flanagan', James K. Baxter; 'Memories of West Street and Lepke', Robert Lowell; 'In Memory of W. B. Yeats', W. H. Auden; 'The Last Words of my English Grandmother', William Carlos Williams; 'Mending Wall', 'Neither Out Far Nor In Deep', Robert Frost; 'My Last Duchess', Robert Browning; 'Holy Willie's Prayer', Robert Burns; 'The Parish Register', George Crabbe; 'Absalom and Achitophel', John Dryden; 'An Horation Ode Upon Cromwel's Return from Ireland', Andrew Marvell.

14

WOMEN'S EXPERIENCE

What do women think and feel? Anything and everything that men do—and with just as much difference between individuals. There are some experiences, like being pregnant or bearing a child, that only women can have. A woman's response to pregnancy or birth may be anywhere from joy to horror, but either way it will be an experience no man can directly have; although Geoffrey Lehmann's poem 'Five Days Late' reminds us that a man can share something of such experiences simply by imagining himself in the woman's place.

In addition there are some feelings and experiences that may equally well belong to either sex, but which may, in a given culture, more commonly happen to women than to men. In our society a woman is still more likely than a man to be asked to pursue her education or her career part-time, or to choose between a career and marriage (or having a child). She is more likely to find herself becoming a single parent; and, as Rosemary Dobson reminds us, she is probably also more likely to find herself caught with the duty of looking after an elderly parent.

In our culture, which until recently gave far more importance to men's activities than to women's, there is always a risk that female activities and emotions will be undervalued. For instance a male editor or reader might feel that Doris Brett's poem about women down the ages talking to each other while keeping an eye on their children was quite clever, but not about anything important. In fact it is about the way half of the human race spends a great percentage of its time.

Since the late 1960s Australian women poets have demanded more attention for female experiences. No two women poets have quite the same ideas or attitudes, but they agree in rejecting the male tendency to see women merely as home makers, or sex objects, or as somebody's wife and somebody else's mum.

They claim the right to describe their own bodies and their own erotic feelings, and in an age when a large percentage of Western housewives are on tranquilizers to help them through the day, they insist on describing the drudgery of housework and the tedium of looking after small child-ren—though we should not assume that motherhood is always as negative an experience as Gwen Harwood's brilliant vignette shows it can be. In addition many female poets have rewritten the traditional myths and fairy stories of our culture, with interesting results.

Many of the poems in this section might equally well belong in other sections. Collected here, they remind us of an important group of issues that women talk about mainly when on their own. Young men in particular may be unaware of these issues; yet sooner or later a man needs to know about them, because he will meet them, even if only indirectly, as a son, brother, friend, colleague, husband, father, grandfather or brother-in-law. For young women, of course, they represent many of the essential choices of life.

The Edge

Three times to the world's end I went,
Three times returned as one who brings
Tidings of light beyond the dark
But voiceless stays, still marvelling.

After great pain I had great joy
Three times that never else I knew;
The last reflection of its light
Fades from the pupils of my eyes.

Webbed by the world again I walk
The mazy paths that women tread
Watchful lest any harm should come
To those who journeyed back with me.

But still, as Lazarus who was born
Again beyond the edge of death,
I see the world half otherwise
And tremble at its mysteries.

Rosemary Dobson

Once When She Thought Aloud

I've had all of the apple, she said,
Except the core.
All that many a woman desires—
All and more.
Children, husband, and comfort enough
And a little over.
Hungry Alice and Bitter Anne
Say I'm in clover.

I've had all of the apple, she said.
—All that's good.
Whiles I feel I'd throw it away,
The wholesome food,
Crisp sweet flesh snowy-cool, and skin
Painted bright—
To have a man that I couldn't bear
Out of my sight.

Dorothea Mackellar

Smalltown Dance

Two women find the square-root of a sheet.
That is an ancient dance:
arms wide: together: again: two forward steps: hands meet
your partner's once and twice.
That white expanse
reduces to a neat
compression fitting in the smallest space
a sheet can pack in on a cupboard shelf.

High scented walls there were of flapping white
when I was small, myself.
I walked between them, playing Out of Sight.
Simpler than arms, they wrapped and comforted—
clean corridors of hiding, roofed with blue—
saying, Your sins too are made Monday-new;
and see, ahead
that glimpse of unobstructed waiting green.
Run, run before you're seen.

But women know the scale of possibility,
the limit of opportunity,
the fence,
how little chance
there is of getting out. The sheets that tug
sometimes struggle from the peg,
don't travel far. Might symbolise
something. Knowing where danger lies
you have to keep things orderly.
The household budget will not stretch to more.

And they can demonstrate it in a dance.
First pull those wallowing white dreamers down,
spread arms: then close them. Fold
those beckoning roads to some impossible world,
put them away and close the cupboard door.

Judith Wright

Emily Brontë

The bell of my loneliness is
a note so high and pure
it leaves you breathless:

these windy slopes are shorn
of the things which make life comfortable:
broad trees, broken bread, the swell

and supple curve of a lover's back.
These come only in dreams,
fade achingly before the besom dawn

Which sweeps away sleep's comforts. I
can sit here in my window, catch
the rough, sweet scent of heather in my nostrils

and write of death and love entwined
destructively together. The poetry
lies wild in my veins, the poetry

of granite skies stabbed by rocky outcrops,
the giving spring of turf, the taste
of solitude like aloes on my tongue

and all the death around me made meaningless
by these which are unchanging, which take
my sisters and myself with mute indifference
and conquer all our passion under soil.

Alison Croggon

Woman to Man

The eyeless labourer in the night,
the selfless, shapeless seed I hold,
builds for its resurrection day—
silent and swift and deep from sight
foresees the unimagined light.

This is no child with a child's face;
this has no name to name it by;
yet you and I have known it well.
This is our hunter and our chase,
the third who lay in our embrace.

This is the strength that your arm knows,
the arc of flesh that is my breast,
the precise crystals of our eyes.
This is the blood's wild tree that grows
the intricate and folded rose.

This is the maker and the made;
this is the question and reply;
the blind head butting at the dark,
the blaze of light along the blade.
Oh hold me, for I am afraid.

Judith Wright

Woman to Child

You who were darkness warmed my flesh
where out of darkness rose the seed.
Then all a world I made in me;
all the world you hear and see
hung upon my dreaming blood.

There moved the multitudinous stars,
and coloured birds and fishes moved.
There swam the sliding continents.
All time lay rolled in me, and sense,
and love that knew not its beloved.

O node and focus of the world;
I hold you deep within that well
you shall escape and not escape—
that mirrors still your sleeping shape;
that nurtures still your crescent cell.
I wither and you break from me;
yet though you dance in living light
I am the earth, I am the root,
I am the stem that fed the fruit,
the link that joins you to the night.

Judith Wright

Andromeda

She was the first pin-up.
Naked and bejewelled,
she was chained to a rock,
then thrown by heavy-breathing
winds into wild postures:
at each new angle, lightning
popped like a photographer's flash.

The gold circling her neck
matched her hair, the emeralds
her eyes, the rubies her nipples,
and the amethysts those bruises
covering her skin, once pearl-
white as for all princesses.

In lulls of wind, she pulled
against iron, stood almost straight.
The sky was a mouth swallowing her,
the sun a glimmering eye;
lolling in the tide, a sea-dragon
slithered and gargled like
some vast collective slob.

From afar, Perseus saw her first
as a creature writhing on a rock;
close up, she was a whirlpool
of rage and terror and shame.
The dragon he changed to stone
with hardly a thought. But
his strength almost failed him
in breaking those chains.

Looking away from her nakedness,
he smooths her ankles, wrists.
She waits for the moment
when he will meet her eyes.

Diane Fahey

Breasts

As I lean over to write
one breast warm as a breast from the sun
hangs over as if to read what I'm writing
these breasts always want to know everything
sometimes exploring the inside curve of my elbow
sometimes measuring a man's hand
lying still as a pond
until he cannot feel he is holding anything
but water
then he dreams he is floating

in the morning my breast is refreshed
and wants to know something new
although it is soft it is also ambitious
we never speak
but I know my breast knows me more than I do
prying hanging over fences
observant as a neighbour
or eager as a woman wanting to gossip
they tell me nothing
but they say quite a lot about me

there is a dark blue river vein here
straggling down taking its time
to the little pale strawberry
picked too soon and left too long
in the punnet in a warm shop

when I lie
these breasts spread like spilt milk
and standing naked in the sea
float like figs
as you will realise
these are my body's curious fruit
wanting to know everything
always getting there first
strange as white beetroot
exotic as unicorns
useless as an out of order dishwasher
more of a nuisance than anything else

some men seem to think highly of them
peering and staring
what they don't know is the breast stares straight back
interested as a reporter

some love them
and invest them with glamour
but like life they are not glamourous
merely dangerous

Kate Llewellyn

Five Days Late

Late, five days late. At night in sleep they fumble
To feel the cool gold ring which is not there,
The space beside them which is sometimes man,
The single girls who laughed and ran from Daddy.
The wind-chimes stir. From their high rented rooms
The city is a wave of black stars breaking
In violet abysses, clouds of gasoline.
Pads of rouge, scent bottles, eyelash brushes
Are mummified in the dressing table mirror.
They travel nightmare elevators up
And down with flimsy shift fanned by ozone.
In an empty building, buttons pressed by no one.
Memories of kisses hang around their necks
Like stones, dolls fall from burning aeroplanes,
And ghosts of children crawl in moonlit playpens,
Clamber and strain for milk from dormant breasts.
Breasts which have never existed, dangling playthings
Craving the press of life, the tug of lips,
Anguished wombs twisting, curving to be filled
With Baby and his big blind head of bread,
The bawling nightmare spilling porridge on floors,
The handful of tears blowing a paper trumpet,
The bib daubed with chocolate kissing the stars goodbye.
In rented rooms the coffee cups are cold,
And single girls toss in their night of doubt.
When morning wakes with blood, they weep, are safe.

Geoffrey Lehmann

Theatre

With my legs in stirrups
I pushed you out—
it was like a race
with life the prize
(and as tricky as knitting under water)

I felt glad but that's all

they wheeled in the Father
and the Doctor said his reward
was in such scenes

a starfish of embarrassment
shrank
beached
I was a prop in their play

I wept all night
because no one had mentioned
responsibility
my face began to fall
in frightened pieces
on the floor

at my parent's home
ten dressing-gowned days later
a whiskey bottle beside the bed
and a baby
and a dummy
and me the Mummy

after your bath
my Father took out the scales
and like a lump of butter
half ounce anxious
my Mother weighed you

the petals of your soles
fluttered on the edge

now with a top hat
and swinging hair
you're on the stage
and wowing them
and they clap
and slowly I begin to clap
a stranger

Kate Llewellyn

In the Park, Looking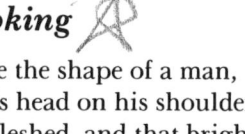

I'm not too old to like the shape of a man,
his walk, the set of his head on his shoulders,
the strong legs, well fleshed, and that bright,
dark-browed glance. There's a nose that I like,
admiring blank-faced. If you should
see me looking, if you saw me at all,
you'd think I'm reminded of someone,
husband, son, grandson, not that I look at you
as a woman looks at a man who stirs her.

The heart lifts, it's good to see a fine man,
to think—there goes a man I could love.
I'm looking at you, not remembering.
But as I well know, you don't see me,
old women are almost invisible. If I do catch your eye,
likely enough you'll be thinking, 'She has a look of my mother.'

Barbara Giles

Play Group

Here we are all
women, gathered in this
faded yard in sunlight.
None of us virgins
we have given
birth to non-
immaculate conceptions
and they run
among us echoing our
faces, while we sitting
in our circle are
echoing other things
sifted through centuries
of women, of mothers
also sitting in circles
listening to children
and each other.

We have had many
faces and we will
have more. We are
all signs of the
stars, have been
called more names
than man remembers,
for he has felt
the velvet selvedge
of our selves but
we know this
from the inside.

Far from the dust
and bark of this
untidy yard are
other selves we left
behind us—lawyers,
doctors, teachers, clerks—

they do not matter
here in this charmed
unfurled circle that
we sit in. Here
we are women, we
are making the world.

Doris Brett

In the Park

She sits in the park. Her clothes are out of date.
Two children whine and bicker, tug her skirt.
A third draws aimless patterns in the dirt.
Someone she loved once passes by—too late

to feign indifference to that casual nod.
'How nice,' etcetera. 'Time holds great surprises.'
From his neat head unquestionably rises
a small balloon... 'but for the grace of God...'

They stand awhile in flickering light, rehearsing
the children's names and birthdays. 'It's so sweet
to hear their chatter, watch them grow and thrive,'
she says to his departing smile. Then, nursing
the youngest child, sits staring at her feet.
To the wind she says, 'They have eaten me alive.'

Gwen Harwood

Couples

this is a song an epithalamium it is also
a requiem this is a poem about couples it
is called *racked and ranked*
the title comes from william faulkner
who said

'and thank God you can flee, can escape from that
massy five-foot-thick maggot-cheesy solidarity which
overlays the earths, in which men and women in couples
are racked and ranked like ninepins.'

this is a poem for couples from which i cannot escape
this is a poem for people who are not couples but who
want to be couples from which i cannot escape a poem
for all you out there people who are coupling up or
breaking up just to couple up again and giving me
second prize because

kate jennings, lose him, weep him, couldn't catch a man
much less keep him

couples create obstacle courses to prevent me from doing
all sorts of things easily
couples make sure i'm not comfortable with myself because
i'm only half a potential couple
couples point accusing right index fingers at me
couples make me guilty of loneliness, insecurity, or
worse still, lack of ambition.

what do i do at the end of the day?
lose him, weep him, think of catching a man,
and eating him.

Kate Jennings

NOTES

'The Edge'
those who journeyed back with me: i.e. her children. **Lazarus:** See the New Testament, the Book of John, Ch. 11.
Companion Piece: 'Cock Crow', Rosemary Dobson.

'Smalltown Dance'
Companion Pieces: 'The Woman', Mary Gilmore; 'Folding the Sheets'*, Rosemary Dobson.

'Emily Brontë'
my loneliness: The speaker is Emily Brontë. **besom:** a country broom made from bundles of twigs. **turf:** 1. peat, 2. grassy sward. **aloes:** a bitter drug made from aloe plants, much used in the Brontës' day.

'Woman to Man'
This is...: 'This' is perhaps not merely the fetus but everything that the child or posterity may grow to be. **afraid:** For what reasons?

'Andromeda'
Andromeda: In Greek mythology Andromeda's parents were forced to chain her to a rock so she could be eaten by a sea-monster. She was rescued and married by the hero Perseus who possessed the Gorgon's head which would turn to stone any creature that looked at it. The rescue of the naked girl fascinated and perhaps titillated painters for 2000 years. Renaissance painters sometimes thought this story was about Heroic Virtue rescuing Innocence from Evil or from the Devil. What does Fahey suggest it is about? Why does Andromeda hope Perseus will meet her eyes?
Companion Piece (Andromeda myth): 'Agony Column', A. D. Hope.

'Breasts'
How does the poet's attitude to her breasts differ from that a man might have? How seriously can you take the image of breasts as curious observers? **merely dangerous:** why dangerous?

'Theatre'
Note that the line-endings replace punctuation—each line is a unit. **the Father... Doctor... Mummy... Mother:** Why the capitals?
Companion Pieces: 'With My Sons at Boarhill', Anne Stevenson (UK/USA); 'Parenthood', Geoffrey Lehmann.

'In the Park, Looking'
The metre is free verse or a loose mix of iambic and anapestic. Does the very long last line work?

'Play Group'
non-immaculate: In Catholic theology the Virgin Mary is believed to have been conceived 'immaculate' (lit. 'spotless'), that is, free from any stain of Original Sin. **selvedge:** probably with a further pun on the derivation from *self + edge*. **unfurled:** not closed, spread out.

'In the Park'
The rhythm is iambic pentameter.
Companion Piece: 'Suburban Sonnet', Gwen Harwood.

'Couples'
epithalamium: a wedding song.
Leaving out capitals and fullstops was quite common in poems of the 1970s. Often, as here, it helps to create a tone of rebelliousness. Does it make the poem harder to read?
Companion Piece: 'I'll Shoot the Man', Gig Ryan.

Activities

1 Choose a poem you particularly like. Singly, or in groups, prepare a short statement of what experiences you feel it captures. Then devise an effective way of reading it out. With 'Couples' you may be able to use a chorus; and 'Theatre' may suggest a playlet or a mime.

2 Write a parody or imitation of one poem in this section, or else write a poem inspired by the same feelings.

3 **Project:** Collect and compare examples of female poets reworking traditional stories: Dorothy Hewett ('Rapunzel in Suburbia'), Fay Zwicky ('Mrs Noah Speaks'), Jennifer Strauss ('Bluebeard Re-scripted'), Judith Wright ('On Adam and Eve'), Sylvia Plath, Anne Sexton.

4 **Discussion:** 'When society is fully liberated it will seem as pointless to have a special section on women's experiences as one on men's experience.' 'Yes, but women have more experiences that a man can't share than vice versa.' What do you think?

5 **Discussion:** Which experiences in these poems do you think are easiest, and which most difficult, for men to share?

6 Research the Brontë family and their environment. How well does Alison Croggon's poem capture Emily Brontë's story? Write an explanation of this 'migrant poem' for an Australian penfriend who knows nothing of Britain or British literature.

7 **Project:** Research the Andromeda story in European painting and sculpture and literature.

8 Does Harwood gain or lose by writing in the third person in 'In the Park'?

9 Pat Makeham in her book *The Poetry of Gwen Harwood: An Intro-duction* sees 'In the Park' as partly a 'situation comedy'. She explains that 'There is bitterness expressed in the poem but it is tempered by humour... The final, so seemingly bitter, utterance is lost on the wind, so that the exaggeration of her situation in "They have eaten me alive!" at once relieves her feelings and yet does no one any harm.' Can you argue for or against this view of the poem?

10 Is it true in our culture that 'old women are almost invisible'? What about in other countries?

11 **Library Project:** Investigate Dorothy Hewett's collection *Rapunzel in Suburbia*. Identify those passages where she uses romantic legends or fairy stories to express the stages of a woman's life, and decide which examples you think are most successful.

12 **Discussion:** Are males or females under most pressure to submerge themselves in a couple?

13 Compare the personal 'voice' and concerns of one or more Australian female poets with those of either Sylvia Plath, Margaret Atwood, Fleur Adcock, Carol Rumens, or Erica Jong.

14 **Activity:** A challenge to both sexes: re-read 'Five Days Late'. Write a poem or paragraph on some aspect of your lifestyle that could be as deeply disturbing to you.

Relevant poems from other sections

'After the "Ball"', 'The Brides', 'Naked Girl and Mirror', 'Weights', 'Ladies and Gentlemen', 'A Simple Story'.

Poems for further study

*'Eskimo Occasion', Judith Rodriguez; 'The Female Transport', Anonym-ous; 'The Blowflies Buzz...', Aboriginal Song; 'Suburban Song', Elizabeth Riddell.

†'Morning Song', Sylvia Plath; 'Woman with Girdle', Anne Sexton; 'An Impromptu for Ann Jennings', Gwen Harwood; 'Aurora Leigh', Elizabeth Browning; 'In Reference to Her Children, 23 June 1656', Anne Bradstreet.

15

LOVE

The poet W. H. Auden once wrote in a lonely moment that 'Millions have lived without love, not one without water'. Yet love in some form is almost a necessity to human beings. Luckily, this dangerous emotion has many forms, from the love that is three-quarters sexual fascination, to the love of siblings, to the love of stamps. Love may well be as necessary to human survival as mother's milk—and as hard to define or divide up into components.

Love's Coming

Quietly as rosebuds
Talk to the thin air,
Love came so lightly
I knew not he was there.

Quietly as lovers
Creep at the middle moon,
Softly as players tremble
In the tears of a tune;

Quietly as lilies
Their faint vows declare
Came the shy pilgrim:
I knew not he was there.

Quietly as tears fall
On a wild sin,
Softly as griefs call
In a violin;

Without hail or tempest,
Blue sword or flame,
Love came so lightly
I knew not that he came.

John Shaw Neilson

Love and Complacency

At Christmas, sometimes, even for unbelievers,
Angels come slanting down across the firebreak
Over flecks of summer grass on the sheep-tracked hill.
Dragonflies mirrored in the dam, weavers
Of transparencies, gyrate
Cerulean and ruby images of free-will.

Dipping and drifting, they couple in mid-air
like helicopters refuelling, carrying on
Mutual flirtations with the bronze face
Of the deep dam, their fuselages clear
As noon sky in the desert, or the red clarion
Venus sometimes flashes through black space.

They float through the branches of the mirrored trees.
A trout rises. They cross the concentric rings,
Wings transparent as angels', though the treasure
Of sex ballasts their jewelled bodies.
They brush the water's gum-blossoms with their wings.
The trout leaps. At least they died for pleasure.

Geoffrey Dutton

Finished

There'll be no more
lying on your shoulder love
or listening for your car

there'll be no more
drinking on the verandah love
or eating roasted veal

there'll be no more
my legs around your neck love
and howling at the moon

there'll be no more
hits across my mouth love
and crawling on the floor

there'll be no more
smoking listening to you curse love
or smiling drinking more

there'll be no more
crying because you rage love
or dancing up your drive

there's no more
love love

Kate Llewellyn

Sassy

She screws up the pages
they write on in restaurants
as she doesn't want him to know
she wants to keep them

she strides in tall boots
very sassy
round the park
because she wants to keep him thinking
she doesn't care too much

when she's ill
she uses rouge and wine
so he can't tell

she has other lovers
so he won't guess
it's him she wants

she calls him Pisspot and Wild One
and hits him on the back
to keep him guessing
she flops in chairs
and sticks her boots out
so he won't see she's nervous

she drinks up and slams her glass down
so he won't see she's trembling

all in all it's a tremendous effort
and it doesn't fool him

Kate Llewellyn

Pas de Deux for Lovers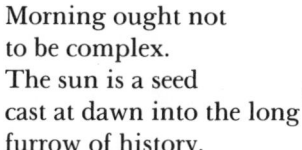

Morning ought not
to be complex.
The sun is a seed
cast at dawn into the long
furrow of history.

To wake
and go
would be so simple.

Yet

how the
first light
makes gold her hair

upon my arm.
How then
shall I leave,
and where away to go. Day
is so deep already with involvement.

Michael Dransfield

A Simple Story

A visiting conductor
  when I was seventeen,
took me back to his hotel room
  to cover the music scene.

I'd written a composition.
  Would wonders never cease—
here was a real musician
  prepared to hold my piece.

He spread my score on the counterpane
  with classic casualness,
and put one hand on the manuscript
  and the other down my dress.

It was hot as hell in the Windsor.
  I said I'd like a drink.
We talked across gin and grapefruit,
  and I heard the ice go clink

as I gazed at the lofty forehead
  of one who led the band,
and guessed at the hoarded sorrows
  no wife could understand.

I dreamed of a soaring passion
  as an egg might dream of flight,
while he read my crude sonata.
  If he'd said, 'That bar's not right,'

or, 'Have you thought of a coda?'
  or, 'Watch that first repeat,'
or, 'Modulate to the dominant,'
  he'd have had me at his feet.

But he shuffled it all together,
  and said, 'That's *lovely*, dear,'
as he put it down on the washstand
  in a way that made it clear

that I was no composer.
  And I being young and vain,
removed my lovely body
  from one who'd scorned my brain.

I swept off like Miss Virtue
   down dusty Roma Street,
and heard the goods trains whistle
    WHO? WHOOOOOO? in aching heat.

Gwen Harwood

Time of Waiting

He will sit at the bare table, reading a dictionary,
Glancing at his watch, waiting for time to begin,
As it has already, on some heat-struck pavement
Contradicted by a cool summer dress
Disguising an urgency of limbs, till at last
Through the heavy semi-silence of the city
 Breaks her light step along the empty corridor
And words and minutes fall like clothing to the floor.

Geoffrey Dutton

Vows

Nay, ask me not. I would not dare pretend
   To constant passion and a life-long trust.
   They will desert thee, if indeed they must.
How can we guess what Destiny will send—
Smiles of fair fortune, or black storms to rend
   What even now is shaken by a gust?
   The fire will burn, or it will die in dust.
We cannot tell until the final end.

And never vow was forged that could confine
   Aught but the body of the thing whereon
Its pledge was stamped. The inner soul divine,
   That thinks of going, is already gone.
When faith and love need bolts upon the door,
Faith is not faith, and love abides no more.

Ada Cambridge

Going Down. With no permanence

I'm finding it impossible to begin, as you've ended so little. Last night my heart was a cheap flag waving to the nearest mirror in sight. I couldn't believe anything, seeing you drive away into others' arms. I'm no sweet virgin sock-washer either. So it's a matter of priorities I guess, just who wants to gamble. Talk of loving when there is no goal. Of belief when there is no road. My shoes are off and I'm walking barefoot. Down a long avenue of arms and kisses like knots. I'm getting tired and angry and thinking hell, I'm no sock-washer but there must be some other venue. I say my heart's big enough, it is. Every time it's eaten and collapses like a cough.

Today I'm trying to be reasonable. You're having breakfast with her. And there's no wedding ring, baby, fidelity, photo. No day to week token of what we have, a visible future. Crazy thing, it's happening everywhere. You waft into my room bringing delicious words, eyes, every other love you're still attached to, claim.

'I want all love-rites simultaneously.'

'I don't want to negate anything.'

Yes I understand. Incredible egotist! that one cracked heart is your own, gyrating in its uncertainty. Adoration. Adulation. Your heart seeks to reflect itself. Narcissus in the bath. How many loves do you want? Are you never full, leaky bucket?

And now you turn to your sock-washer reasoning socks are better than none. So you're surrounded again. Pursued and claimed. A shroud of outrage going up. Thinking of numbers and lines. It sharpens your humour. While I love this one the others must love me too. I'll keep my heart spinning. You think you're responding, keeping all the doors open. Yes. Yes.

This is the road my bare feet touch. Going down. The avenue with few affirmatives. Going down. With no permanence. This is the alternative to restrictions. So we assume. Without end.

Vicki Viidikas

Stars

The stars have so far to go
alone or in harness
across a window-pane.

Hour after hour tonight
I've journeyed with them, steady
the waves of your breath.

Dark space between our beds.
On the table a full tumbler
splits the light of stars

to stars, or floats a leaden
column of dead water,
dead sky. From centuries

away, out of the reign
of one of nineteen pharaohs
a planet's dust, metallic,

alive, is sifted down,
hovers in a bright
arc upon your cheek.

Miraculous! I lean
across the dark and touch it,
you smile in your sleep....

How far, how far we've come
together, tumbling like stars
in harness or alone.

David Malouf

NOTES

'Love and Complacency'
Angels: i.e. dragonflies. **cerulean**: sky blue; azure. **Clear as noon sky etc.**:
their bodies are bright blue or red. **the treasure of sex**: i.e. eggs and sperm.

'Sassy'
Would the third line be better as 'so he won't know'?

'Pas de Deux for Lovers'
pas de deux: a dance or figure for two performers.

'A Simple Story'
Roma Street: in Brisbane.
Companion Piece: 'David's Harp', Gwen Harwood.

'Vows'
never vow was: no vow was ever. **Aught but**: any more than. **inner soul
divine**: divine soul within. **abides**: stays, endures.
Does the poem work despite its out-of-date language? If so, why?

'Stars'
a planet's dust: meteorites, presumably.

ACTIVITIES

1 **Discussion**: If you agree that all the poems in this section are in some
sense about love, can you find anything they all have in common?

2 What is love? Here are two possible definitions: 'Love is when another
person's welfare matters more to you than your own.' 'Love is an obsessive
and possessive erotic admiration for another person perceived as having
qualities that are lacking in one's self.' Do they fit any of the poems
collected here? Can you devise better definitions?

3 Memorize any one of these poems, and then work out an effective way
to recite it, perhaps against a musical background. Or try turning it
fully into a song.

4 Imagine you are editing a picture book called *Love in Australia*. Choose
photos or paintings (they can be abstract if you like) to go with these
poems, or with others of your choice.

5 Use one of these poems as an inspiration for a poem, painting, sketch,
or short story.

6 'Women's love poems seem to be much more about the need for caution
in love than men's.' Why? Is it true of this sample?

7   Many people, trapped in the throes of jealousy, have tried to thrash out an explanation of their loved one's behaviour. How successful is the woman in Viidikas's 'Going Down. With no permanence?' What is her diagnosis of her boyfriend?

8   Ada Cambridge and Vicki Viidikas take different positions in the old argument between freedom and commitment. What are they?
Discussion: Female writers often complain about the male ego and the tendency of men to want more than one girlfriend. Is this an inborn difference between the sexes?

9   **Library Project**: Research Judith Wright as a love poet, either making your own anthology of favourite passages from her *Collected Works*, or preparing a report on her attitudes to love.

Relevant poems from other sections

'Louise and Alessandro', 'In the Park', 'Woman to Man'.

Poems for further study

*'Poems', Lesbia Harford; 'A Sweet Disorder in the Dress', Harry Hooton; 'Graffiti', Julian Croft; 'Heritage', Dorothea Mackellar; 'Wings', Judith Wright.

†'She Considers Evading Him', Margaret Atwood; 'In Love', Kamala Das; 'Soliloquy for One Dead', Bruce Dawe; 'The Wine is Drunk', 'I Knew a Woman', Theodore Roethke; 'As I Walked Out One Evening', 'Since', W. H. Auden; 'The River-Merchant's Wife: A Letter', Ezra Pound; 'Remember', Christina Rossetti; 'Meeting at Night', Robert Browning; 'Bright star would I were stedfast as thou art', John Keats; 'John Anderson My Jo', A Red Red Rose', Robert Burns; 'A Letter to her Husband, absent upon Publick employment', Anne Bradstreet; 'A Song', Anne Finch; 'Upon Julia's Clothes', 'To Dianeme', Robert Herrick; 'The Good-Morrow', 'Song', 'The Sunne Rising', John Donne; 'Let me not to the marriage of true mindes', 'My mistres eyes are nothing like the sunne', William Shakespeare; from 'Idea', Michael Drayton; from 'Amoretti', Edmund Spenser; 'And if I did what then?', George Gascoigne; 'I grieve and dare not show my Discontent', Queen Elizabeth I; 'They fle from me that sometyme did me seke', Sir Thomas Wyatt: 'Westron Wynde, When Wyll Thow Blow', Anonymous.

16

MORTALITY

Here are two lines from very different poems: 'As the leaves of trees are the lives of men' (Homer), and 'I stood and looked and knew mortality like an old wound' (Bruce Beaver).

A great proportion of the poetry of any nation is about mortality—the fact that human life is a temporary thing and ends in death. Relative to British or European poets of the past, recent Australian poets have been less inclined to offer religious consolations or to assume an afterlife. Most accept death as painful but necessary; but some, like Gwen Harwood, defy death, while others agonize over the meaning of a human life that ends in death.

To Kill an Olive

Nobody knows how long it takes to kill an olive.
Drought, axe, fire, are admitted failures. Hack one down,
grub out a ton of mainroot for fuel, and next spring
every side-root sends up shoots. A great frost
can leave the trees leafless for years; they revive.
Invading armies will fell them. They return
through the burnt-out ribs of siege machines.

Only the patient goat, nibbling his way down the ages,
has malice to master the olive. Sometimes, they say,
a man finds a dead orchard, fired and goat-
cropped centuries back. He settles and fences;
the trunks revive. His grandchildren's family prosper
by the arduous oil-pressing trade. Then wars
and disease wash over. Goats return. The olives
go under, waiting another age.

Their shade still lies where Socrates disputed.
Gethsemane's withered groves are bearing yet.

Mark O'Connor

Popular Statesman

Brought back from the tedium of dying,
From the work of holding skin and bone
And memories together, from a life
Pottered at like a never-ending hobby
Down the soft lanes of second childhood, he
Stands a while, head tremulous with events,
Like a boy fetched out of nightmare
Blinking light away in the sudden doorway.
Someone takes his hat, raises his hand
In promise, or blessing, or to gain a respite.
Is it himself, or the People,
Or the bodyguard with the belted coat?
He neither knows nor cares; the grand old man
Blinks on a surfeit of smoky light,
Ducks his head to the tidal wave of cheering.
The armoured cars point away from him;
The committees meet in other rooms;
The pickpockets move among the crowds.

Vincent Buckley

Meditation on a Bone

A piece of bone, found at Trondhjem in 1901, with the following
runic inscription (about A.D. 1050) cut on it:
*I loved her as a maiden; I will not trouble Erlend's detestable wife; better
she should be a widow.*

Words scored upon a bone,
Scratched in despair or rage—
Nine hundred years have gone;
Now, in another age,
They burn with passion on
A scholar's tranquil page.

The scholar takes his pen
And turns the bone about,
And writes those words again.
Once more they seethe and shout,
And through a human brain
Undying hate rings out.

'I loved her when a maid;
I loathe and love the wife
That warms another's bed;
Let him beware his life!'
The scholar's hand is stayed;
His pen becomes a knife

To grave in living bone
The fierce archaic cry.
He sits and reads his own
Dull sum of misery.
A thousand years have flown
Before that ink is dry.

And, in a foreign tongue,
A man, who is not he,
Reads and his heart is wrung
This ancient grief to see,
And thinks: When I am dung,
What bone shall speak for me?

A. D. Hope

Ulinda

There was a duck egg as green as the evening sky.
Trout hovered in the horse-trough. The road was white
And vanished like a headache in sheets of light
And pale blue mountains. The homestead creek was dry
And warm with pebbles. Grandfather said that *Why?*
Was a crooked letter. His beard got in his plate.
'Milk grandfather. Sugar grandfather.' 'Now that
Is just what I can't have.' And he winked the bluest eye.
It was like the duck egg. We were only playing a game,
But mother left the table; so we ran along.
One sundown they butchered a pig and I saw it scream.
I held my ears and it went on screaming. 'What's wrong?'
They said. 'It's only a dream.' But I sang in my dream:
'Grandfather's dying. He's going to die,' I sang.

David Campbell

Starting from Central Station

A moon hangs in the air,
Its hands at ten past ten:
My father leaps alive
And I shrink to his son.

My father strides ahead
And stops to have a word
With men in caps who laugh.
He slips them a reward.

The trolley rolls behind
With boxes stacked like bricks:
Smoke and a whistle blow
And I am fifty-six.

Houses move through the parks,
Streets run with greens and reds:
Night conjures up the same
Old promises and dreads.

The train is on its way
And daylight gets to work,
Puts father in a box
And shoves him in the dark.

David Campbell

Green Hands

I have lain on my back in caves
Studying the hands of dead people
Stencilled in coloured ochres
On the smoky ceilings—
Long slender hands and
The small hands of children.
This morning under
An overhanging scanner
There were two hands on the screen
Mossed with a green lichen.
One had the little finger missing.

David Campbell

To David Campbell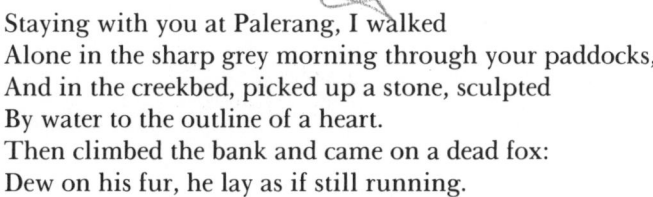

Staying with you at Palerang, I walked
Alone in the sharp grey morning through your paddocks,
And in the creekbed, picked up a stone, sculpted
By water to the outline of a heart.
Then climbed the bank and came on a dead fox:
Dew on his fur, he lay as if still running.

Later, you and I walked in the sun. Joe Gullett,
The young collie, ran up a leaning tree,
Barking with pleasure. You too climbed a tree.
No branches within reach: knees, feet and arms
Gripping the trunk, bark-stains on your white trousers
As you slid down again.

           And at the end
Of your long strip of earth, there were the graves:
The earliest settlers, quiet under their headstones,
Inside your boundary, close to the old road
Grassed-over many years. And you grew silent.
Tall powerful body, broken nose, fair hair,
You stood beside me, yet you stood apart,
In a moment's piety towards the dead, and towards
The earth they knew, and were.

           Speech is good,
But silence also. Let me do as you did.
Standing in thought by your grave, I fall silent.

Philip Martin

Song be Delicate

Let your song be delicate.
  The skies declare
No war—the eyes of lovers
  Wake everywhere.

Let your voice be delicate.
  How faint a thing
Is Love, little Love crying
  Under the Spring.

Let your song be delicate.
  The flowers can hear:
Too well they know the tremble
  Of the hollow year.

Let your voice be delicate.
  The bees are home:
All their day's love is sunken
  Safe in the comb.

Let your song be delicate.
  Sing no loud hymn:
Death is abroad... Oh, the black season!
  The deep—the dim!

John Shaw Neilson

Mid-Channel

The days shall come upon you, that he will take you away with hooks,
and your posterity with fishhooks.

Amos, IV, 2

Cod inert as an old boot,
tangling dance of the little shark,
perch nibble, flathead jerk—
blindfold I'd know them on my line.

Fugitive gleam on scale and fin,
lustrous eye, opalescent belly
dry and die in the undesired
element. A day will come,

matter-of-fact as knife and plate,
with death's hook in my jaw, and language
unspeakable, the line full out.
I'll tire you with my choking weight

old monster anchored in the void.
My God, you'll wonder what you've caught.
Land me in hell itself at last
I'll stab and swell your wounds with poison.

Not here, not now. Water's my kingdom
tonight, my line makes starspecks tremble.
My dinghy's decked with golden eyes
and still the cod boil round my bait.

Gwen Harwood

Goya Paints a Portrait of a Child

The boy is made of gold, almost: close
to the perfect child, with satin cummerbund
and bows on spotless shoes, lace at cuffs
and neck. He'll never muck in mud.

He is all of an innocent eye. His mouth
is a childish bud, he stands a doll
among his living toys. The caged things crouch
in their palace, rich with balconies and dome.

A larger bird, with unmistakeable claws
and vicious bill, is tied to a string,
possessed. The house and garden cats pause
with eyes on fire, trained not to spring

and bring blood to the nursery floor.
The boy's father is paying good money for this
reminder of innocence: there are years more
of protected youth, of the nurse's kiss

before the toys and the pets are set free
and the boy goes out to the world. Expect
him to lead an army, a cat unleashed
at provinces, blood on his boots in some town's wreck.

John Griffin

The Apparition

After the entertainments of the night,
  Somewhere in limbo he had lost his way,
A dark empty suit in a dark street
  Swinging toward another nameless day.

Discarded leaves ran murmuring from his feet
  And agonies of perfume round his head
Drifted from shrubs he could no longer name:
  From petal, stem and calyx of the dead.

A Norfolk pine sprang skyward as he came.
  He knew it well—had climbed it as a child—
So when he saw a pale shape quit its port
  Of shade, he was already reconciled

To the small bent figure with collar caught
  Beneath her chin by a massive cameo;
To fragile glasses crooked on their bridge;
  To the known voice, its unperturbed hello.

'Robert', she said. Light as a hovering midge
  She moved beside him now through vacant air.
'Those cannas which you planted are in bloom.
  The daisies too. But weeds are everywhere.

'For seven months I wilted in a room;
  It was your name that rose upon my breath
And yet my favourite grandson never came
  Into the narrow chamber of my death.'

As early-woken starlings cried for shame
  And a dry twig snapped where his footstep fell,
Robert addressed the hostile universe:
  'I was only a child. How could I tell?'

Her ghost had faded. Deep grey like a hearse,
  The sky bore downward with its close-webbed net
And every shaken leaf was echoing,
  'You always found it easy to forget.'

Chris Wallace-Crabbe

Death
From *Letters to Live Poets*

Three images of dying stick in my mind like morbid transfers
of the other side of life. First, a cow on my uncle's farm
had broken a leg calving. My uncle held a shot-gun to its poll
and fired both barrels. The dogs ran in to lick the blood welling
    from
the nostrils. We hauled the carcas behind a wooden sled to the
    burial ground,
a small island of dark trees centring a wide field.
On the way the top of the cow's head came loose and left a trail.
Heifers followed us and shrieked with eyes rolling at the blood.
We piled the heavy carcas high with old tyres and lit the pyre.
Sleeping and waking I saw the shattered head for many years to
    come.

The second incident occurred years later in a goods yard.
Near to a storage shed I came across a group of cats surrounding
such a scrawny bag of fur and bone it wasn't a bit funny.
This cat had eaten poisoned corn or a rat poisoned.
At first I'd thought it starving and had brought bacon from the
    galley.
The other cats moved back from me while I offered it the bacon.
It stretched out a claw at the meat, hooking it towards its mouth
then died before it bit. I watch the twitch of life pass up its spine
centre, then go out like a light snuffed. Its eyes had closed before
its life. Blinded. Starved with poison. The other cats began to move
away. I stood and looked and knew mortality like an old wound.

The third time clawed me in a room filled with smoke and proof-
    readers.
The air clanged with advertisements read aloud like crazy psalms.
A man was dying at his desk. His heart was broken and the kiss
of life rejected. As he died his fellow workers chanted on
and he was left with a handkerchief over his face where he lay dead
in his chair in a room full of the loud chanting of the living.
No one pleaded for silence while he remained or when he was
    gone stayed
their tongue. I read on then, knowing not a minute's silence will
the rest of us get. When they rang his ninety-year-old mother all
    she asked for
were his keys. Tomorrow we'll talk of life and sundry other things.

Bruce Beaver

The Electors

There were three voters, one, two, three,
went into a polling booth, left, right, left,
and their names were Heart and Tongue and Death.

Said Heart: We are living in stirring times.
Never felt like this since the world was good.

Said Tongue: I am tripping on anthems now.
I hear their words and I know they're true.

Said Death: I have just come with these two.

John Griffin

Individualist

Splitting firewood I often found
Fat white grubs in the grain
And would toss them on the ground—
The fowls learned this, and a vain
Old crow who posed apart in liberty
Used to wait for me to throw
The juicy ones under his special tree,
Where he would stab them straight
Before the frantic fowls arrived—
Bird-brain, they were in such a state,
The brown contentious crowd that lived
In a clucking strain of imitation.
But then, a cackling hen, meanly
By cunning, running to look
Would try to beat the mob to it again,
Push up, put her head on the block,
Staring, arrogant, stupid, plain,
And I would cut it off, throw
It to the black and elegant crow
Who did not rely on my offering—
There was no change in the fowlyard cries,
They were indifferent to headless suffering,
And he would peck out its beady eyes.

B. R. Whiting

Brother and Sisters

The road turned out to be a cul-de-sac;
stopped like a lost intention at the gate
and never crossed the mountains to the coast.
But they stayed on. Years grew like grass and leaves
across the half-erased and dubious track
until one day they knew the plans were lost,
the blue-print for the bridge was out of date,
and now their orchards never would be planted.
The saplings sprouted slyly; day by day
the bush moved one step nearer, wondering when.
The polished parlour grew distrait and haunted
where Millie, Lucy, John each night at ten
wound the gilt clock that leaked the year away.

The pianola—oh, listen to the mocking-bird—
wavers on Sundays and has lost a note.
The wrinkled ewes snatch pansies through the fence
and stare with shallow eyes into the garden
where Lucy shrivels waiting for a word,
and Millie's cameos loosen round her throat.
The bush comes near, the ranges grow immense.

Feeding the lambs deserted in early spring
Lucy looked up and saw the stockman's eye
telling her she was cracked and old.
                              The wall
groans in the night and settles more awry.
O how they lie awake. Their thoughts go fluttering
from room to room like moths: 'Millie, are you awake?'
'Oh John, I have been dreaming.' 'Lucy, do you cry?'
—meet tentative as moths. Antennae stroke a wing.
'There is nothing to be afraid of. Nothing at all.'

Judith Wright

NOTES

'To Kill an Olive'
Gethsemane: a garden outside Jerusalem, scene of the agony, betrayal and arrest of Christ in the New Testament. The olive trees there today are said to be the original ones.

'Ulinda'
Ulinda: the farm's name? **duck egg... green... bluest**: the boy notices that the same object can be both green and blue. Perhaps he also notices that his family is both secure and not secure. **only playing a game**: grandfather pretends his severe diet is a game, but mother takes the children away from the table. Why?
In what phrases does Campbell best capture the world of a small child?

'Starting from Central Station'
Central Station: the terminus of country trains in Sydney. **And I am fifty-six**: Note the effect of the strong rhyme in making the jump to the present seem natural and inevitable. In other stanzas Campbell prefers the gentler effect of imperfect rhymes (e.g. **work/dark**).

'Green Hands'
hands of dead people: Aborigines often 'stencilled' their handprints on the walls of caves. Campbell wrote this poem after learning that he had a fatal cancer in his arm.
Companion Pieces: 'The Crab', 'Crayfish', David Campbell.

'To David Campbell'
Palerang: the farm.
Are the details in the first two stanzas as random as they seem?
Companion Piece: 'The Man and The Tree'*, Philip Mead.

'Mid-Channel'
Amos: a book of the Old Testament. **undesired element**: air. **stab... with poison**: as many fish spines do.
Who is the old monster anchored in the void?

'Goya Paints a Portrait of a Child'
Goya (1746–1828): Spanish painter.

'The Apparition'
Why are the first two stanzas necessary? Note how the indented lines tend to have falling intonations.

'Death'
poll: head or back of the head.
Would this poem work equally well as prose?

'Individualist'
Discussion: Compare 'Individualist' with other poems about 'nature red in tooth and claw'. Ted Hughes's 'Crow' series, or 'Hawk Roosting', would be good choices, also Beaver's 'The Big Web'.

'Brother and Sisters'
pianola: a type of piano that plays recorded music from a sheet of perforated paper.

ACTIVITIES

1 As each poem in this section is read aloud, write an 'instant reaction'. Then exchange it with your neighbour and write a brief comment on each other's reaction.

2 **Discussion**: At what age does it 'hit' people most strongly that they are mortal? Does it depend on whether you had a close friend or relative die when you were young? Do older people think as much about being mortal as young ones do?

3 Classify the poems in this section according to their different attitudes to death. Which do you find most honest and realistic? What do *you* think is the best consolation against death?

4 **Research Project**: Have people always felt mortality in the same way? What did Shakespeare have to say about it? or Homer? You might even like to go as far back as 'The Epic of Gilgamesh'. What about other cultures—Asian, European, African, Aboriginal, Polynesian, for instance? Philosophers? You might get a quick sample by looking up a dictionary of quotations. What do different cultures think about whether there is life after death? Will science ever conquer ageing and death?

5 Produce your own artistic or literary response to any or all of the poems in this section.

6 Memorize one poem from this section.

7 **Library Project**: Investigate Philip Hodgins's poems in his book *Blood and Bone* (Angus & Robertson, 1986) as a record of a young person's response to the news that he is dying.

Relevant poems from other sections

'Mute Conversations: Conversazioni Mute', 'So Quietly', 'Death of a Whale', 'Natural Increase'.

Poems for further study

*'June Fugue', Thomas W. Shapcott; 'Night Flight', Marion Alexopoulos; 'The Crafty Butcher', Susan Hampton; 'Behind the Veil', Andrew Lansdown; 'Ad Infinitum', Joan Aronsten; 'Self Pity', Philip Hodgins; 'Turtles Hatching', Mark O'Connor; 'Five Bells', Kenneth Slessor; 'Death Has No Features of His Own', Gwen Harwood.

†'The Soho Hospital for Women', Fleur Adcock; 'The Ikons', James K. Baxter; 'Body of John', R. A. K. Mason; 'Going', 'The Explosion', Philip Larkin; 'Mr Edwards and the Spider', 'Terminal Days at Beverly Farms', Robert Lowell; 'Do not go gentle into that good night', Dylan Thomas; 'Devonshire Street W. 1', John Betjeman; 'Sailing to Byzantium', W. B. Yeats; 'On Wenlock Edge the wood's in trouble', A. E. Housman; 'I heard a Fly buzz–when I died', 'Because I could not stop for Death', Emily Dickinson; 'A Toccata of Galuppi's', Robert Browning; 'Tears, idle tears, I know not what they mean', 'In Memoriam *A.H.H.*', 'Tithonus', Alfred Tennyson; 'Ode to a Nightingale', 'When I have fears that I may cease to be', John Keats; 'Ozymandias', Percy Bysshe Shelley; 'To his Coy Mistress', Andrew Marvell; 'Church-Monuments', George Herbert; 'Song', Thomas Nashe; 'Since Brasse, nor Stone, nor Earth', 'Fear no More the Heate o'th'Sun', William Shakespeare; 'What is our Life?', Sir Walter Ralegh; 'Tychborne's Elegy', Chidiock Tichborne; 'I that in heill wes and gladnes', William Dunbar.

17

THE WORLD WITHIN

Poets write to communicate, but they cannot always confine themselves to those experiences or feelings that are common to everyone, or even to many other people. Sometimes a successful poem may deal with experiences so private and personal that it was intended at first not for publication but purely for the writer's diary. Some poets develop special skills for turning personal experience or private states of mind into something that will make sense to a wider audience. For example...

Faith

And is the great cause lost beyond recall?
Have all the hopes of ages come to naught?
Is life no more with noble meaning fraught?
Is life but death, and love its funeral pall?
Maybe. And still on bended knees I fall,
Filled with a faith no preacher ever taught.
O God—*my* God—by no false prophet wrought—
I believe still, in despite of it all!

Let go the myths and creeds of groping men.
This clay knows nought—the Potter understands.
I own that Power divine beyond my ken,
And still can leave me in His shaping hands.
But, O my God, that madest me to feel,
Forgive the anguish of the turning wheel!

Ada Cambridge

The Inspector of Tides

I had gone for a walk
dressed in clouds
& with the wind
& with some friends

we were swift & slow
the sun entered us & went away
the moon hid in a tree

from a prison window
I watch go by
all but myself

my life
in a mirror
too near

reflections in an eye
or the morning
a snail on a stone rainbow

Michael Dransfield

The Land I Came Thro' Last

The land I came thro' last was dumb with night,
a limbo of defeated glory, a ghost:
for wreck of constellations flicker'd perishing
scarce sustain'd in the mortuary air,
and on the ground and out of livid pools
wreck of old swords and crowns glimmer'd at whiles;
I seem'd at home in some old dream of kingship:
now it is clear grey day and the road is plain,
I am the wanderer of many years
who cannot tell if ever he was king
or if ever kingdoms were: I know I am
the wanderer of the ways of all the worlds,
to whom the sunshine and the rain are one
and one to stay or hasten, because he knows
no ending of the way, no home, no goal,
and phantom night and the grey day alike
withhold the heart where all my dreams and days
might faint in soft fire and delicious death:
and saying this to myself as a simple thing
I feel a peace fall in the heart of the winds
and a clear dusk settle, somewhere, far in me.

Christopher Brennan

Sea Children

When the sun blew over the hills on the dry east wind
and the town was lit with sunflowers; when the sea
grew flat and green in the harbour, and blue beyond,
and Pietro sang in his dinghy of Sicily:
   then the children would lie in the sand
   and bar with a lazy hand
the glare of the stunning sun, and all time to be.

For the children the sea was deeper, and the dive
longer, the things to be found in the tangled weed
richer and stranger: coral, writhing, alive;
a hairclip formed like a bow, or a coloured bead
   —rare things. And at times they saw,
   brown on the pale sea floor,
the flat threat of a stingray stopped to feed.

And beyond the arm of the harbour, on the banks
of teased and surf-washed seaweed, there would be
frail sea-eggs, and sponges, and shells with curious marks;
and the lighthouse, when night came, branching with light
    like a tree,
   made horses and flowers of the foam
   on the reefs, and the boats coming home
from the islands bucked like Pegasus over the sea.

Randolph Stow

So Quietly

Who would have thought that you, so quietly,
who could set any dark room blazing with that
voluptuary innocence, who froze the candy-apple
against our teeth when Gregory Peck leaned over
and kissed your mouth, whose every movement
kept us awake till dawn while the first fuzz
thickened on our jowls, so heated the blood
in aging professors that they leapt across twenty
starved years and took their astonished wives
savagely, without a word, in kitchens and in
sewing-rooms, right after church, their boots half on,
turned hordes of copper-skinned Italians
up to the Arctic riffling Swedish grammars
while you flew South to the sputterings of
a second-rate volcano, taught ambitious virgins
from Omaha and Melbourne to tilt
back their heads, hesitate, feign a lilt
when they said 'No—not yest now,' set Congress
raging for loving so carelessly, your thought
plain as a running river, and as difficult,
would rise on your birthday, late at night,
toss back a glass of Veuve Clicquot, chuckle,
stride to your room, pull up the sheet
and without a word to any of us who in our labyrinths
whispered always to you and only you
widowed by that slow disease, turn
your face quickly to the dark and,
most privately, burp, and die.

Keith Harrison

The Wandering Islands

You cannot build bridges between the wandering islands;
The Mind has no neighbours, and the unteachable heart
Announces its armistice time after time, but spends
Its love to draw them closer and closer apart.

They are not on the chart; they turn indifferent shoulders
On the island-hunters; they are not afraid
Of Cook or De Quiros, nor of the empire-builders;
By missionary bishops and the tourist trade

They are not annexed; they claim no fixed position;
They take no pride in a favoured latitude;
The committee of atolls inspires in them no devotion
And the earthquake belt no special attitude.

A refuge only for the shipwrecked sailor;
He sits on the shore and sullenly masturbates,
Dreaming of rescue, the pubs in the ports of call or
The big-hipped harlots at the dockyard gates.

But the wandering islands drift on their own business,
Incurious whether the whales swim round or under,
Investing no fear in ultimate forgiveness.
If they clap together, it is only casual thunder

And yet they are hurt—for the social polyps never
Girdle their bare shores with a moral reef;
When the icebergs grind them they know both beauty and terror;
They are not exempt from ordinary grief;

And the sudden ravages of love surprise
Them like acts of God—its irresistible function
They have never treated with convenient lies
As a part of geography or an institution.

An instant of fury, a bursting mountain of spray,
They rush together, their promontories lock,
An instant the castaway hails the castaway,
But the sounds perish in that earthquake shock.

And then, in the crash of ruined cliffs, the smother
And swirl of foam, the wandering islands part.
But all that one mind ever knows of another,
Or breaks the long isolation of the heart,

Was in that instant. The shipwrecked sailor senses
His own despair in a retreating face.
Around him he hears in the huge monotonous voices
Of wave and wind: 'The Rescue will not take place.'

A. D. Hope

Poetry and Religion

Religions are poems. They concert
our daylight and dreaming mind, our
emotions, instinct, breath and native gesture

into the only whole thinking: poetry.
Nothing's said till it's dreamed out in words
and nothing's true that figures in words only.

A poem, compared with an arrayed religion,
may be like a soldier's one short marriage night
to die and live by. But that is a small religion.

Full religion is the large poem in loving repetition;
like any poem, it must be inexhaustible and complete
with turns where we ask Now why did the poet do that?

You can't pray a lie, said Huckleberry Finn;
you can't poe one either. It is the same mirror:
mobile, glancing, we call it poetry,

fixed centrally, we call it a religion,
and God is the poetry caught in any religion,
caught, not imprisoned. Caught as in a mirror

that he attracted, being in the world as poetry
is in the poem, a law against its closure.
There'll always be religion around while there is poetry

or a lack of it. Both are given, and intermittent,
as the action of those birds—crested pigeon, rosella parrot—
who fly with wings shut, then beating, and again shut.

Les A. Murray

Third Song of Pop-Eye the Sailorman

Sun and clear air today as I scrape
the barnacles from this beached boat's hull.
Singing because my heart is full,
no longer searching now to find escape.
Such small things can fill the heart—a letter
that makes no promises, and yet reminds one
of things too long forgotten. A tentative hand,
a few well-chosen words. This day is better
at last because of small things. The sun
fires the river, the water laps the sand
limpid and bright. I sing at my scraper,
warm in my shorts, under the boat's red side.
Transparent shrimps quest the lip of the tide.
Nothing is promised. Nothing on paper.

Hal Colebatch

Semi-conductors are also semi-insulators

Yes, my room's a mess. 'Alfred', Carlyle is reputed
to have said of Tennyson, 'is always carrying a piece
of chaos with him, turning it into cosmos'. I hope
I'm not so cosmetic as Alfred, but that, roughly,
is my work too. Better, then, to be surrounded by mess.
You, of course, are a tidy soul: a neat body, too.
But what things lurk in swamps, under rotting logs,
in deep scrub, live under water, or move on dark nights,
you prefer not to think on: sometimes, though, your
well-lit, disinfected, clockwork, deodorised life gets
dull. So you come to look in my room, remind
yourself of some of those unthinkable thoughts you
wish to live safely insulated from. That's why all
civilised minds keep a tame poet or two on their
bookshelves. So, in a large view, I'm neatly pigeonholed
in a role, too. Besides, it's a carefully chosen,
cunningly fabricated mess: else I would have to walk
outside, and who knows what waits out there?

R. G. Hay

NOTES

'Faith'
own: acknowledge. **can leave me**: can leave myself. **the turning wheel**: i.e.
the clay on the potter's wheel.
Would the poet have written *clay* rather than *wheel* if it had rhymed?

'The Land I Came Thro' Last'
thro': through.

'Sea Children'
The rhythm is a mixture of iambic and anapestic.
dry east wind: The setting seems to be Stow's home town, Geraldton, in
WA. **Pegasus**: the winged horse of Greek mythology.

'So Quietly'
The poem refers to the career, controversies and films of the actress Ingrid
Bergman. The poem is one long sentence ending with a deliberate shock
of anti-climax. **a second-rate volcano**: The literal reference may be to
Stromboli in Italy, the site of her film *Stromboli* (1949–50). There was
enormous publicity and criticism in the world's press of her adulterous
affair with its director, Roberto Rossellini, by whom she had a child. *yest*;
i.e. just. **Congress**: the US Senate and House of Representatives. **Veuve
Clicquot**: an expensive brand of French champagne, literally 'Widow
Clicquot'.

'The Wandering Islands'
What do you think the wandering islands stand for? and the shipwrecked
sailors?
the social polyps: coral polyps.

'Poetry and Religion'
concert: to bring together, either in co-operation, or debate, or struggle.
figures: makes sense? participates? **poe**: a verb created from poem?
Can Murray's poem be translated into a prose argument? Would the argu-
ment be a valid one?
Companion Piece: 'Equanimity'*, Les A. Murray.

'Third Song of Pop-Eye the Sailorman'
Pop-Eye: This seems to be Colebatch's name for himself.

'Semi-conductors are also semi-insulators'
What does the title mean?
Carlyle: Thomas Carlyle (1795–1881), Scottish historian, philosopher and
essayist.
'Hay has fascinating ideas, but his free verse is so prosy it might just
as well be prose.' What do you think? Examine the poem's line-endings.
Do they tend to come at significant points? Try reading the poem as prose.
Is the effect different?

ACTIVITIES

1 Read the first six poems aloud. Pass around six sheets of paper on which each person in turn writes a reaction. Then read out all the reactions. On which poems is there most agreement?

2 Write a poem or a few paragraphs of prose, perhaps inspired by 'Sea Children', in which you try to recapture your own childhood.

3 What do you think 'The Wandering Islands' is saying? Do you have to agree with the poem in order to enjoy it?

4 Paraphrase the poem 'Semi-conductors are also semi-insulators'.

5 **Discussion**: 'The Land I Came Thro' Last' and 'The Inspector of Tides' are poems of a highly personal, somewhat obscure sort. Compare these two poems with examples of the carefully explained personal poem like Buckley's 'Parents' or McAuley's 'Because'. Do the more obscure poems offer qualities that would suffer by being fully explained?

6 **Project**: Select a sample of poems that are highly personal and apparently obscure. Working on the principle that in poetry, as in all the arts, 'what you feel is what you get', see if you can identify lines or sections of poems that don't make anyone in the class feel anything. Conversely, can you find lines in which everyone agrees there is a certain charge or 'kick'?

7 Investigate recent numbers of at least two poetry magazines. What percentage of poems would you place in the 'obscurely personal' category? What do you think makes the difference between a personal poem that is of interest only to the author and his or her friends, and one that will interest a larger audience? Write a poem purely for your own bottom drawer, without bothering to explain the things that other people won't understand.

8 Look over a poem or piece of prose that you wrote some months (or years) ago, and that seemed right at the time. Can you now see things that need improving? Select one or two people who seem to have much the same tastes as yourself when looking at other poets' work. Show them the piece, and see if they suggest similar improvements. Now show them a piece you've recently finished and from which you are not yet distant. Ask them to put their comments in a sealed envelope. In a month's time open the envelope and see if what you now think about it agrees with what they could have told you then.

Relevant poems from other sections

'Prague 1968', 'Post Card', 'Bringing the Cattle'.

Poems for further study

*'Cows', 'An Inmate', Peter Kocan; 'The Horizon', 'The Members of the Orchestra', Kevin Hart; 'Act Six', Peter Goldsworthy; 'A Dream', Evan Jones; 'Night Flight', Marion Alexopoulos; 'The World of Dreams', Philip Salom; 'The Mother-in-Law of the Marquis de Sade', Jennifer Maiden; 'Sound Waves', Andrew Sant; 'The Cliff', David Rowbothan.

†'Tulips', Sylvia Plath; 'An Angel in Blythburgh Church', 'What I Have Written I Have Written', Peter Porter; 'The Sea Anemones', Gwen Harwood; 'Conversation', Louis MacNeice; 'Not Waving but Drowning', 'Away, Melancholy', Stevie Smith; 'The Love Song of J. Alfred Prufrock', 'The Waste Land', 'Marina', T. S. Eliot; 'Not, I'll not, Carrion comfort, Despair not feast on thee', 'I wake and feel the fell of dark, not day', Gerard Manley Hopkins; 'To Marguerite', 'Dover Beach', Matthew Arnold; ' "I Am" ', John Clare; 'Surprised by Joy—Impatient as the Wind', William Wordsworth; 'To Heaven', Ben Jonson.

IT'S IN OUR HANDS!

18

WORLD IN PERIL—THE FUTURE

Many times in the past our ancestors have believed they were facing the end of the world. Each time they were wrong. To have your nation decimated by one of history's innumerable plagues, or to have everyone who spoke your language carried off into slavery by the Romans, or massacred by Attila the Hun, may have seemed like the end of the world; but in the grand panorama of history such episodes were almost too trivial to mention. Only in this century has it become truly possible for the human race to destroy itself—along with the five million other species on the planet.

Ironically, it is only in this century that we have learned, thanks partly to film and television, about the vast richness and complexity of the planet we possess.

Behind nuclear war comes the second great spectre of the twentieth century. Overpopulation has already reduced great areas of the planet to ecological deserts, devoid of their native species; and it also helps keep hundreds of millions of human beings in poverty. A mathematical calculation will show that if the human race had begun from just two ancestors a mere 10,000 years ago, and had been able to grow at a steady average of 1% a year, it would by now be a ball of flesh several light-years across and expanding at the speed of light! Yet many countries today consider it desirable to increase their population by several per cent each year.

Overpopulation increases the risk of war and of nuclear war by leading nations to squabble over scarce resources. At the same time nations are forced to rely on nuclear power, with all its dangers, because there is not enough oil and gas to go around. Wealthy countries like Australia and the United States use up far more of the world's resources per person. Now the millions of China and India are beginning to claim their share.

The world's political system is not well adjusted to cope with these problems. In many countries there is no free press, and dissent is suppressed by imprisonment, torture, or murder, so that the faults of leaders can go unchecked. In the Western democracies the free enterprise system has been spectacularly successful in delivering the goods, but unfortunately it tends to judge projects largely by whether they make a profit. Ships sail to remote Pacific islands to chop down their rainforests, which reappear as furniture in our shops. Worse still, short-sighted politicians can justify almost any commercial activity as creating jobs for the population. Free enterprise sometimes seems like the broom started by the sorcerer's apprentice: a marvellous machine that somehow has to be turned off—or at least turned down—before it sweeps the world bare.

It is no wonder that many poets are pessimistic about the future. Yet the truth is we know almost nothing about it. As Les Murray reminds us, we see 'a small living distance' into the future, but 'all our projections fail to curve where it curves'.

One cause for hope has been the success of the conservation movement in making people more aware of what there is to protect in Australia. Poets like Judith Wright have been important in this. More recently, the Australian conservation movements have begun to press for action on the nuclear and population issues, arguing that if these two environmental problems are not solved all others become irrelevant. Nevertheless, a glance at the daily paper will show how much of today's news is still made up of the greedy squabblings of pressure groups who want to exploit the Earth *now* without care for the future. Perhaps it is because the nuclear and conservation issues have seemed so urgent that poets as yet have concentrated on them, leaving the more distant and optimistic panoramas of the future to the science-fiction writers in prose.

Package for the Distant Future

Dear Inheritor,
Since you have dared to open this container
you must be living in some far-distant,
unimaginable future,
and I am writing from a time of earth
before your world began—
we call it the era of Modern Man
(a bit after the Cro-Magnon).
Enclosed you will find evidence
of our existence:
a skein of yellow silk;
a carving of a child of unknown origin
with normal limbs and features;
a violin;
some lilac seeds;
the Song of Solomon.
The selection is not scientific, just
flotsam and jetsam of our civilisation.
I hope you like them.
We had a lot of things we did not like
and could have lived without.
Do not invent gods.
I hope the earth is nearly clean again.
Sow the lilac seeds in damp soil
and if they grow and flower, and if you can,
smell them after rain.

Sylvia Kantarizis

Your Attention Please

The Polar DEW has just warned that
A nuclear rocket strike of
At least one thousand megatons
Has been launched by the enemy
Directly at our major cities.
This announcement will take
Two and a quarter minutes to make,
You therefore have a further
Eight and a quarter minutes
To comply with the shelter
Requirements published in the Civil
Defence Code—section Atomic Attack.
A specially shortened Mass
Will be broadcast at the end
Of this announcement—
Protestant and Jewish services
Will begin simultaneously—
Select your wavelengths immediately
According to instructions
In the Defence Code. Do not
Take well-loved pets (including birds)
Into your shelter—they will consume
Fresh air. Leave the old and bed-
ridden, you can do nothing for them.
Remember to press the sealing
Switch when everyone is in
The shelter. Set the radiation
Aerial, turn off your television now.
Turn off your radio immediately
The services end. At the same time
Secure explosion plugs in the ears
Of each member of your family. Take
Down your plasma flasks. Give your children
The pills marked one and two
In the C. D. green container, then put
Them to bed. Do not break
The inside airlock seals until
The radiation All Clear shows
(Watch for the cuckoo in your
perspex panel), or your District
Touring Doctor rings your bell.

If before this, your air becomes
Exhausted or if any of your family
Is critically injured, administer
The capsules marked 'Valley Forge'
(Red pocket in No. 1 Survival Kit)
For painless death. (Catholics
Will have been instructed by their priests
What to do in this eventuality.)
This announcement is ending. Our President
Has already given orders for
Massive retaliation—it will be
Decisive. Some of us may die,
Remember, statistically
It is not likely to be you.

All flags are flying fully-dressed
On Government buildings—the sun is shining.
Death is the least we have to fear.
We are all in the hands of God,
Whatever happens by His Will.
Now go quickly to your shelters...

Peter Porter

Death of a Whale

When the mouse died, there was a sort of pity:
the tiny, delicate creature made for grief.
Yesterday, instead, the dead whale on the reef
drew an excited multitude to the jetty.
How must a whale die to wring a tear?
Lugubrious death of a whale: the big
feast for the gulls and sharks; the tug
of the tide simulating life still there,
until the air, polluted, swings this way
like a door ajar from a slaughterhouse.
Pooh! pooh! spare us, give us the death of a mouse
by its tiny hole; not this in our lovely bay.
—Sorry we are, too, when a child dies;
but at the immolation of a race who cries?

John Blight

Natural Increase

From *Conversation with Calliope*

'A plague like locusts, lemmings, lice
Breaks out like fire, typhoon, or flood,
And swiftly as it grows, it dies;
The human plague, less understood
Through slow millennia takes its rise,
At every step, so far so good!
And yet as each divide is crossed,
Some measure of the whole is lost.

'Man wants but little, even so
By little wants he is misled:
'Man wants but little here,' you know,
'Nor wants that little long,' was said
By Edwin just about to throw
Fair Angelina on his bed;
Which lost the girl her pilgrim's permit,
And left him an unlicensed hermit.

'Their vows abandoned with their habits
The "Law of Measure" set aside
Alas, the phrase is Irving Babbit's,
This precious hermit and his bride
Bred, as you might expect, like rabbits
And had produced before they died,
Counting great-grandchildren as well,
Two hundred from that single cell.

'But death by then was just the stitch in
Time devoutly wished by both.
They'd seen the life their love was rich in
Imperilled by its very growth.
It is not only in a kitchen
Too many cooks can spoil a broth,
And families perish by inflation
Into a tribe, a horde, a nation.

'What Edwin found to be the case
Proves true in history's arena:
Huntress or victim of the chase,
Angelica or Angelina,

Each future mother of the race
So ravishing in her demeanour,
By instinct still, and natural bent, is
Another Sorcerer's Apprentice.

'No hunter of the Age of Fable
Had need to buckle in his belt;
More game than he was ever able
To take ran wild upon the veldt;
Each night with roast he stocked his table,
Then procreated on the pelt.
And that is how, of course, there came
At last to be more men than game.

'No matter: man's invention can
Snatch triumph from his worst mistakes.
Soon cuts of beef and pork began
To take the place of feral steaks,
Next bread, and sifting out the bran
He turned his plain loaf into cakes.
—And as for cake, mankind will do
Their best to eat and have it too.

'It does not work: a time must come
—A fact that man is slow to learn—
Patch, plan, put off, explore and plumb,
You face the point of no return;
The Providential Voice is dumb,
And Wisdom, weeping by her urn,
Proffers in place of Nature's fruits
Synthetic pulps as substitutes.

'Effects of over-population
Converge, no matter where you start;
The economics of inflation
Follows the same curve on the chart
To where *ersatz* provides the ration
Alike for belly, mind or heart.'

A. D. Hope

The Future

There is nothing about it. Much science fiction is set there
but is not about it. Prophecy is not about it.
It sways no yarrow stalks. And crystal is a mirror.
Even the man we nailed on a tree for a lookout
said little about it; he told us evil would come.
We see, by convention, a small living distance into it
but even that's a projection. And all our projections
fail to curve where it curves.
                                   It is the black hole
out of which no radiation escapes to us.
The commonplace and magnificent roads of our lives
go on some way through cityscape and landscape
or steeply sloping, or scree, into that sheer fall
where everything will be that we have ever sent there,
compacted, spinning—except perhaps us, to see it.
It is said we see the start.
                                  But, from here, there's a blindness.
The *gouffre Avenir* that will swallow all our present
blinds us to the normal sun that may be imagined
shining calmly away on the far side of it, for others
in their ordinary day. A day to which all our portraits,
ideals, revolutions, denim and deshabille
are quaintly heartrending. To see those people is impossible,
to greet them, mawkish. Nonetheless, I begin:
'When I was alive—'
                            and I am turned around
to find myself looking at a cheerful picnic party,
the women decently legless, in muslin and gloves,
the men in beards and weskits, with the long
cheroots and duck trousers of the better sort,
relaxing on a stone veranda. Ceylon, or Sydney.
And as I look, I know they are utterly gone,
each one on his day, with pillow, small bottles, mist,
with all the futures they dreamed or dealt in, going
down to that engulfment everything approaches;
with the man on the tree, they have vanished into the Future.

Les A. Murray

A Document

'Sign there.' I signed, but still uneasily.
I sold the coachwood forest in my name.
Both had been given me; but all the same
remember that I signed uneasily.

Ceratopetalum, Scented Satinwood:
a tree attaining seventy feet in height.
Those pale-red calyces like sunset light
burned in my mind. A flesh-pink pliant wood

used in coachbuilding. Difficult of access
(those slopes were steep). But it was World War Two.
Their wood went into bomber-planes. They grew
hundreds of years to meet those hurried axes.

Under our socio-legal dispensation
both name and woodland had been given me.
I was much younger then than any tree
matured for timber. But to help the nation

I signed the document. The stand was pure
(eight hundred trees perhaps). Uneasily
(the bark smells sweetly when you wound the tree)
I set upon this land my signature.

Judith Wright

Outback

When your skin is worn away
by wind, by time, like the Macdonnell Ranges,
what will emerge
what will be left to face the sun?
Worthless quartz stripped back
may reveal an opal. But you are an island,
your shores are fences built by foreign cash,
you are ripped into beef roads and investments;
the abos move to the cities, their homesickness
cauterised by cheap wine and promises of jobs.
Speculators will ruin this last wild place,
few will protest, for profit eases consciences.
In thirty years
there will be nothing to distinguish this
from mined and gutted countries anywhere.
Our leaders betray us, sell our heritage,
what remains is not worth stealing,
and so becomes an Army weapons-range.

Michael Dransfield

NOTES

'Your Attention Please'
Polar DEW: The distant early warning system which was designed to detect Russian missiles coming over the North Pole to Britain or the USA. **C.D.**: Civil Defence. **Valley Forge**: a village in Pennsylvania where Washington and his troops dug in for the winter of 1777–8 during their successful War of Independence. What is the irony of this name?
What does this poem make you feel? and how does it do so?

'Death of a Whale'
immolation: sacrifice.
Companion Piece: 'The Stranded Whales', Geoffrey Dutton.

'Natural Increase' from **'Conversation with Calliope'**
Man wants but little: The full quote is 'Man wants but little here below, / Nor wants that little long.' The quotation is from 'Edwin and Angelina' (a.k.a. 'The Hermit'), a ballad by Oliver Goldsmith (1730–74). Edwin the hermit tries to convince an unhappy young traveller to ask less from life. But the traveller turns out to be his lost love Angelina in male disguise. **Measure**: i.e. restraint, balance. **Irving Babbitt**: (1865–1933) an influential American educator, critic and author. **feral steaks**: i.e. from wild cattle. **sifting out the bran**: i.e. producing white flour. **Providential**: 1. looking to or providing for the future; 2. wise or prudent; 3. expressing the benign guidance of God or nature; 4. of or related to a lucky escape from disaster. **Wisdom**: Wisdom or science. Hope is imitating Goldsmith's eighteenth-century use of abstract nouns with capital letters. **urn**: jar or container for liquids, or sometimes for cremation ashes. Abstract figures like Wisdom are often depicted leaning on an urn. **ersatz**: any low-grade substitute used in time of scarcity or rationing. **economics of inflation**: the way prices go up faster and faster once inflation is out of control? **for... mind or heart**: Elsewhere Hope claims 'The Great Society produces / Only the arts it can afford, / Stamped, sterilized and tinned and tested / And standardized and predigested.'
Companion Piece: 'Going, Going', Philip Larkin (UK).

'The Future'
yarrow: a herb used in medicine and magic. **crystal is a mirror**: i.e. crystal balls, like mirrors, only reflect ourselves? **on a tree**: on the cross? Perhaps with a side reference to the tree-sacrifices described in Sir James Frazer's anthropological study *The Golden Bough*. **scree**: a steep pile of rock-fragments, often found near cliffs. *gouffre Avenir*: future abyss. **weskit**: an informal word for waistcoat. **duck trousers**: i.e. made of heavy plain cotton fabric.
Companion Piece: 'A History of the Future', Kevin Hart.

'A Document'
coachwood: a.k.a. *Ceratopetalum* or Scented Satinwood. This tree is sometimes the dominant species in southern Australian rainforests. During World War II Mosquito fighter-bombers were built in Australia using plywood sheets made from tough light coachwood. **calyces**: plural of calyx, the outer whorl of leaves or sepals at the base of a flower. **socio-legal dispensation**: social and legal system (of distribution of ownership, or of exemption from restrictions). Does Judith Wright get away with using this mouthful in a poem?
In what sense is this poem a plea for conservation? How does it avoid preaching? Has there been any significant reform of our 'socio-legal dispensation', as regards nature, in this century?

ACTIVITIES

1 John Blight points out that it is easier to make people shed tears for an individual than for 'the immolation of a race'. How does each poem in this section solve the problem of expressing large issues through particular cases?

2 A large percentage of verse published today is about conservation. Investigate recent editions of nature magazines like *Habitat* or *Wildlife Australia* and determine what themes and styles they prefer. Type and submit one or more poems from the class to one of these magazines, enclosing a stamped self-addressed envelope and a note to the editor asking for a brief comment on the poem.

3 Write your own note (in free verse) to enclose with a 'package for the distant future', trying to make each line a new unit of thought or information. Later divide into groups and let each group make its own selection of the best lines from everyone's version. See if either groups or individuals can combine these lines into a poem with a striking beginning, a steady development and strong ending.

4 Do the same thing, based on 'Your Attention Please'.

5 Memorize at least two stanzas of 'Natural Increase', using the rhymes as memory pegs.

6 **Library Project**: Investigate A. D. Hope's use of scientific understanding in his poem 'Clover Honey', or else in his work as a whole. Does it allow him to make more sense of the modern world than when he uses classical mythology?

7 Write someone's reply (e.g. an economist's) to Dransfield's 'Outback'.

8 Write to the Australian Conservation Foundation (672B Glenferrie Road, Hawthorn, Victoria, 3122) for copies of their current nuclear, conservation and population policies. Examine them carefully. Which clauses in these policies do you think represent compromises between different ideals, or pressures? Do any clauses correspond to points made by the poets in this section? Write your own argument that these policies go too far, or not far enough, using at least three quotations from the poets.

9 **Activity**: With notebook in hand, visit one 'spoiled' and one successfully preserved natural area. Write a short article, radio talk, TV script or poem, about one or both places.

10 Copy out your own private anthology or list of the most memorable lines and passages of poetry you have studied this year. Which poets in this anthology have meant most to you. Have they necessarily written the best poems? Do you respond to their work as individual poems or as the expression of a personality.

Poems for further study

*'Epitaph for a Scientist', Lex Banning; 'Flames & Dancing Wire', Robert Gray; 'Radiation Victim', Colin Thiele.

†'Who Tests Today?', Hone Tuwhare; 'The Road to Newfoundland', Al Purdy.

BIOGRAPHICAL NOTES

BIOGRAPHICAL NOTES

This section provides some basic information on most of the younger poets in this volume. Information on poets born before 1930 can be found in *The Oxford Companion to Australian Literature* (1985) and in the most recent edition of the Australian *Who's Who*.

ALEXOPOULOS, MARION. Born 1948, London. She was a school teacher there before meeting her Australian-born husband and coming to live in Melbourne in 1975. Has published *Baby at a Tram Stop* (1986).

BRETT, DORIS. A clinical psychologist, she is married with one daughter. *The Truth about Unicorns* (1984) won the Anne Elder prize for the best first book of poetry, and also the Mary Gilmore prize.

COLEBATCH, HAL. Born 1945, into a well-known West Australian family. He has been a journalist, lawyer, director of a publishing company, radio-scriptwriter and yachtsman. Has published *Outer Charting* (1985) and *In Breaking Waves* (1979).

CROGGON, ALISON. Born 1962 in South Africa of a British family, but grew up mainly in Ballarat, Vic. A journalist in Melbourne for seven years, her poems have as yet appeared only in magazines. She is currently completing her first collection.

DAWE, BRUCE. Born 1930 at Geelong, Victoria. He has worked in a factory, sawmill and on a farm, as well as a labourer, handyman–gardener, postman and clerk. He joined the RAAF in 1959 and served for nine years. He was a secondary teacher from 1969 to 1971. At present he is a lecturer in literature at Toowoomba, Queensland.

DRANSFIELD, MICHAEL. Born Sydney, NSW, in 1948, died 1973. By the time of his death he was something of a cult-hero. His association with drugs, with bisexuality, and with the 1960s 'counter-culture' was part of the reason, but Dransfield's poetry also denounced an Australia that had lost its ideals and become obsessed with commercialism.

DURACK, DAME MARY. Born 1913 at Adelaide, of a pioneering pastoral family. She lived for some years in the Kimberleys helping to run the family properties, and married the pioneer aviator Horrie Miller. She is the author of many books, including the story of her family, *Kings in Grass Castles*. She lives in Nedlands, Perth.

DUTTON, GEOFFREY. Born 1922 at Anlaby station, South Australia. He was a pilot in the RAAF 1941–45. After lecturing at various universities he has been a full-time writer and editor since 1962. He has written more than 40 books, including nine books of poetry. After many years in South Australia, he now lives in Sydney.

ENCARNAÇÃO, J. J. Born East Timor, 1940. He came to Australia in early childhood as a refugee from the Japanese invasion of East Timor. He has had two short stories published in an anthology. His poems are often performed in public readings in Portugal and Australia, and may have been translated into Portuguese.

FAHEY, DIANE. Born Melbourne, 1945. After a period spent abroad she returned in 1986 to live in South Australia. Her poetry has won numerous awards, and her first book of verse *Metamorphoses* has been published by the Danish-Australian international publisher Dangaroo Press.

GILBERT, KEVIN. Born Condobolin, NSW, 1933, to an Irish father and a part-Aboriginal mother. Both parents died when he was seven. He left school after fifth class in primary school, and for some years worked as a station hand. In 1957 he was sentenced to life imprisonment for the murder of his wife, and spent fourteen and a half years behind bars. He had been almost illiterate, but prison gave him access to books, and he began writing. Today he is a writer who campaigns to improve the lot of Aborigines. His books include *Living Black* (1978) and *People and Legends* (1979).

GILES, BARBARA. Born 1912 in Manchester, England, she came to Australia in 1923 and later taught in Victoria. She has also been involved in migrant education. Her books of poetry include *Eve Rejects Apple* (1978) and *Earth and Solitude* (1983). She is strongly interested in children's literature.

GOULD, ALAN. Born London, 1949. A novelist and poet, he has spent most of his life in Australia and is one of the leading figures in the 'Canberra School' of poets. His father is a former British army officer, his mother Icelandic.

GRAY, ROBERT. Born 1945. Robert Gray grew up in Coffs Harbour on the north coast of New South Wales. He left school early and has worked in Sydney, in advertising agencies and bookshops. The main preoccupation of his poetry is the relationship of man to nature, and he has been attracted to Taoist and Buddhist philosophy. His *Selected Poems* was published in 1985.

GRIFFIN, JOHN. Born 1935. He is a schoolteacher by profession, and lives in Adelaide. He has published two books of poetry: *A Waltz on Stones* and *Menzies at Evening*.

HARRISON, KEITH. Born Melbourne, 1932. He has taught in Victoria and England before taking up an academic career in North America. Harrison is well-known internationally as a poet, editor, academic and critic.

HART, KEVIN. Born 1954 in London, Hart came to live in Brisbane at ten years of age. He graduated in philosophy from the Australian National University in Canberra, taught at Geelong College, and now teaches literature at Deakin University. His work, since his conversion to Catholicism, reflects a Christian attitude to experience.

HEWETT, DOROTHY. Born Perth, 1923. Playwright, novelist and poet. Books of poetry include *Windmill Country* (1965), *Rapunzel in Suburbia* (1979), *Greenhouse* (1979). She now lives in Sydney.

JENKINS, JOHN. Born Melbourne, 1949. Associated with a group of poets who sometimes called themselves the 'Generation of '68' and with several of the magazines they produced. There is a selection of his work in *The New Australian Poetry*, edited by J. Tranter.

JENNINGS, KATE. Born 1948 near Griffith, NSW. Edited a well-known collection of feminist verse *Mother I'm Rooted* (1975), and has published a collection of her own poetry, *Come to Me My Melancholy Baby* (1975). She now lives in the USA.

JONES, EVAN. Born 1931, Preston, Vic. Educated at the University of Melbourne and Stanford University, USA. Jones has taught history and English at the University of Melbourne and the Australian National University. In the 1950s he was one of a group of writers at the University of Melbourne which included Vincent Buckley and Chris Wallace-Crabbe.

JURGENSEN, MANFRED. Born 1940 in Flensburg. He came to Australia in 1961 after living in Germany, Switzerland and the USA, was educated at the Universities of Melbourne and Zurich, and is now a Professor of German literature at the University of Queensland. He writes in both English and German.

KANTARIZIS, SYLVIA (a.k.a. KANTARIS). Born Derbyshire, UK, 1936. Lived in Australia from 1962 to 1973. Published *Time and Motion* (1975), *News from the Front* (with D. M. Thomas, Harry Chambers 1983), *The Tenth Muse* (1983), *The Sea at the Door* (1985).

KEFALA, ANTIGONE. Born 1935, Braila, Romania, of Greek parents, she has lived in Romania, Greece, NZ, and Australia. She graduated from Victoria University, Wellington, in 1960 and has worked as a librarian, migrant English teacher and as an arts administrator.

KOCAN, PETER. Born Newcastle, NSW, 1947. He spent his childhood in Melbourne, and after leaving school returned to NSW and worked in country areas as a labourer and station hand. He spent 10 years in prison after attempting at the age of 19 to assassinate the Labor leader Arthur Calwell. Since his release he has become a successful novelist and poet.

LEHMANN, GEOFFREY. Born Sydney, NSW, 1940. Graduated in Arts and Law, and worked for some years as a solicitor. He is now a lecturer in tax and law at the University of N.S.W. His books include *Selected Poems* (1976) and *Ross Poems* (1978).

LLEWELLYN, KATE. Born 1940 at Tumby Bay, South Australia. She has a BA in history and classics, and has worked as a nurse and as owner-director of an art gallery. She now lives at Leura in the Blue Mountains.

LEWITT, MARIA. Born in Lodz, Poland, 1924. She came to Australia in 1949, and began to write in English in 1967. She has written four books: *Just Call Me Bob, Come Spring, Grandmother's Yarn*, and *No Snow in December*. She won the Alan Marshall award in 1979 and the NSW Premier's award in 1986.

LOEWALD, UYEN. Born in Vietnam in 1940, she moved to the South in 1951. She studied mathematics and literature and was imprisoned by the Diem government in 1962. In 1964 she married and moved to the USA, but settled in Australia in 1970.

MALOUF, DAVID. Born Brisbane, 1934, of British and Lebanese parents. He was brought up and educated in Brisbane, lived in Europe 1959–68, but now divides his time between Australia and a house he owns in Italy. His novels have brought him international reputation. His *Selected Poems* was published in 1980.

McDONALD, ROGER. Born 1941. Son of a Presbyterian minister, McDonald spent his childhood in country towns, and is a graduate of the University of Sydney. He was poetry editor for the University of Queensland Press's innovative series of Paperback Poets. His novel *1915* was made into a TV series. He lives now on a farm near Braidwood, NSW.

MARTIN, PHILIP. Born 1931, Richmond, Vic. He graduated from the University of Melbourne in 1958 and now teaches English Literature at Monash University in Melbourne. He has also been a script-writer of literary programs for ABC radio and television.

MURRAY, LES. Born 1938 in Nabiac, a rural village on the north coast of NSW, Murray spent his childhood and adolescence on his father's dairy farm in the nearby Bunyah district, a remote, dairying community. He left the University of Sydney in 1960 without a degree but with an abiding love for its Fisher Library. After being a professional translator, and then a public servant, he is now a professional poet, and has returned to live at Bunyah.

O'CONNOR, MARK. Born 1945, Melbourne. Mark O'Connor abandoned a career as a university teacher, and began writing poetry in 1972 while working as a diver on the Barrier Reef. He went to Europe 1977–81 on a Marten Bequest Writing Fellowship. At differing times he has lived in most states of Australia. His *Selected Poems* was published in 1986.

PAGE, GEOFF. Born 1940. Grew up on a property near Grafton, NSW, part of a family with rural and political traditions. He was educated at the University of New England at Armidale. He has published five volumes of poetry, and edited an anthology of poetry about the First World War. He is now a high school teacher in Canberra.

PAPERTALK-GREENE, CHARMAINE. Born Eradu, via Geraldton, Western Australia. Lives in Canberra, and works at the Australian Institue of Aboriginal Affairs.

ROBERTS, NIGEL. Born 1941. From New Zealand, he has lived in Australia for over 20 years, and teaches art at a Sydney high school. Many of his poems are designed for public performance.

SHAPCOTT, THOMAS. Born 1935. Educated at Ipswich, Qld, he left school at fifteen and worked as a clerk in his father's accountancy business. A public accountant until 1978, he has since worked as a poet, novelist, editor, and arts bureaucrat. His works include *Selected Poems* (1978).

SKRZYNECKI, PETER. Born Europe, 1945, he came to Australia at the age of four. He has published *There, Behind the Lids* (1970), *Head-waters* (1972), *Immigrant Chronicle* (1975), *The Aviary* (1978), and has worked as a teacher.

SMITH, VIVIAN. Born Hobart, 1933. Studied at Hobart and Sydney Universities. He teaches English Literature at Sydney University, and has published *The Other Meaning* (1956), *An Island South* (1967), *Familiar Places* (1978), *Tide Country* (1982).

STRAUSS, JENNIFER. Born 1933, Heywood, Vic. Has published *Children and Other Strangers* (1975), *Winter Driving* (1981). Currently lectures in English at Monash University.

TIPPING, RICHARD. Born 1949 in Adelaide. He now lives in Sydney, and has worked as a director or freelance writer on documentary films, including a series on Australian writers. He has been editor and co-editor of a number of magazines.

TOTARO, PAOLO. Born Naples. He came to Australia in 1963, and later became founding chairman of the first Ethnic Affairs Commission in Australia, set up by the NSW government in 1977. His occasional poems in English or Italian are not available in book form.

VIIDIKAS, VICKI. Born 1948, Sydney, NSW, of an Estonian father and Australian mother. She left school early, and after an unsettled childhood, worked in many jobs from bookshops to pubs, and pursued the bohemian life in Balmain, and then in India. Her books include *Condition Red* (1973) and *Knäbel* (1978).

WALLACE-CRABBE, CHRIS. Born Richmond, Melbourne, in 1934. He was educated at the University of Melbourne where he now teaches English Literature. An anthologist, poet and critic, his books include *Selected Poems* (1973).

WHITING, B. R. Born Melbourne, 1923, educated Geelong Grammar. Enlisted in Army, held all ranks to Captain, Paratroops. Enjoyed the end of the British Raj as ADC to Governor of Bengal. Settled in Rome in 1955. He has published two books: *The Little Desert* (1978) and *Winter for Quiet* (1979).

ACKNOWLEDGEMENTS

MARION ALEXOPOULOS: 'Lines from a Factory' from *Baby at a Tram Stop* (1986), © Marion Alexopoulos, reprinted by permission of Angus and Robertson Publishers.

BRUCE BEAVER: 'The Big Web'; 'Death', reprinted by permission of the author.

JOHN BLIGHT: 'Mangrove'; 'Death of a Whale' from *Selected Poems 1939–75* (1976), © John Blight, reprinted by permission of the author.

CHRISTOPHER BRENNAN: 'Fire in the Heavens' from *The Quest of Silence*; 'The land I came thro' last' from *Selected Poems*, reprinted by permission of Angus and Robertson Publishers.

DORIS BRETT: 'Playgroup' from *The Truth about Unicorns* (1984), © Doris Brett, reprinted by permission of Jacaranda Wiley.

VINCENT BUCKLEY: 'Parents'; 'Return of a Popular Statesman' from *Selected Poems* (1981), © Vincent Buckley, reprinted by permission of Angus and Robertson Publishers.

ADA CAMBRIDGE: 'Faith'; 'Vows' from *The Hand in the Dark and Other Poems* (1913), Heinemann UK.

DAVID CAMPBELL: 'Harry Pearce'; 'The Australian Dream'; 'Starting from Central Station'; 'Snake'; 'Ulinda' from *Selected Poems* (1978), © Judith Anne Campbell, reprinted by permission of Angus and Robertson Publishers; 'Green Hands' from *The Man in the Honeysuckle* (1979), © Judith Anne Campbell, reprinted by permission of Angus and Robertson Publishers.

HAL COLEBATCH: 'Third Song of Pop-eye the Sailorman' from *Outer Charting* (1985), © Hal Colebatch, reprinted by permission of Angus and Robertson Publishers.

ALISON CROGGON: 'Emily Brontë', reprinted by permission of the author.

BRUCE DAWE: 'Life-Cycle'; 'Weapons Training'; 'Homecoming' from *Sometimes Gladness: Collected Poems 1954–82* (1983); 'Doctor to Patient' from *Towards Sunrise* (1986), © Bruce Dawe, reprinted by permission of Longman Cheshire Pty Ltd.

ROSEMARY DOBSON: 'Child with a Cockatoo'; 'The Bystander'; 'The Scarecrow'; 'Painter of Antwerp'; 'The Edge' from *Selected Poems* (1973), © Rosemary Dobson, reprinted by permission of Angus and Robertson Publishers.

MICHAEL DRANSFIELD: 'Wine Tasting' from *Voyage into Solitude* (1978); 'Prosperity' and 'The Inspector of Tides' from *The Inspector of Tides* (1972); 'Outback', 'That Which We Call a Rose' and 'Pas de Deux for Lovers' from *Streets of the Long Voyage* (1970), reprinted by permission of University of Queensland Press.

MARY DURACK: 'Lament for the Drowned Country', reprinted by permission of the author.

DOROTHEA MACKELLAR: 'Once When She Thought Aloud' from © The Estate of the Late Dorothea Mackellar, reprinted by permission of Curtis Brown Pty Ltd.

DAVID MALOUF: 'Stars' from *Bicycle and Other Poems* (1970), © David Malouf, reprinted by permission of University of Queensland Press.

ERN MALLEY (James McAuley and Harold Stewart): 'Petit Testament', reprinted by permission of Max Harris.

PHILIP MARTIN: 'To David Campbell', reprinted by permission of the author.

JAMES McAULEY: 'An Art of Poetry'; 'Because' from *Collected Poems 1936-70* (1971), © James McAuley, reprinted by permission of Angus and Robertson Publishers.

ROGER McDONALD: '1915' from *Airship* (1975), © Roger McDonald, reprinted by permission of University of Queensland Press.

LES A. MURRAY: 'The Conquest'; 'Folklore'; 'The Breach'; 'The Future'; from 'The Budelah-Taree Song Cycle' from *The Vernacular Republic Poems 1961-81* (1982); 'Weights'; 'The Fishermen at South Head'; 'The Bulldozer' from *The People's Otherworld* (1983); 'Poetry and Religion' from *The Daylight Moon* (1987), © Les A. Murray, reprinted by permission of Angus and Robertson Publishers.

JOHN SHAW NEILSON: 'Love's Coming'; 'Song Be Delicate', reprinted by permission of Lothian Books.

MARK O'CONNOR: 'The Beginning' from *Reef Poems* (1976); 'Pozières Cemetery'; 'To Kill an Olive' from *The Eating Tree* (1980), © Mark O'Connor, reprinted by permission of Curtis Brown (Aust.) Pty Ltd and the author.

GEOFF PAGE: 'Brothers'; 'Christ at Gallipoli' from *Cassandra Paddocks* (1980), © Geoff Page, reprinted by permission of Angus and Robertson Publishers.

PETER PORTER: 'Mort aux Chats'; 'Your Attention Please' from *Collected Poems* (1983), © Peter Porter, reprinted by permission of Oxford University Press.

NIGEL ROBERTS: 'The Gull's Flight' from *Steps for Astaire*, © Nigel Roberts, reprinted by permission of Hale and Iremonger.

PETER SKRZYNECKI: 'Post Cart' from *Immigrant Chronicle* (1978), © Peter Skrzynecki, reprinted by permission of University of Queensland Press.

THOMAS W. SHAPCOTT: 'Near the School for Handicapped Children' from *Shabbytown Calendar* (1978), © Thomas W. Shapcott, reprinted by permission of University of Queensland Press.

KENNETH SLESSOR: 'Beach Burial'; 'Crow Country' from 'Five Visions of Captain Cook'; 'The Night-Ride' from *Selected Poems* (1944), © Paul Slessor, reprinted by permission of Angus and Robertson Publishers.

VIVIAN SMITH: 'At an Exhibition of Historical Paintings, Hobart' from *Selected Poems* (1985), © Vivian Smith, reprinted by permission of Angus and Robertson Publishers.

DOUGLAS STEWART: 'Brindabella'; 'Lament' from *Selected Poems* (1973), © Margaret Stewart, reprinted by permission of Angus and Robertson Publishers.

RANDOLPH STOW: 'Sea Children' from *Selected Poems* (1969), © Randolph Stow, reprinted by permission of Angus and Robertson Publishers.

JENNIFER STRAUSS: 'Migrant Woman on a Melbourne Tram' from *Winter Driving* (1981), © Jennifer Strauss, reprinted by permission of the author.

LILIAN TAIT: 'After the "Ball"', permission of the author.

RICHARD TIPPING: 'Mangoes' from *Domestic Hardcore* (1975), © Richard Tipping, reprinted by permission of University of Queensland Press.

PAOLO TOTARO: 'Mute Conversations: Conversazioni Mute' © Paolo Totaro, reprinted by permission of the author.

DMITRIS TSLOUMAS: 'Postponement: Anavolee' from *The Book of Epigrams* (1985), © Dmitris Tsaloumas, reprinted by permission of University of Queensland Press.

VICKI VIIDIKAS: 'Going Down. With no permanence.' from *Condition Red* (1973), © Vicki Viidikas, reprinted by permission of University of Queensland Press.

KATH WALKER (OODGEROO OF THE TRIBE NOONUCCAL): 'We Are Going' from *My People* (1970, second edn 1981), © Kath Walker, reprinted by permission of Jacaranda Press.

CHRIS WALLACE-CRABBE: 'The Apparition', reprinted by permission of the author.

B. R. WHITING: 'Individualist', © B. R. Whiting, reprinted by permission of Hub Publications Ltd.

WONGURI-MADJIGAI PEOPLE: 'Harvesting Lily Roots' from *Song-Cycle of the Moon-Bone*, fist published in *Oceania*, 1949, vol. 19, no. 1, song no. 13, pp. 47–50. Translated by and reprinted with the permission of Professor R. M. Berndt.

JUDITH WRIGHT: 'At Cooloolah'; 'The Old Prison'; 'South of My Days'; 'The Cycads'; 'Naked Girl and Mirror'; 'Woman to Man'; 'Woman to Child'; 'Brothers and Sister'; 'A Document' from *Collected Poems 1942–70* (1971), © Judith Wright, reprinted by permission of Angus and Robertson Publishers. 'Lake in Spring', © Judith Wright, reprinted by permission of the author.

Details for the acknowledgements are as supplied by copyright-holders. Every effort has been made to trace the original source of all material contained in this book. Where the attempt has been unsuccessful the editor and publisher would be pleased to hear from the author/publisher concerned, to rectify any omission.

INDEX OF TITLES
AND FIRST LINES

1915   102

A freedom fighter, she said   81

A graveyard grows re-cycling
myths   100

A moon hangs in the air   210

'A plague of locusts, lemmings,
lice   240

A post card sent by a friend   84

A visiting conductor   200

Adieu   97

Adieu, the years are a broken song   97

After the 'Ball'   140

After the entertainments of the
night   215

After the fingernails   140

All afternoon I've lain about this
illuminated country   147

All day, day after day, they're bringing
them home   105

And a Good Friday Was Had by All   55

And is the great cause lost beyond
recall?   224

And when I say eyes right I want to
hear   104

Andromeda   183

Apparition, The   215

Art of Poetry, An   130

As I came down Talbingo Hill   37

As I lean over to write   184

As if the entire population but you   80

*At an Exhibition of Historical
Paintings, Hobart*   28

At Christmas, sometimes, even for
unbelievers   197

A Cooloolah   27

At the Last Judgement, as the final
batch   169

Australian Dream, The   44

Be Good, Little Migrants   89

Be good, little migrants   89

Beach Burial   99

Because   158

Before the glare o'dawn I rise   39

Beginning, The   72

Beneath the moon in the standing corn
at midnight   129

Big Web, The   133

Bit weird at first   100

Black greyed into white a nightmare
of bicycling   117

Bonegilla 1961   82

Breach, The   53

Breasts   184

Brides, The   124

Brindabella   131

Bringing the Cattle   147

Brother and Sisters   218

Brothers   103

Brought back from the tedium of
dying   208

Budelah-Taree Song Cycle, The   30

Bulldozer, The   132

Bullocky Bill   37

Bystander, The   124

Child with a Cockatoo   4

Christ at Gallipoli   100

Cod inert as an old boot   213

'Consultation'   19

Conquest, The   2

Conversations with Calliope   241

Convicts' Rum Song, The   124

Cook was a captain of the Admiralty   5

Couples   190

Cricket   166

Crow Country   66

Cut yer name across me backbone   124
Cycads, The   70

Daybreak: the household slept   156
Dear inheritor   237
Dear one, forgive my appearing before
    you like this   144
Death   216
Death of a Whale   239
Dedication, A   65
Doctor to Patient   115
Document, A   243
Down the assembly line they roll and
    pass   125
Drought in the Mallee, 1940   70

Edge, The   179
Egrets   69
Electors, The   217
Emily Brontë   181
Empty people   20
English Queen, The   42
Epitaph, World War I   97
Evening Star, The   17
Exile, The   80

Faith   224
Father and Child   156
Finished   198
Fire in the heavens, and fire along the
    hills   66
Fisherman at South Head, The   167
Five Days Late   185
Five Visions of Captain Cook   5
Folklore   51
For David Campbell   169
Freedom Fighter   81
Future, The   242

Garrakeen   145
Garrakeen, the parakeet, is slim and
    swift   145
Gas flaring on the yellow platform;
    voices running up and down   143
Generations   133
God himself   72
*Going Down. With no
    permanence*   202
Gone. No words of parting or rejection
Goya Paints a Portrait of a Child   214
Green hands   211
Gull's Flight, The   143
Gutted of station, noise alone   66

Halfshadowed hospital room   86
Harry Pearce   38
He crouches, and buries his face on his
    knees   26
He will sit at the bare table, reading a
    dictionary   201
Here let me rest me feet!   56
Here we are all   188
His hat is rammed on   172
Homecoming   105

I am a policeman   53
I am the one who looks the other
    way   124
I go to see my parents   133
I had gone for a walk   224
I have lain on my back in caves   211
I sat beside the red stock route   38
I saw its periscope in the tide   68
I'm finding it impossible to begin, as
    you've ended so little   202
I'm not too old to like the shape of a
    man   187
I've a good nose for perfumes but no
    head   133
I've had all of the apple, she said   179
Impossibly black   83
Inspector of Tides, The   224
In the Park   189
In the Park, Looking   187
In the twenty-fifth year of my age   145
Individualist   217
Inscription for a War   97
Iris has her hands full   113
It is the season of the Long Narrow
    City; it has crossed the Myall   30
It was somewhere in September, and the
    sun was going down   40

Jim Jones   35

Kangaroo, A   71
Kangaroo, Kangaroo!   6
Kangaroo, The   6

Ladies and Gentlemen   166
Lake in Spring   161
Lament   131
Lament for the Drowned Country   14
Land I Came Thro' Last, The   225
Last of His Tribe, The   26
Late Ferry   110

Late, five days late. At night in sleep they fumble 185
Let your song be delicate 212
Letter from Rome 126
Life-Cycle 52
Likeness of sound 141
Lines from a Factory 113
Linger not, stranger; shed no tear 97
Living Dangerously 116
Louise and Alessandro 126
Love and Complacency 197
Love's Coming 196

Machine Portraits with Pendant Spaceman 132
Malta 58
Mangoes 141
Mangoes are not cigarettes 141
Meat Works, The 112
Me, mate? 19
Meditation on a Bone 209
Mid-Channel 213
Migrant Woman on a Melbourne Tram 81
monday to friday at the plant 111
Morning ought not 199
Mort aux Chats 142
Most of them worked around the slaughtering 112
Mute Conversations: Conversazioni Mute 86
My father and my mother never quarrelled 158
My father asks me how I stand it all 155
My man took off yesterday 20

Naked Girl and Mirror 160
Natural Increase 241
Nay, ask me not. I would not dare pretend 201
Near the School for Handicapped Children 172
Ned knew I was short of tobacco one day 42
Ned's Delicate Way 42
Night-Ride, The 143
Nobody knows how long it takes to kill an olive 208
Not owning a cart, my father 155
Note on Rhyme 141

O to live dangerously again 116

O, listen for a moment lads, and hear me tell my tale 35
Observing that Kanakas pined 28
Old, The 184
Old Prison, The 36
Once as I travelled through a quiet evening 69
Once on a silver and green day, rich to remember 131
Once When She Thought Aloud 179
Outback 244

Package for the Distant Future 237
'Paid by my Lord, one portrait, Lady Anne, 4
Painter of Antwerp 168
Parents 155
Pas de Deux for Lovers 199
Petit Testament 145
Phillip was a kindly, rational man: 2
Play Group 188
Please sit down. I'm afraid I have some 115
Plod homeward, peasant, north-bound from Italy 168
Poetry and Religion 229
Popular Statesman 208
Post Card 84
Postponement (Anavolee) 89
Pozières Cemetery 100
Prague, 1968 80
Prosperity 111

Quest of Silence, The 66
Quietly as rosebuds 196

Religions are poems. They concert 229
Regulars, The 98
Reverie of a Mum 56

Sassy 198
Sea Children 226
Scarecrow, The 129
Semi-conductors are also Semi-insulators 230
She sits in the park. Her clothes are out of date 189
She was the first pin-up 183
Shearer's Wife, The 39
Shells 20
Sigh, wind in the pine 132
'Sign there.' I signed, but still uneasily 243

Simple Story, A   200
Since all our keys are lost or
  broken   130
Smalltown Dance   180
Smugglers   79
Snake   148
So Quietly   227
Softly and humbly to the Gulf of
  Arabs   99
Song be Delicate   212
South of My Days   67
South of my days' circle, part of my
  blood's country   67
Splitting firewood I often found   217
Stars   203
Starting from Central Station   210
Staying with you at Palerang, I
  walked   211
Sun and clear air today as I scrape   230
Sweeney   40

Take lead figures pushed across a
  map   98
Terra Australis   69
That evening I had dinner with a
  man   126
That hungry face   71
That Which We Call a Rose   117
The bell of my loneliness is   181
The blue crane fishing in Cooloolah's
  twilight   27
The boy is made of gold almost:
  close   214
The bulldozer stands short as a boot on
  its high-heel ripple soles   132
The dead-weight of years crushing
  down, down   43
The doorbell buzzed. It was past three
  o'clock   44
The dunes slide to swallow   70
The eyeless labourer in the night   181
The gull's flight   143
the heat of burnt grass   82
The land I came thro' last was dumb
  with night   225
The late ferry is leaving now   110
The lights in strange houses   80
The Polar DEW has just warned
  that   238
The road turned out to be a cul-de-
  sac   218
The rows of cells are unroofed   36

The sadness in the human visage
  stares   28
The shallow reaches of the lake   161
The sky was carpeted with Italian flak.
  Crump!   58
The stars have so far to go   203
The tiger snake moves   148
Theatre   186
There is nothing about it. Much science
  fiction is set there   242
There was a duck egg as green as the
  evening sky   210
There were three voters. one. two.
  three   217
There will be no more cats   142
There'll be no more   198
There's an ordinary woman whom the
  English call 'the Queen'   42
They are rhymes rudely strung with
  intent less   65
They came in to the little town   18
They have walked out as far as they can
  go on the prow of the
  continent   167
*Third Song of Pop-Eye the
  Sailorman*   230
This is a song a epithalamium it is
  also   190
This is not I. I had no body once—
  160
Three images of dying stick in my mind
  like morbid transfers   216
Three times to the world's end I
  went   179
Thud of leather on willow—and the
  ball   166
Time of Waiting   201
To David Campbell   211
To Kill an Olive   208
Two days beyond the Last Post
  dawn   103
Two women find the square-root of a
  sheet   180

Ulinda   210
Up and up soars the Evening Star,
  hanging there in the sky   17
Up they go, yawning   102

*Victorian Hangman Tells his Love,
  A*   144
Vows   201

Voyage within you, on the fabled
    ocean   69

Wandering Islands, The   228
Wanna Be White   20
We Are Going   18
We were met   79
Weapons Training   104
Weights   155
Welcome to this poem. Why you?
    Because   59
What are the sights of our town?   51
When children are born in Victoria   52
When the mouse died, there was a sort
    of pity   239
When the sun blew over the hills on the
    dry east wind   226
When your skin is worn away   244
Where did I study, you ask—to send
    your son there too   89
Who would have thought that you, so
    quietly   227

Wine Tasting   43
With my legs in stirrups   186
Woman to Child   182
Woman to Man   181
Words scored upon a bone   209

Yes, my room's a mess. 'Alfred', Carlyle
    is reputed   230
You are such a gentleman   166
You cannot build bridges between the
    wandering islands   228
You cannot forget the old   154
You hear them kids over there laugh
    this old woman?   14
You men there, keep those women
    back   55
You who shall come, exalt these
    childless dead   97
You who were darkness warmed my
    flesh   182
You're Great!   59
Your Attention Please   238

INDEX OF POETS

Alexopoulos, Marion 113
Anonymous 35, 37, 97, 124
Beaver, Bruce 133, 216
Blight, John 239
Brennan, Christopher 66, 225
Brett, Doris 188
Buckley, Vincent 155, 208
Cambridge, Ada 201, 224
Campbell, David 38, 44, 148, 210, 211
Colebatch, Hal 230
Croggon, Alison 181
Dawe, Bruce 52, 55, 104, 105, 115, 144
Dobson, Rosemary 4, 124, 129, 169, 179
Dransfield, Michael 43, 111, 117, 199, 224, 244
Durack, Mary 14
Dutton, Geoffrey 197, 201
Encarnação, J. J. 80
Esson, Louis 39
Fahey, Diane 183
Field, Barron 6
Gilbert, Kevin 19
Giles, Barbara 70, 187
Gould, Alan 98
Gordon, Adam Lindsay 65
.Gray, Robert 71, 110, 112, 147
Griffin, John 214, 217
Harrison, Keith 227
Hart, Kevin 80, 154
Harwood, Gwen 156, 189, 200, 213
Hay, R. G. 230
Hewett, Dorothy 116
Hope, A. D. 97, 124, 126, 169, 209, 228, 241
Hughes, Selwyn 20
Ingamells, Rex 145
Jenkins, John 58
Jennings, Kate 190
Jones, Evan 133
Jurgensen, Manfred 82
Jury, C. R. 97
Kantarizis, Sylvia 237
Keesing, Nancy 56
Kefala, Antigone 81

Kendall, Henry 26
Kocan, Peter 160
Lawson, Henry 40, 42
Lehmann, Geoffrey 185
Lewitt, Maria 79
Llewellyn, Kate 166, 184, 186, 198
Loewald, Uyen 89
Mackellar, Dorothea 179
Malley, Ern (James McAuley and Harold Stewart) 145
Malouf, David 203
Martin, Philip 211
McAuley, James 69, 130, 145, 158
McDonald, Roger 102
Murray, Les A. 2, 30, 51, 53, 132, 155, 167, 229
O'Connor, Mark 72, 100, 208
Oodgeroo of the tribe Noonuccal 18
Page, Geoff 100, 103
Papertalk-Greene, Charmaine 20
Porter, Peter 142, 238
Roberts, Nigel 143
Shapcott, Thomas W. 172
Shaw Neilson, John 196, 212
Skrzynecki, Peter 84
Slessor, Kenneth 5, 66, 99, 143
Smith, Vivian 28
Stewart, Douglas 131
Stewart, Harold 145
Stow, Randolph 226
Strauss, Jennifer 83
Tait, Lilian 140
Tipping, Richard 141
Totaro, Paolo 86
Tsaloumas, Dimitris 89
Viidikas, Vicki 202
Walker, Kath (Oodgeroo of the tribe Noonuccal) 18
Wallace-Crabbe, Chris 215
Whiting, R. B. 217
Wickham, Anna 141
Wonguri-Madjigai People 17
Wright, Judith 27, 36, 67, 70, 160, 180, 181, 182, 218, 243